BOWMAN'S STORE

A JOURNEY TO MYSELF

Bowman's Store, aerial view, 1952. Middle Grove Road
runs from the upper left of the photo to the lower right, where
it intersects with the State Road, Route 9N.

BOWMAN'S STORE

A JOURNEY TO MYSELF

Joseph Bruchac

Lee & Low Books
New York

Printed in Canada

The text is set in Latin 725

10 9 8 7 6 5 4 3 2 1
First LEE & LOW Edition, 2001

Library of Congress Cataloging-in-Publication Data
available upon request.

ISBN 1-58430-027-2

To the memory of my grandfather,
Jesse E. Bowman

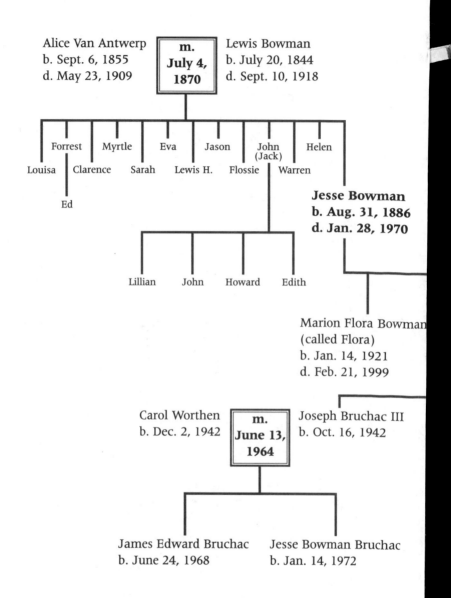

Alice Van Antwerp
b. Sept. 6, 1855
d. May 23, 1909

m.
July 4,
1870

Lewis Bowman
b. July 20, 1844
d. Sept. 10, 1918

Forrest   Myrtle   Eva   Jason   John   Helen
                                  (Jack)
Louisa   Clarence   Sarah   Lewis H.   Flossie   Warren

Ed

Jesse Bowman
b. Aug. 31, 1886
d. Jan. 28, 1970

Lillian   John   Howard   Edith

Marion Flora Bowman
(called Flora)
b. Jan. 14, 1921
d. Feb. 21, 1999

Carol Worthen
b. Dec. 2, 1942

m.
June 13,
1964

Joseph Bruchac III
b. Oct. 16, 1942

James Edward Bruchac
b. June 24, 1968

Jesse Bowman Bruchac
b. Jan. 14, 1972

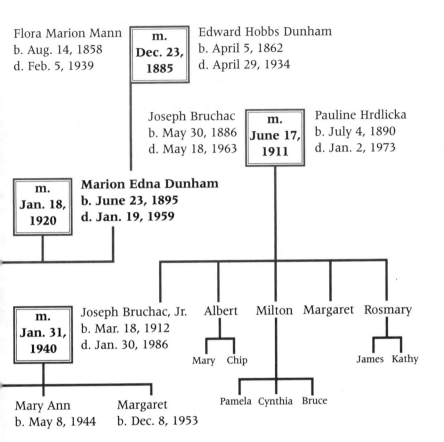

Flora Marion Mann
b. Aug. 14, 1858
d. Feb. 5, 1939

**m.
Dec. 23,
1885**

Edward Hobbs Dunham
b. April 5, 1862
d. April 29, 1934

Joseph Bruchac
b. May 30, 1886
d. May 18, 1963

**m.
June 17,
1911**

Pauline Hrdlicka
b. July 4, 1890
d. Jan. 2, 1973

**m.
Jan. 18,
1920**

**Marion Edna Dunham
b. June 23, 1895
d. Jan. 19, 1959**

**m.
Jan. 31,
1940**

Joseph Bruchac, Jr.
b. Mar. 18, 1912
d. Jan. 30, 1986

Albert

Milton

Margaret

Rosmary

Mary   Chip

James   Kathy

Mary Ann
b. May 8, 1944

Margaret
b. Dec. 8, 1953

Pamela Cynthia Bruce

BOWMAN'S STORE

A JOURNEY TO MYSELF

GHOSTS ALONG
THE RIVER

Bowman's Store. That is what everyone called the place where I spent my childhood. A little gas station and general store in the Adirondack foothills town of Greenfield Center, New York. A town where at least a third of the people were Slovak immigrants—like my father, whose name I bear—who desperately wanted their children to be real Americans. A town where fully another third were of American Indian ancestry—real Americans, though few of them would admit it openly. And one of them was my mother.

Though my parents' home was less than half a mile away from Bowman's Store, I never spent a single night under their roof. Instead, I was raised by my maternal grandparents, Jesse Bowman and Marion Dunham Bowman.

Jesse Bowman was a dark-skinned man who tried to hide his Abenaki Indian ancestry. I know now that he did this because of the prejudice against Indians that his family and many other Native families in the Northeast had experienced. Though his looks and demeanor were those of a Native person, he always referred to himself not as Indian but as French. And when anyone asked him why he was so dark-skinned he would simply say, "Us French is always dark."

"But if you are French, Grampa," I said to him once, "what am I?"

My grandfather with my mother as a toddler, *above,*
and with me at the age of four months, *right*

"Yer a mongrel," he said. Then he smiled. "Jes' like me. Mongrels is tough."

Jesse Bowman raised me to manhood without ever admitting his heritage, yet today I am known as an American Indian storyteller and writer. People in many parts of this country and other countries read my words. Some even think of me as a teacher, of sorts. My own children have followed the path that I now walk; and they too, adults now, tell the traditional stories, sing the old songs in Abenaki, and know the American Indian view of the world as their own. It is a Native view of the world that their father only fully realized was his own when he became an adult.

How did this happen? How did I get from this childhood, in which my grandfather denied our shared Indian heritage, to my life today? This process was not linear or orderly. But I know where it begins. It begins in Bowman's Store, a place where small seeds of love and trust, of belief and sharing, were planted—a place that was the home of my childhood, and the place where I live to this day.

There are ghosts along the river. That is what the woman who is close by my left shoulder says in a soft voice. We are standing in that dusky light only experienced on a late fall evening. There is a house behind me, but it is not one with windows or one made of boards and nails. Built with bent poles and bark, it is as round as the circle of sky above us, that same circle of sky which will soon be brilliant with the light of the full autumn moon. The full moon we call *Mzatonos Kisos*, the "Frost-Coming Moon." When I was a child I did not know how to say those words in the Abenaki language. Nor did the grandparents who raised me ever speak of the Abenaki blood that was in my veins and in the veins of my grandfather.

There are ghosts along the river. And so I go to walk alone beside its flow. There is a light with me, a light that I hold in my hand, and I can see clearly for a long, long way. Before me, behind me, to either side, above and below, I can see. The light helps me to see those six directions and also the seventh direction within. I walk downstream.

I look across the river and I see them. A wolf is running there. Its coat is black and gray, almost blue, as I see it in this light made of moon and shadow. A man runs behind the wolf, not chasing it, but following it. His feet are bare and his only clothing is a deerskin loincloth. In his hand he carries a firebrand. He moves with the ease of one used to running great distances, and as I see that he and the wolf are one, I see him no longer. Now only a great gray wolf is running there on the other side.

I stop, knowing what the wolf will do. It will cross the river at the place ahead of me where the swift stream runs shallow over the stones. I hear its feet splashing the water, and then I see it in front of me, running toward me. I stand there, unafraid, as the wolf brushes by me and then leaps into the deep water of the lake behind me. The light that I hold shines into the wolf's eyes, two bright eyes glowing out of the dark shape of its head, as it turns from the place where it sits in the water, turns to look at me.

It is still looking at me when I wake. Dawn and a feeling of great peace are in my heart.

That was the dream which came to me on my third night in Washington, D.C., where I had gone to promote a new book and to tell traditional Abenaki stories at the American Folklife Center. The morning when I woke from my dream was that of Saturday, November 19, 1994, the morning when I began to write this memoir. Somewhere, that same morning, my older son Jim was also waking with the dawn. He was camped by the waters of Lake Champlain with my younger sister, Marge, and others who had made a sacred vow to take a difficult journey. They were going north by canoe from Montpelier, in the center of Vermont, to Swanton, by the Canadian border. Down the Winooski, the "Onion-Land River," they went, past Burlington and into the windswept waters of Champlain, the big lake we call *Petonbowk*, "The Waters Between."

They would go up the lake to Grand Isle and then cross to the Black River, making their way upstream, past ancient campsites and places where our fires had burned for thousands of years and where our ancestors were still buried. They would travel like this, perhaps a hundred miles by water, to return—in the old way—the remains of Abenaki ancestors who had been taken from the earth by archaeologists when my son, then twenty-six, was a small child. These old ones, these *ktsiak*, were from the time of pre-Contact; some had been placed in the arms of the earth more than 5,000 years ago, before their rest was disturbed by the archaeologists. Now their grave goods, their bones, and their bone spirits were being brought home.

I called home. Carol, my wife, answered the phone in the

old house on Splinterville Hill where I had been raised. She told me about the message she had received from Jim. The journey was going well, even though they were tired and cold and their tents were full of frost in the morning. There had only been one mishap the day before. One of the other canoes had capsized when they reached the end of the river and entered the rough waters of the lake. Nothing had been lost and they had built a fire to warm up the two people who had been in the canoe: Wolf Song and Tom Obomsawin. Obomsawin appears to have been the name of my great-grandfather's family, before it was "Americanized" to Bowman. *Obomsawin*, which means "Keeper of the Fire."

There are those who think our lives and even our memories go in an unbending line. They say too that truth is a straight and a narrow path. If I ever believed that, I no longer think it to be true. Our memories, our dreams, and what truth we do know, may better be seen as a great circle. That great circle, like the beautiful spiraling web of the orb-spider, is filled with lines of connection which move between circles within circles. So it is that both this breathing moment and what is called "the future" are always linked with what is called "the past." So it is that dreams become reality, that memories move back and forth between dreams, and that our stories are a swaying, dancing bridge between them. And there are ghosts along the river which is itself a great circle, a circle that moves between cloud and ocean, between rain and snow and the breath-thin mist of evaporating water which rises like a spider's web to catch the sun.

Like the Native American stories that have guided me through my adult life, this book is not strictly linear in terms of time. It does begin with my earliest memories of childhood and it continues in more or less chronological order through the twenty-eight years that I shared of my grandfather's life—from my birth in 1942 to his death in 1970. However, because it draws on memory and on dreams to guide its course, each chapter—like memories and dreams—is linked to that which is long ago and that which is today.

As my older son Jim journeys to return the spirits of ancestors to rest, ancestors as distant and yet as close to our lives as the highest clouds which return as rain, my younger son Jesse walks into a classroom to begin another journey. It is a journey of song. He has given a great part of his life over to that Abenaki language which I have never learned to speak fluently, though its words shape the flow of my own voice. After long seasons of study with the elders at Odanak, he has begun to teach the language to high-school students in the Abenaki community at Swanton, Vermont.

Jesse taps the heartbeat drum and sings the words of Abenaki songs that had been hidden for long decades. The time when the sound of a drum in Swanton would bring a visit from the police is still well within living memory. He speaks aloud the Prayer of the Lord, "*Nemitokusena, spemkik aian, sogmowalmegawdets aliwizian,*" in those lilting words which my grandfather, Jesse Bowman, never spoke to me. "Our Father," it says, "in the Sky Land are you; sanctified like a chief is your name." Yet in the voice of his great-grandson I hear the old man's gentle tones. Circles within circles.

So it is that when I walk, wherever I walk, I know that I have only to hold out my hand to feel it held once again by the strong grasp of an old man with hair as white as snow, with a face as brown as the good earth. I close my eyes and the fifty years that have passed are no more than one heartbeat, one drumbeat. I am still there, there with my grandfather at Bowman's Store.

FITTING THE GROUND
TO PLANT

There is a story about corn. It is one of the stories that my grandfather never told me. There was hardly any mention of Indians at all when the old men gathered around the potbellied stove in my grandfather's general store, sitting in the wooden chairs my grandfather had made of pine cut from his woods. Even though more than one of those old men, like my grandfather, had the dark tanned skin and features that hinted at something more than the Scotch-Irish or French ancestry that most of them claimed, they were careful about how they mentioned Indians. One never knew who might be listening.

But I think of this story as one of his stories too. I learned it two decades ago from my friend and teacher Maurice Dennis, as he stood behind his house in the Adirondack village of Old Forge, carving into a cedar pole the shapes of Bear and Turtle—the two main clan animals of our Abenaki people.

Maurice's parents had come down from Odanak, the Abenaki reserve in Quebec, when he was a small child. Like my great-grandparents, they were basket makers. A number of Abenaki families made their way from that town of refuge in the far north to return to upstate New York or Vermont or New Hampshire—new European names grafted onto the land their ancestors once called simply Ndakinna, *"Our Land." They came now as either "French-Canadian" loggers or as "Canadian" Indians, playing the role of fishing and hunting guides and makers of souvenirs for tourists. They were no longer people who belonged to this land, not in the eyes of those who held pieces of paper that proved ownership. But their stories still remembered a long connection with an earth that would never forget those who loved it. Maurice Dennis was telling me such stories that day, stories of canoes that could cross the sky, stories of the meaning of the thirteen plates on the back of Turtle, stories of how some things came to be.*

Long ago, he said, the Abenaki people had no knowledge of corn. They gathered plants from the forest, hunted, and fished. But one year the game grew scarce and the fish were few, and when they went to gather berries and roots and nuts, those too were hard to find. The people made it through the winter, but when the spring came they worried that they would not survive.

One man went out hunting and this happened to him. He saw no game, but when he entered a clearing in the forest, he saw a woman there. One moment there was no one, and then there was this woman. Her long hair was a strange yellow color.

That woman with hair as yellow as the sunrise stood there, looking at the hunter. Her clothing was all green and her thin blonde hair blew in the wind. The hunter came closer to her, and though she swayed back and forth, dancing in the wind, she still did not move from the place where she stood. It was as if she had grown up out of the earth there in front of him. As he looked at her, feelings of great love swept over him—not the kind of love a man feels for a woman, but more like that grateful love a child feels for a caring grandparent.

"I have come to help your people," she said. "I am going to die. When I die, you must loosen the earth all around this clearing. Then drag my body over that earth and bury me. Keep my grave

clean and protect it from the birds and animals. If you do this, you will see me again and I will feed your people. Care for me well and I will never leave you."

Having spoken those words, the beautiful maiden fell to the earth. The hunter tried to wake her, but he soon saw that she no longer breathed. So he did as she had told him to do. He took his spear and used it to loosen the earth all around the clearing, and he dragged her body around and around. As he did so, she became smaller. When he was done, all that was left of the maiden were her green clothes, which had begun to turn brown.

Day after day he returned to the clearing to keep her grave clean and drive away the birds and animals. Now small plants were growing. When he saw they were as green as the clothing the maiden had worn, he understood they were her children. They grew taller and taller until they were as tall as a man. Late summer came and silky strands like hair, hair as yellow as the sunrise, grew from the tops of those plants and from the ears of corn that formed on their sides. That corn was the gift which helped the people survive. So it was that the Corn Maiden gave herself to the Abenaki people a thousand years ago.

I picture my grandfather when I think of this story, picture him in the one place where he always mentioned Indians. He spoke of them in a way both reverent and bemused, almost the way a person might say the name of a parent he had been separated from not long after birth. *My mother? My father?* Always with a hint of uncertainty. That one place where my grandfather always mentioned Indians was in his garden.

My grandfather's name was Jesse Bowman. Jesse E. Bowman. The E was for Elmer, though no one outside the family was allowed to say that middle name to him. He and my grandmother ran their little gas station and general store on the corner of Middle Grove Road and State Route 9N. The road rose

Grampa and Pudgie, 1950

up the hill so steeply from Saratoga Springs, three miles to the southeast, that the iron-shod hooves of the horses straining to pull wagons up the hill would splinter the wood of the plank road that had once been there. So the hill where the store was located was called Splinterville Hill. Fifty yards behind their store was another road, named for the mill that used to be located on it—a mill and a now-vanished pond that had belonged to my grandmother's parents, the Dunhams. Bell Brook, the stream that had powered that mill and filled the pond, still rippled down over the stones.

Sometimes, in my dreams, I am walking again down Mill Road with my grandfather. He carries in his arms the black-and-white fox terrier that he named Pudgie, a wiry little dog that never growled at me. The closest that she came was an indignant yip one day when I was two years old and she was eight—getting on to be an elder in dog years. My grandparents turned to look and saw that I had just bitten off one of her whiskers. My grandfather liked fox terriers. Though they were little, bigger dogs stepped aside from them. They lived a long time—for a dog. They were compact and tough.

"They be almost as smart as a mongrel," my grandfather said.

When I was a very small child, as soon as I could walk, I was following my grandfather. In addition to running the gas station and store, he was still doing other work. He worked on the road crews, especially in the winter when he drove a snowplow. He had done that since the days when the plows were pulled by horses, and there were times when he would whisper "Gee" and "Haw" as he drove one of those big vehicles, smiling to himself as he felt the truck answer his commands to turn, just as teams of horses had done three decades before.

He worked too at the butter plant down the road. His job there was a good one. I was old enough to know that. Without him that plant would not have been able to run, for he was the man who shoveled the coal into the boilers. Grama had taken me to see him working there. I was proud of the way he looked, his brown arms glistening with sweat and with gleaming dust from the hard coal that flew into the open maw of the great boiler, as he bent and dug the blade in, lifted it up, and tossed it with no more effort than another man would expend to take a deep breath. And the fire breathed back its thanks to him with each shovelful it swallowed.

He had a strong relationship with fire, my grandfather did. So many memories of him are around the fire. Around the woodstove in the kitchen, where our lives centered in the cold seasons. My grandfather and I kept the wood box, with its hinged lid, filled with split ash and maple. Since my grandmother cooked on that stove, it was warm most of the day; and as soon as the leaves began to turn colors, it was kept burning day and night.

It was behind that stove that the cats had their kittens. There was just enough space for me to crawl back in there with them to feel their little claws hooking into my shirt and my pants as they crawled over me, mewing in their tiny, insistent voices. And it was there behind that woodstove that Grampa placed the chilled calf which had strayed from its mother, warming it back to life wrapped up in his red flannel shirt.

Each spring he would burn the grass in the field—the way his father had taught him to do it. Clearing the way for new green growth, burning back the dry tangles of berry bushes at the edge of the field so that fresh, strong canes would rise up to be covered with blackcaps in late summer. I followed behind him, helping him make a circle of fire that would feed on itself, the circle growing smaller and smaller until it became a single ember at the blackened heart of the field. Our feet would be black with the soot of burned grass, and it would be on our faces and in our hair.

There were times, though, when the wind would change. Then the fire would turn and run ahead of us in directions that we did not expect. We had rakes and shovels in our hands and we would beat the burning grass, making sparks fly up so high that I was certain they became stars. But we could not stop that burning grass, and more and more smoke filled the air.

Then my grandfather would stop and lean on his rake. I would do the same.

"Guess the fire department'll get here soon," he would say.

"I guess," I would answer.

And we would listen for the familiar sound of their siren, coming down from Greenfield after the fire spotter in his tower on Spruce Mountain, eight miles to our north, had seen the rising smoke and called it in to them. We knew what he probably said: "Them Bowmans is burning that field again."

Distant and then closer the sound of the siren would come, a sound that was exciting to me not just because I knew I'd soon see the red truck of the Greenfield Volunteer Fire Department and the men dressed in boots and slickers and hats. It was exciting because I knew, even as a small boy, that open burning like this was illegal without a permit. My grandfather never went to get one and I wondered if this would be the time that they would come with guns and handcuffs, and—just the way they did to the criminals I saw in the movie serials at the Congress Theatre—take my grandfather away. If they did, they would have to take me too. I would show them the pack of matches in my hand and tell them I was the one who started the fire.

But, while the time would come when I would see my grandfather handcuffed and taken away in a police car, it never happened when he burned his field and the fire truck arrived.

Instead, big smiling men would climb off the pumper truck and begin to wet down the edges of the fire.

"Jess, you old firebug!" one of them might yell.

My grandfather would not answer. Sometimes, though, he might lean over to me and say in a soft voice, "This here is one way to keep them firemen in business."

I would nod, understanding his words. You couldn't have firemen if you didn't have fires.

Just as I remember those fires every spring, so too I remember my grandfather's garden. It was around back, between my grandparents' house and the small two-room building we called "the Little House" and used for storing things. It was in the Little House that my grandmother's parents spent their last impoverished years, cared for by my grandmother and the husband they'd looked down on when he was their hired help.

Another of my earliest memories is walking through the furrows of that newly plowed garden with my grandfather—who seemed taller than the biggest trees then—holding my hand. I could barely walk, even on level ground, but he wouldn't let me fall. I wore the same kind of overalls that he did, and people were already calling me "Jess's Shadow."

That was how Lawrence Older put it one day when he was buying gasoline at my grandparents' filling station. I was following behind my grandfather, my tiny hand holding onto his overalls because his hands were too busy to hold mine.

"Jess," Larry said, with a twinkle in his eye, "that grandson of yours stays so close to you he don't hardly leave room enough for your shadow."

Jess's Shadow? I didn't quite understand that name. My name was Sonny. I knew that for sure. That was the name my grandparents called me by. I never heard either of them speak to me or about me by any other name.

I remember the day—I could not have been more than two and a half years old—when my grandfather said to me, "Sonny, cup out yer hands." I held them out together, trying to make a really good cup. Carefully, taking the seeds out from the cloth sack he had slung over his shoulder, he filled my hands with kernels of golden corn. I stood there holding those seeds for him, watching as he took them, four at a time, to plant them.

"Yer turn now," he said when those seeds were gone, and he held out one leathery hand filled with corn. I'd watched

On the steps of my grandparents' house in 1944, at age two

really carefully, so I knew what to do. I did it so well that my grandfather allowed that I was already better at it than he was. Then, as I planted my first hills of corn, he talked to me about things. He always talked more when he was in his garden.

There in his garden, as he spaded or began to hoe, he would talk about the different plants, about the birds we heard singing, about how we had to watch for the woodchucks or the rabbits or the raccoons. Sometimes he would talk about the old way of plowing with a team of horses, and he would tell me the names of the horses he'd loved—the last of them dead and gone a decade before I was born. He told me how, as their plows cut their way down into the rich earth that was the same color as his face, he and his father used to turn up arrowheads.

"Indian arrowheads," he would say.

FITTING THE GROUND TO PLANT

He had a name for that work of preparing his garden for the sweet corn and green beans and butternut squash we always put in. I never heard anyone else say it just the way he did until I met Grampa's younger brother Jack, many years later, when I was a grown man. "Fitting the ground to plant." That is what Grampa called it. That is what Jack called it. That is what their father, Lewis Bowman, had called it. Fitting the ground to plant.

Another spring day, perhaps a year later, I was following my grandfather while he worked in the garden. He had made a small hoe for me that year, and I was, as always, trying to do exactly what he did. Then he stopped hoeing. I stopped too and waited. I remember that I heard a bird sing just then, a long ululating song.

"Oriole," my grandfather said. Then he bent over and picked something up. He brushed soil from it and went down on one knee next to me.

"Sonny," he said, "looky here."

I leaned close to look at the dark, blocky piece of flint that filled my grandfather's broad hand.

"Indian," my grandfather said. "Axhead."

He hefted it first in one hand and then the other. He did it with the same care that my grandmother used when she was gathering eggs in the henhouse and putting them into the basket hung over her arm. Then he placed that axhead into my hands.

Thirty years after that day when my grandfather put the stone axhead in my hands, I understood at last why, as I held that stone, my mind had filled with images of tall corn swaying in the wind, images of slender women dancing as they held the season's harvest in their hands. Hearing Maurice Dennis tell the story of the coming of corn was the last stroke of the hoe that fit my own mind to the earth my grandfather had given to me. And I knew that as long as my hands had the strength to hold a hoe, I would work that garden where corn had been cared for by my grandparents and by my great-grandparents before them. I would listen to that land just as it had once been listened to by other men and women, generations of Abenaki people and Mohawk people whose stories were told in a tongue as old as the soil. Spring would find me preparing the earth for the Corn Maiden, find me fitting the ground of my grandfather's garden to plant.

CLIMBING THE LADDER

In the photograph that stands on top of the old up-right piano, there are two people. One of them is a man whose thick gray hair was once as jet-black as a raven's wing. His face is clean-shaven, for he would never abide any kind of a beard, and he is smiling. He wears overalls, the kind with straps over the shoulders and brass buttons, and a light-colored workshirt under that. He is slightly bent—not from the years, but because his right hand is holding the left hand of a very small child. That little boy, whose terribly serious face is not yet two years old and much paler than that of the old man, is dressed exactly the same as his grandfather. The same overalls, the same shirt. Behind them you can see part of a 1940 Ford pickup truck, and the side of the small gas station and general store on the corner.

That picture of my grandfather and myself is on the piano in the living room of the house where my grandparents raised me, and where Carol and I raised our two sons. I look at that piano and remember the day when it was carried up the concrete steps and placed on the screen porch. I was eight years old and awed by the way Steve Sadlon, our neighbor across the road, was able to lift one whole end of it himself, while Dick Arnold and my grandfather took the other side. I wondered if I would ever be as strong as Steve Sadlon.

With Grampa in May 1944, behind Bowman's Store

My grandmother had bought the piano for ten dollars with the idea that, as she put it, "one of us in the house would play it." My grandfather was musical. He could sing and play the fiddle or pick out almost any tune on a harmonica. The piano, though, was too much for him. Grama's idea, of course, was that I would be the one to learn piano. But I was not pushed into lessons, and the piano stayed untuned on the unheated porch for more than twenty years.

I never learned to play it, but our son Jesse, who carries the musical gifts and the name of the great-grandfather he never met, does play that now well-tuned piano. He fills the house with music that ripples and flows as sweetly as the waters of Bell Brook in the spring, completing another circle that my grandparents started to draw long before he was born.

I look at that piano and the picture on top of it and think of how links are made, how things started long ago may be completed in another generation. But not always without pain. Pain was part of the bona that placed my hand so firmly in my grandfather's. It is a pain that, as I trace it back, goes farther and farther, wider and deeper. It is like digging up the roots of the spruce which are used for sewing together a birch-bark basket. If you do not cut them off, those hidden roots spread out farther and farther. When you pull them, other nearby trees—which seemed unconnected before—may tremble, or even fall, themselves.

As I look at that photograph and the smile on my grandfather's face, I think of the day I climbed the ladder. The story of me and the ladder is a tale both my grandfather and grandmother told me so often that I feel my memory of it is completely my own.

My grandfather was never afraid of heights. I've heard it said, and even read it in a place or two, that the Indian people of the Northeast are born without a fear of high places, that it is something genetic. I don't know if I believe that. It might be more that non-Indians are taught, as children, to be afraid of so many things that might hurt them—sharp objects, fire, high places, wild animals, the woods, strangers—that they grow up scared of everything. Do this and don't do that.

There was little of "do this and don't do that" in my grandfather's growing up, from what he told me. If he stuck his hand in the fire, that fire would burn him. No need for any adult to teach a kid that. If he climbed a tree and fell out, then he'd learn on his own that high places were dangerous. Neither his father nor his mother ever struck him—or even shouted at him.

Perhaps it was that he was only one of thirteen brothers and sisters, and so there was less time, up there in their homestead on the heights of Cole Hill, for his parents to spend watching over each and every one of them. Maybe they just had to let experience be the final teacher, because they couldn't always be there. Or maybe the old Abenaki way was so deep in their family that, though they didn't talk about being Indian, they just did things Indian. In the Abenaki way you learn better by doing than by being told. People are allowed to make their own mistakes. In the Abenaki way, you never strike a child, for fear that a blow might break their spirit. It might take away their self-respect, make them sad and fearful, and teach them that it is right for those who are big to bully those who are small.

The self-respect that was nurtured by his parents was so much a part of my grandfather's upbringing, he would never allow anyone to tell him what to do—unless he felt in his heart that it was right for him to do it. His mother died when he was thirteen and his father remarried—marrying his wife's widowed sister. My grandfather left his father's home shortly after that, never to return. I once asked him why.

"I didn't like her," he said, referring to his stepmother.

"Why not, Grampa?"

"She jes' yelled at me," he said. "I told my father, if he ever needed help, all he had to do was ask and I'd do it. But I wasn't a-going to stay under the same roof with her."

And that was it. That same year he left home and went off to work. He worked first at the store of Seneca Smith and then as a logger in the woods. He was on his own, but not afraid to be there. That was just how he was with heights too.

There was this thing my grandfather used to do every now and then, even when he was eighty years old. He called it "checking the peak." He would go outside, look up at the roof of the house, and then declare, "I got to check the peak." He'd take the wooden extension ladder and place it against the south side of the house. That house rises up three stories and more. When you stand on the peak you can see Saratoga Lake, ten miles to the south, and the hills of Vermont, thirty miles to the east. That was what my grandfather would do. He would climb that ladder and then make his way up the steep metal roof to stand on the very peak, to walk along it with easy, balanced steps, and then lean against the brick chimney and look out. Checking the peak.

The autumn day I remember, the day my grandparents lodged so firmly into my memory by telling and retelling the story, my grandfather decided to check the peak. It was October and I had just turned three. It was just over a year since my mother and father and my sister Mary Ann, seventeen months younger than me, had moved out of my grandparents' house. In that house, my mother and father had spent the difficult first years of their marriage. Those angry years had included the stillborn death of my mother's first child, whose name would have been my name—my father's name—had he ever drawn breath. That brother I never knew was like the nameless son born to my grandmother, whose second and only other child was my mother. I do not know where those two little ones were buried. I do not know if words were said to either of them, those spirit twins who have always been a part of my life, the two first sons whose destinies I carry. For I was the one who took the place of them both, a son for two generations of mourning women, a link and a wedge between mother and daughter.

My face intent and serious, I followed my grandfather as he took out the ladder that day. I was quiet. I had already learned that it was easier to go unnoticed when one was quiet. When my parents lived in this house, it had usually been safest for me to be unnoticed. My grandfather set the base of the ladder firmly onto the ground and stomped on the bottom rung with his foot. He shook it to make sure it was steady, and then went up. Even though he was over sixty, he moved as quick as a cat up that ladder. I watched every step to see how he did it. He reached the top and then went up the silver-painted roof to stand on the peak and look out, shading his dark-browed eyes with his left hand. Then he heard a sound. It was a little voice saying "Aaah!"

He turned and looked down to see me at the very top of the ladder, swaying back and forth a bit and looking out. There was so much to see from up there! I was happy.

"Aaah," I said again.

Another man might have yelled then or tried to grab me, but that was not my grandfather's way. Instead, in his calm, soft voice he just said, "Well, I'll be! Fergot my hammer. Got to go back down and get it. Sonny, you go first."

I started down the ladder, but before I had gone more than a rung or two, my grandfather was there with me. He was climbing down the ladder with his hands a rung above me and his feet two rungs below me. I had heard my grandmother talking to him so often about how he was "getting on in years" and needed "to be more careful." She was worried about him doing such things as climbing high ladders. I remembered that, and so I guessed that he must have wanted my help when he came down. I took it slow and was really careful.

But when we got to the bottom the strangest thing happened. Grampa forgot all about the hammer he'd needed. Instead, he just took that ladder, laid it down on the ground, and then sat there himself with one arm around me and one hand patting his chest. I put my hand on his shoulder to reassure him. I didn't know what "getting on in years" was, but I figured that must have been the reason for him being so upset. Whatever it was, I hoped he would recover from it soon.

SOMEBODY'S
OUT THERE

My grandparents never locked the door of their house. Day or night, it was open to whoever came; and when they closed up their little general store and gas station at night, all they did was turn out the lights.

Long ago, among the Abenaki, there were no such things as locked doors. If people left a wigwam and didn't want anyone to enter it while they were gone, all they had to do was lean a stick across the door. If they wanted privacy when they were at home, that same stick leaned across the doorway would ensure that no one would disturb them. Few of the histories written about the Abenaki people mention this, but everyone who was Abenaki knew it. Without locks or keys, without jails or police, they lived in a culture remarkably free of crime.

The histories of Native people on this continent, their histories as individuals and as nations, have often been secret histories. There are histories found in books written by non-Indian experts, in which the Abenaki people are referred to as the "bloodthirsty and savage St. Francis Indians." In school Indian children are taught about events that have little connection with the realities of their lives and the lives lived by their people, either those of long ago or those of today. It is that way with the Abenaki people. It is that way.

The histories written—and unwritten—about the Abenaki people are, however, an eloquent explanation why my grandfather, whose relatives would openly acknowledge their Native heritage to me years later, described himself as French.

To be French, French-Canadian, was a way of surviving. Surviving not only the stereotypes and the deeply-held prejudice against Indians in the Northeast, but physically surviving, not being killed as an Indian—an easy target. We see this in the histories the Abenaki people did not write, but held in oral tradition. Those histories influenced the living of my grandfather's life, and the things that his life taught me.

"Somebody's out there!"

How many thousands of times did I say those three words or hear my grandfather or grandmother call them out?

"Filling station" was the phrase used back then for a gas station. Because there were three Flying A Gasoline pumps out in front of our general store—two for regular, one for high-test—we always referred to our store as "the station." Middle Grove Road came from the west to end there at Route 9N, and the T those roads shaped made Splinterville Hill a perfect location for a filling station and general store.

Our house was right next to the store building. It had been built on the stone foundation of an older house, the one my great-grandparents had owned. The first floor of our house was raised up four feet above the ground over the old foundation. Splinterville Hill, like most of Greenfield, was bedrock only a few feet down, and that was the only way my great-grandparents had been able to build a cellar with any depth to it.

A cellar is what it was and remains, not a basement by any stretch of the imagination. Even today, when I go down into that cellar, the one smell stronger than any other is that of the moist earth, despite the worn, age-darkened concrete floor. I look to the right, into the recess in the wall behind the new furnace we put in four winters ago, and see the old stone steps that end at the floorboards.

These steps belonged to the older house. Carrying beets and carrots, winter squash and potatoes, carrying bottles of relish and tomatoes to store in the cellar for the winter, my great-grandparents came down those stairs thousands of times. Now only ghosts come down those stairs, but the ghosts in my grandparents' house, even in that dark cellar, have never been angry ones. Despite three generations of pain, there was always too much gentleness and too much laughter here for anger to win out. It was gentleness and laughter that finally opened a smile from the face of the frightened little boy I was in my first two years in that house, in the second-floor rooms where my parents spent the first storm-cloud years of their marriage.

Our house was large, even larger than the old one which had first stood on that foundation. But the station started off being small. When I was three years old, not long after my parents had left me to stay "for a while" with Grama and Grampa, the station was one single ten by twelve-foot room, with a long overhang in front of the building to cover the two concrete islands for the gas pumps. One pump for regular gas was on the inner island. It was, like the outer pump, topped by a white globe bigger than a man's head, with a light bulb inside. When we turned the lights on at night, those two gas pumps looked a little like the space aliens who threatened Buck Rogers in the serials at the Congress Theatre. When we turned on the lights that went around the inner edge of the overhang covering the pumps, twenty-eight lights in all, it was a little like being inside one of those flying saucers that carried Buck's greatest adversaries. And from the age of three on, I was the one who got to flick the three switches in the panel box which either turned on all those lights or plunged that corner of Splinterville Hill into a deep darkness.

My grandfather kept adding on to the station. The first addition was another regular pump on the outside island, next to the high-test. Then he began to make the building bigger. On the wall between the house and the station were three doors. The first two led to the men's room and the women's room, each the size of a closet just big enough for a toilet and a sink. The third door, farther back from the road, was the back way to the station. This door led into the next addition, a room laid across the back of the original building that made the station a full six feet longer. When you walked in through that back door you saw the cash register right there in front of you, on a shelf built into the wall. It was a convenient location for a cash register, especially if you wanted to make it easy for someone to rob it.

Right next to it was yet another door, this one leading out into the one-car garage that was built onto the back of the station. When you added on the front door, the big front window where we displayed the long glass bread box, the two original side windows and the two new windows on the Middle Grove Road side—not to mention the garage door that my grandfather always kept open—there were eleven windows and doors. There were more ways in and out of that little building than holes in a sieve.

In the warm months of the summer and early fall, my grandparents would sit in their chairs out in front of the station, waiting for customers. But in the winter, despite the radiator that ran the length of the inside wall of the station, it was too cold in there to sit and wait, especially for old people.

It had always been warm in the station in the days when a potbellied stove heated the building, but radiators were more modern and thus much better. However, since the hot water for

Grama and Grampa in their house in the 1950's

those radiators came from the cellar of our house—and that water had to go underground for thirty feet before hitting the radiators—they were seldom more than lukewarm. The thermostat was in the house, and the two buildings were connected to a single heating system. It had to be hotter than the Sahara in our living room before the station went much above freezing on a dark January day.

So my grandfather put in "the buzzer." When the front door of the station was closed, a button was depressed. When it was opened, the button clicked out and closed a circuit, and the buzzer—which my grandfather placed over the door between the dining room and the kitchen—went off with a sound like a hundred bumblebees.

"Somebody's out there," the person closest to the buzzer would yell. And then whoever was closest to the front door would go out to wait on the customer—if there actually was anyone there. Ingenious as my grandfather was, he was never the world's most efficient handyman. He figured that a hammer and lots of nails could solve about any problem. Adjusting the buzzer was one of his main pastimes.

Hammer in hand, Grampa would climb up the rickety stepladder, itself patched more than once with black tape and nails, to readjust the buzzer which had loosened to the point where it went off at random intervals whether the door opened or not. A nail here, a nail there, and it was done. Usually it worked for a while, unless the problem was not the buzzer itself but the positioning of the screen door or the lack of tension left in the stretched-out spring that was supposed to hold the door tightly shut.

A wind would come up and the door would swing open and the buzzer would go off. Grampa would pull the spring tighter, take his tin snips, and cut off the straightened piece of metal that had been the end of the spring. Then, unless the screw that had held the spring was still in place—less than likely in a door whose wooden sections had almost as many holes as the screen itself—Grampa would reposition the hook that held the end of the spring, add another nail for good measure just to hold that hook in place, and step back. The door would then slam so hard because of the tension on the shortened spring that it would knock the buzzer clean off the door frame and leave it hanging with a distant sound like a nest of angered hornets emanating from the house.

Since the cry of "Somebody's out there" was, as often as not, more hopeful prophecy than certainty, neither of my grandparents was all that quick to be the first out the door. By the time I was six, I was always the first to go out to the station, a bright-faced emissary delivering the message "They're coming."

Then came television. I was in second grade before I saw it for the first time. Some of the other kids in my class said they

had seen it. One girl, known for her drastically imaginative exaggerations, even swore that her parents had one—although no one was ever allowed to visit her house to verify that assertion. Television was a far-off and distant thing in our world, as unlikely for us to have, it seemed, as a heliport on your roof would be today.

One autumn day, though, I got off the big yellow bus and my grandmother was not there to greet me. That was unusual, for I had been having trouble with the bigger boys on the bus. I was a small child with a big vocabulary and as fond as that made my teachers of me, it did not endear me to my classmates. When Mrs. Monthony brought me up front one morning to read the poem aloud that I had written for her, I had done so with some trepidation (a word I had just learned from the dictionary). I saw the look in the eyes of Butch Vasco and Tim Farley. As I came out of Saratoga Springs School Number Two, they escorted me to the edge of the rough stone building and gave me an intimate introduction to the third stone from the left on the west corner. Although my blood was washed away long ago from the dark gray granite and School Two is now an office building, I can still point out that stone, and the scar remains on the back of my head.

So now, tightly clutching my pencil case and my Hopalong Cassidy lunch box, I dashed out the bus door before the other boys who got off at the corner stop could grab my collar. I was across the road and up the concrete steps before their heavy feet crunched the gravel. I pushed open the porch door and stopped. There sat a big cardboard box that I had never seen before. Something had been brought in it. I dropped my pencil case and lunch box and opened the front door. My grandmother was sitting in her chair, but she hardly noticed me. My grandfather was on his knees in front of something as tall as our windup Victrola. But in the place where the doors of the

Victrola would have disclosed shelves to stack 78-rpm records, there was a white, flickering screen. It was . . . a television.

I sat down next to my grandmother. The book she had been reading was set aside on the nearest shelf of the tall, many-windowed cabinet. She placed her hand on my shoulder, then gently touched the tender place on the back of my head.

"Tomorrow we'll take you in to Doc Magovern to get those stitches out," she said.

I nodded, but the beating I had taken from Butch and Tim and the stitches in my scalp were the farthest things from my mind now. We had a television!

Grampa fiddled with the three round controls on the front of the console.

"Mebbe this," he said.

Then, as lights and lines shaped themselves more distinctly on the screen, the high-pitched whirring sounds of static were replaced by a human voice. It was a woman's voice, singing.

" 'When the moon comes over the mountain . . .' "

We sat there in amazement. The picture wasn't much to look at, but that voice was something! We had a television. We sat there watching it, listening to it, for hours. For the first time in her life my grandmother forgot to put supper on the table. People came to the station and I left the room only long enough to shout out to them, "We've got a television, come and see it!"

Before long, our living room was filled with people. No one had ever seen anything like it before. They admired the wood finish of the set, the sound that came from it. There was only one channel, it seemed, but it was a good one for music. Kate Smith just kept singing and singing on it. It came out of Schenectady, so we were looking at something that was going on thirty miles away! It was hard to believe. The picture wasn't all that good, but if we looked hard we could make out the people.

At last, sometime around eight that evening, a car pulled in to get gas and honked its horn.

"We've got a television!" I shouted to the man who stepped out of the car.

He came into the house where my grandparents, their neighbors, and their customers sat entranced on chairs and on the floor.

"Got a Philco, eh?" he said. It was plain that this television thing was nothing new to him. "Mind if I fix your vertical hold?" he asked. Then he leaned over and moved a knob on the side of the set that none of us had noticed before. Immediately the whirring lines on the front of the set adjusted themselves, and where we had seen only the rolling, elongated repetitions of shapes vaguely human, there now stood, black-and-white and distinct as if on a miniature movie screen, a human figure.

In a way, that clarity of image broke the spell. People shifted from their seats and stood up to go back out to their cars. My grandmother went into the kitchen to finally finish making our supper. My grandfather, shaking his head, went out to pump gas into the man's car. Perhaps we would have sat there for days watching those distorted shapes, if that man hadn't come along. But, even though we went about our business that night, things had changed. There was a new center to our lives.

And then came *Gunsmoke*. It became my grandfather's favorite show.

"That Marshall Dillon," he would say, "is a big man."

It seems in my memory as if my grandfather was able to turn on the TV any time of day or night and find *Gunsmoke* there. When Marshall Dillon was on the screen, nothing could make my grandfather move. The buzzer would sound, horns would honk from prospective customers waiting for gas and, if he was alone, my grandfather would go no further than to

My grandmother, Marion Dunham Bowman, in 1957

poke his head out the door and call out: "I be only an old man. Pump it yerself, and put the money in the cash register."

When somebody was out there, it was always my grandmother or me who would go out, if the streets of Dodge City were in sight.

My grandmother was the one in the family with the business sense. She handled all the money and kept all our records. It was just as well. My grandfather could barely read or write.

When he wrote a new account into the Book that recorded all those to whom my grandparents had given credit, he would put down only the person's first name. "Red," it might read, and under the name would follow a list two pages long of purchases of gasoline and bread and milk and canned goods. Those were the accounts that almost never paid up what they owed.

"But I'm better than some," my grandfather once said. "Old Lester who used to run that store over there in Galway, he couldn't write a-tall. He sold cheeses and grindstones, and whenever he sold a grindstone or a cheese, he would have the person write down their name, and then he'd draw a circle under it. Problem was he never could remember later whether that circle stood fer a grindstone or a cheese. I don't think he ever did figger out how to draw two circles that would look different one from the other."

In fact, neither of my grandparents was really that good at making money. The idea of charging interest on an account was farther from their minds than the earth is from the moon. In the summer and early autumn they were just as likely to do such things as sell the vegetables from Cousin Bobby's garden for him from their store, keeping all the receipts in a cigar box and giving every penny to him.

The reason my grandfather was nearly illiterate was a simple one. It was because of the way he'd been treated in the one-room schoolhouse in Porter Corners. Poor, dark-skinned, and dressed in rough homespun linsey-woolsey clothes, he'd found few friends in that little white building. Finally, when he was in fourth grade, something snapped.

"Somebody called me a name," he told me. "I flattened 'em and then I jumped out the window and never come back."

"What did they call you, Grampa?" I said to him.

There was a long pause before he spoke.

"They called me an Indian," he said.

SECRET HISTORIES

There is a dream that I have had more than once. It first came to me twenty years ago, when I began teaching a Native American literature course at Skidmore College. In my dream I could hear something as I walked. It was a deep beat and its rhythm seemed to come from within me as much as it came from around me. I was in a forest of old-growth pine trees. They were as tall as those few giant trees that I saw once in a last stand of ancient pines, which had somehow escaped the loggers, on a hill not far from Lower Saranac Lake in the Adirondack Mountains, a hundred miles north of my grandparents' home. The last time I had been in that place was on a field trip with a Cornell University forestry class in 1963. In the dream I stopped walking, and although the sound did not stop, it grew fainter, deeper. That was when I knew I had been listening to my footsteps on the rocky earth with one ear and to the beat of my heart with the other.

This earth is a drum, I thought. Then, thinking that, I knew I was not alone in that place.

Who are you? a voice said.

Sometimes I tell people that I'm part Indian, I said.

Grandson, said that familiar voice, do you also tell people that you are part alive?

When I woke up, still hearing that voice, still hearing the drum in my heart, I was crying.

By the eighteenth century, the Abenaki found themselves caught between the interests of the two great warring European powers of France and England. Although both the French and the English vacillated between friendship and hostility in their dealings with the various Abenaki communities, there were significant philosophical differences between the way the two European nations approached the "Indian problem." Perhaps it may best be seen as a religious difference.

The Catholic French had courageous and single-minded Jesuit missionaries, linguists *par excellence*, whose first task on meeting a new Native people was to learn and write down that Native language so that they could then translate the Bible into it. The French saw the Abenaki nations as fertile fields for the harvest of souls, potential converts to Catholicism. By the eighteenth century, the majority of the Abenaki people living in the areas of the Northeast under French influence had been baptized as Catholics.

Moreover, there were always relatively few French immigrants to the New World and many more men than women. Intermarriage between French men and Native women was a long-standing French colonial practice. Children from such unions in other places often were acknowledged by their fathers and sent to France. In North America, though, among Native peoples who universally share a deep regard for women, the culture in which those children were raised was almost always the Native one. However, the French last names gained either through baptism or through intermarriage set the stage for later generations, when Abenaki people could call themselves "French-Canadian."

The relatively sparse French populations in North America also made the French even more reliant than the English upon their Native allies. Whether as mercenaries or as full partners in the enterprise, the Abenaki people would make up the bulk of the many French raiding parties and armies that would engage in two centuries of warfare along the New England frontier.

Among the Protestant English, things were different. Although the first person to meet the English at Plymouth Colony in 1621 was Samoset, an Abenaki Indian who walked into their camp saying (in English), "Welcome, English," and although the Pilgrims survived their first New England winters only because of the very active help of the Native people—the English were not in the New World primarily to trade or make allies or convert Indians. They were there to take the land.

Because of the great plague of 1617, an outbreak of some European-introduced disease which killed as much as three fourths of the Native population of New England, there was plenty of room, at first, for the inrushing tide of English settlement. But as more of those new people arrived, they found the Indians in their way. Less than twenty years after being saved by Native people, the Plymouth Colony passed a resolution to exterminate the nearby Pequot Nation of Indians. The destruction or the removal of the Native peoples remained the policy of the English colonies—and the United States that sprang from those colonies. That policy found a name and the name was manifest destiny, a wave which washed across this continent from the Atlantic to the Pacific. The Abenaki Nations and their neighbors were those whose shores first felt its force.

There were thirteen Abenaki Nations: Micmac, Maliseet, Penobscot, Passamaquoddy, Penacook, Cowasuck, Pocumtuck, Nipmuck, Pigwacket, Kennebec, Sokoki, Missisquoi, Arosagun-tacook. This is how the British declared their intentions toward the Penobscots—traditionally allied with the enemy French—in a proclamation "Given at the Council Chamber in Boston this third day of November 1755 in the twenty-ninth year of the Reign of our Sovereign Lord George the Second by the Grace of God . . . King, Defender of the Faith." The words could not be simpler or clearer:

I do hereby require his Majesty's subjects of the Province to embrace all opportunities of pursuing, captivating, killing and destroying all and every of the aforesaid Indians.

As an incentive to do so, at the time when an English pound was worth the equivalent of fifty dollars today, a bounty would be paid:

For every scalp of a male Indian brought in as evidence of their being killed as aforesaid, forty pounds.
For every scalp of such female Indian or male Indian under the age of twelve years that shall be killed and brought in as evidence of their being killed as aforesaid, twenty pounds.

The result of such bounties—and the Proclamation of November 1755 was only one—was that a new and lucrative trade sprang up in New England: scalp-hunting. Best of all, Indian scalps all looked alike. So a scalp taken from a friendly Indian—such as those in the communities of Christian Indians that had chosen to ally themselves with the English, accept Protestant Christianity, and make their settlements close to the towns of the white colonists—was worth just as much as the scalp of an Indian allied with the French. Such scalps were much easier to come by.

By the late 1700's, the Abenaki people of western New England had discovered that their survival depended upon taking one of a few paths. They could fight—and many did so. They could flee—and thousands did flee, seeking refuge in communities that became small united nations, incorporating the survivors of dozens of tribal nations. Or they could become invisible. They could cease being visibly Indian and, in small settlements in the hills and valleys, carry on their lives. Swarthy-skinned, called Gypsy or French-Canadian, they would hide their language and practice their customs only in private. If they were light-skinned enough, they could even pass as white. But they would still hold the secret histories in their hearts.

As a small child I saw it happen. I watched it in a movie called *Northwest Passage*. It documented the eighteenth-century raid of Rogers's Rangers on the "St. Francis Indians"—the Abenaki village of Odanak. Spencer Tracy played Rogers, and he led his men bravely north to attack that village of cowardly, evil, marauding Indians.

In the movie there was a giant drum—a drum such as never existed in real life—big enough to dance on, in the center of that imagined Odanak. The Abenakis played a song of war on the drum until the righteous rangers arrived and silenced its voice. The beat of that war drum and the music played behind it in the soundtrack of *Northwest Passage* is echoed today when the Atlanta Braves play baseball—and thousands of white fans, dressed in burlesque imitations of Indian clothing, wearing headdresses of chicken feathers and garish warpaint, chant and swing their arms in the tomahawk chop. At the end of *Northwest Passage*, after finally making his way back to civilization (which always begins where the lives of Indians end), Spencer Tracy stated, "Sir, I have the honor to report that the Abenakis are destroyed."

I was only six years old when I saw that movie, sitting next to my grandmother. For some reason, my grandfather had refused to see it. People cheered when Spencer Tracy spoke those victorious words. I don't remember cheering and I don't remember my grandmother cheering. But she knew the work of Kenneth Roberts, the author of the book on which the movie had been based. "The book," she said as we left the theater, "was different."

I think she was trying to comfort me, for that movie had made me afraid. I was afraid of many things when I was a little child and I didn't understand why. Loud noises frightened me. Big people who moved quickly frightened me. The dark frightened me—not the dark itself, but what might come out of it.

NIGHTMARES

There is a story told among the Abenaki. A similar tale is told by our Iroquois neighbors, the Mohawk. The story has to do with dreams. Dreams were regarded as sacred messages, sent to people in their sleep. Often a dream revealed, it was believed, a secret wish of the heart which would have to be gratified, or the person who had that dream would become sick, disturbed in mind and spirit. The Mohawk had a special "dream-guessing" ritual. Sometimes the dream would be acted out literally or in a symbolic way.

Among the Abenaki, a man or a woman with a deep, disturbing dream would speak it to the m'teowlin, the deep-seeing one, who could interpret the dream. Such faith in the power of dreams was noted by the French Jesuits, who regarded it as superstition.

In the Abenaki story, an Abenaki man dreamed that he had been given a beautiful shirt by the white man whose cabin was nearby. He had seen that white man wear just such a shirt, and so he went and told him the dream. The white man listened closely. He knew something about the faith the Abenaki had in those spirit messages that came while sleeping.

"I understand," said the white man. Then he went into his

cabin, got out that shirt, and gave it to the Abenaki man, who went happily back to his wigwam.

The next day, though, the white man was at the Abenaki man's wigwam.

"I had a dream last night," the white man said. "In my dream, you gave me all of this tract of land, this wide valley where you and your family hunt."

The Abenaki man looked at the cocked rifle that the white man held in his hands. "I understand," he said. "The land is yours. But let us no longer tell each other our dreams."

When I think back on those early years of my life in my grandparents' house, the same house in which my own sons would grow to manhood, I remember the times that were the worst for me. Those times were the nights. I could not explain why I was afraid of the dark. I remember lying in bed in the downstairs bedroom, which was connected by a door in its northern wall to the room where my grandparents slept. My head was toward the east, my feet toward the setting sun that I could watch as it disappeared behind the line of trees along Mill Road, through the window at the foot of my bed. In the room next to mine, my grandparents' bed was aligned in that same way. Their room was the one my great-grandfather Ed Dunham had died in. His picture was on the wall at the foot of the bed, a picture taken in that very room as he held the happy, smiling baby who was my mother on his lap.

When I was very little, I could not be alone in my bedroom when the darkness came. Even a night-light or doors left open was not enough. My grandfather or my grandmother had to sit in the chair at the foot of the bed where I could see them, see that it was them and not some larger, darker, angrier figure about to loom over my bed and strike me when I cried. Night after night, they would sit there patiently until I finally slept.

By the time I was six, I was able to go to sleep without having them in the room. But the doors had to be open, and there was a litany that had to be gone through each night.

First I would kneel and say my prayers, loud enough for them to be heard.

"Now I lay me down to sleep, I pray the Lord my soul to keep. If I should die before I wake, I pray the Lord my soul to take. God bless Grampa and Grama and Pudgie, our dog, and Snoopy, my cat, and . . . Mom-and-Dad-and-Mary-Ann-and-everybody-and-everything. Amen."

I'd climb into bed then and pull the covers up to my neck, making sure that the sheet and blankets were tucked in good and tight—so that my arms and legs wouldn't stray out from under the bedcovers, so that nothing could come in and get me. Settled at last, I'd turn my head toward my grandparents' door.

"Good night," I'd call.

"Good night," my grandparents would answer from their big bed.

"Sweet dreams," I would say.

"Sweet dreams," they would call back, through that blessedly open door.

Then I would take a deep breath and speak those last words of the charm that I prayed would protect us all in my sleep.

"I love you," I always said.

"We love you," they always answered back.

Then I would close my eyes, hoping that when sleep came the dream would not come with it. It was a bad dream, and sometimes I worried so much about having it that it seemed as if sleep would never come. I would look over to the table near my bed at my illuminated clock and see that no more than five minutes had passed, even though it had seemed to be hours.

"Good night," I would call out again, repeating the litany, reassured by their answering voices. As it grew later in the night, though, sometimes only one of them would be awake to answer me.

Looking back on those endless nights I find myself amazed at the patience they showed. There was never anger, never exasperation in their voices when they answered the small uncertain voice of the child in the next room. There was only caring. There was only love.

As it got later, I would become certain that I would never fall asleep again for the rest of my life. It was usually then that sleep took me, and I found myself in that bad dream once more.

It was a simple dream and it was always the same. I stood next to my grandfather and my grandmother. We were in a wide field. Suddenly, like a crack opening in the ice of a pond, the earth began to separate between us. I called out to them, but it was too late. The earth had broken in half and I was alone, watching that part of the world which held them falling farther and farther away, falling away from me forever. I called to them, but they could not hear me. Then that piece of the earth which held everything that I knew of safety and happiness was lost from sight in a great, cold darkness.

Many nights I would wake up in the midst of that dream, crying silently. Then I would wipe my tears away with one hand and start to listen. If I heard only silence it would frighten me more, because I was listening for the sound of my grandparents' breathing. I knew that they were old people. Even when I was very small I knew what that meant. Ever since the age of four I had been reading the books in that house, even the books that were not written for young children. I knew from stories like Dickens's *A Christmas Carol* that being old meant you were very close to being dead. So I lay there in the dark, hoping to hear the sound of their lives continuing, and terrified of the silence that would one day take the place of their answering voices.

Some nights it was too much for me. I would call out to them, my voice trembling.

"Grama! Grampa!"

"Yes, Sonny?" It was usually my grandmother's voice that answered me when I called out so fearfully to them in the night.

"I had a *bad* dream."

"Do you want to come in with us?"

"Yes."

"Bring your pillow."

Then I would jump out of bed, clutching my pillow to my chest. I would go on tiptoe through the door and climb up the foot of their bed to get under the covers in between them. I was careful as I crawled not to step on Pudgie, the old fox terrier who faithfully slept at the bottom of their bed. Sometimes Pudgie would nuzzle my face or lick my bare foot as I made my way past her. This was a ritual that she knew well.

My grandfather always smelled like pipe smoke and wood, and as I slid up beside him his body was as hard as an ash tree. My grandmother was softer than the pillow I clutched in my arms, and she would always give me a hug with her big arms and kiss me before rolling back over. I would pat first my grandfather's firm back and then hers. Although their bed was big, there was no distance between us. Touching them like that in the darkness took all the fear out of the dark for me. I felt as if I could hold on to them forever, that my being there with them would make it certain that they would never die. Then, so swiftly that it seemed there was not even time enough for me to close my eyes, a peaceful wave of sleep would wash over me as I lay there, the smile on my face a mirror image of my mother's childhood smile in the picture on their wall.

BRINGING IN THE CHRISTMAS TREE

Two years ago, we staged a kind of reunion at our house. We brought together my mother and the four children of my grandfather's brother Jack. It was seven years after my father's final heart attack, and Mom was just back from the hospital where she'd had knee-replacement surgery. Carol and I had been in touch with Jack's children for many years, but my mother said that she had never met her cousins before. She said this even though one of them, Howard Bowman, had been my grandparents' soda delivery man for years when the station was running. Howard's route from the main Coca-Cola bottling plant in Glens Falls ran down through Greenfield Center.

My grandmother had barred my grandfather's family from any social visits to her house. She never said why, but I later understood that part of it was because they were connected to the Indian past my grandparents tried to hide. In all the time we lived together, my grandfather never mentioned any of them in the present tense—with the exception of his nephew Berlin, who lived on Bacon Hill near Schuylerville. Now and then my grandfather would disappear for days at a time, never saying where he was going and sometimes not even telling anyone before he left. He would go off to Vermont or Bacon Hill or Stony Creek, to visit some of those relatives who were *too Indian to come to the house where my grandmother ruled the roost.*

That day we brought my mother and her cousins together was a good one. They all had fond memories of my grandfather. Lillian— who, in her eighties, was the oldest of the four—kept referring to him as "Dad." Although her father Jack was younger and a little lighter-skinned, he and Jesse had looked like twins. Carol and I met Jack for the first time at my grandfather's funeral in 1970, and at first we thought we were looking at my grandfather sitting next to his own coffin. Although their father, Jack, had also called himself "French," Howard Bowman, John Bowman, and Edith Bowman all spoke openly about their Indian blood. They talked about how their grandfather was Abenaki and "had come down from Canada." I could see my grandfather in all their faces. And my mother just kept listening and smiling, smiling a broad smile that made her look so much like the little girl she had been in that long-ago photo.

At one point in the evening, Lillian began to talk about her grandfather, Lewis Bowman. As the oldest, she had known him best. One of his children—perhaps it was Forrest Bowman—had a son named Ed. Her little cousin Ed became, as Lillian put it, "the apple of his grandfather's eye."

Lillian shook her head, remembering. "To Grampa Lewis," she said, "he was always 'my little Eddie.' Grampa Lewis loved him so much and he always followed his grampa around." She paused, thinking about what she was going to say. "When Grampa Lewis was dying, it was the winter and there was an influenza epidemic. Eddie was six then. The night Grampa Lewis died, the last words he said were, 'How's my little Eddie?' No one had the heart to tell him that Eddie had just died that same afternoon of the influenza."

Lillian looked at her hands, folded in her lap. "Later that night, we all saw it, we looked out over the field and we saw a little light out there. It was wandering around like it was lost. Then a bigger light came up, back over the hill. That little light went right up to it and then the two of them, the big light and the little one, they disappeared over the hill together. We all knew those two lights was Grampa Lewis and his little Eddie."

The dirt road is steep to the top of Cole Hill. My first memory of going there, the place where my grandfather was born, was when I was seven years old. It was a few days before Christmas and we still didn't have our tree. But this year Grampa had promised me that I would go with him when he went to cut it up in North Greenfield, seven miles above our house, where the hills rose up into the small mountains of the Kaydeross Range, the foothills of the Adirondacks.

"Well, I guess we better go," my grandfather said that Saturday noon, as he looked outside through the station window and saw that the snow had stopped falling. He stood up from the chair inside the station and put on his coat.

I stood up from the chair next to his, putting on my coat too.

"Where we going, Grampa?"

"We ain't goin' too far," he said.

I followed my grandfather down cellar, where he had his tools in the big wooden box with its iron-bound lid. Whenever he opened it, it always seemed to me as if every tool in the world was in there. There were chisels, files, a brace and bit, a hand drill, pliers and screwdrivers, tin snips and ball-peen hammers, and screws and nails—lots of screws and nails. Grampa needed them, and the older he got, the more he seemed to need them. There wasn't much that he couldn't fix without putting in a few more nails and screws, even though some of the things he repaired probably weighed twice as much from the added iron, after twenty years of his carpentry.

Aside from wedges, which he was always tapping into the heads of his axes, hammers, and sledges—"jes' to tighten 'em on"—nails were his favorite things, and he would never throw a used nail away if it could still be straightened. I was glad of that, for I had my own hammer he had given me for that express purpose. I knew just how to use it to straighten out a nail, holding the nail carefully balanced against the concrete of the front steps for that first hit to get it back into whack, and then tapping all around it to true it up.

The lid of the toolbox creaked, and I leaned forward. I loved the smell that came out when the lid was first opened. It was a mixture of the smells of leather—from the old pieces of horse harness he still kept in the bottom of the toolbox—and oil-soaked wood, and a faint hint of rust. Grampa reached in and pulled out a curved handsaw, which he gave to me. I loved the way he would always trust me with things that were sharp-toothed or razor-edged. It was the way he was brought up and the only way he knew how, as he put it, to "learn it to me."

"You got to learn it by hand," he'd say. And when I cut my palm or sliced a fingertip he was there quick enough to sympathize with me and take me in—my hand wrapped in his red kerchief. My grandmother would wash it out, put in the Mercurochome (and though I winced, I didn't cry, because I was her brave boy), put on a Band-Aid strip, and let my grandfather take me back out again.

"We be goin' to get us a tree," he said as he gave me the saw, "from up on Cole Hill."

I put the saw on the floor of the backseat of the car, and then ran in the house to kiss my grandmother good-bye.

"We'll be right back," I said.

"You two take your time," she said. "I'll watch the station."

Then I went and took two sodas out of the cooler—one for each of us, though my grandfather always seemed to need a good deal of help with the drinking of his—before I got into the front seat of the blue Plymouth.

As we drove up through Greenfield my grandfather took the long way that led along North Creek Road, paralleling Kaydeross Creek.

"Now that there is a good spring," he said, pointing out a concrete trough below a pipe that brought water out in a steady stream from the base of a hill. "I'd water the team there many a time."

"I see it," I said. He had showed it to me before, just as he showed me the springs on the road up to Lake Desolation, or pointed out to me the places where the old Indians, the ones that "been gone," had ground their corn in samp mortars that were worn like potholes a foot or more deep into exposed bedrock. There was one below Woodlawn Park, another near King's Station, still another just off the North Greenfield Road before it came to Route 9. Up there on that hill was a good place to camp. Way back in there was a cave that you could sleep in or hide in if you didn't want to be found. My grandfather knew where all those places were. It is only now that I realize those words he spoke to me, guiding me to those old spots which had once been so vital to survival, were probably the same words his own father had spoken to him, seventy years before they were spoken to me.

There was a dead-end sign at the base of Cole Hill, and the road was plowed only part way up. There was more snow up here than down on Splinterville Hill, where only an inch or two was on the ground.

"It's like that up here," Grampa said, "snow ever' day in the winter. But we kin walk it."

He pulled the car over, put on the parking brake, and got out.

Holding the saw, I followed him as he left the road and went into the woods. I knew what we were looking for. It had to be a spruce and it had to be shaped just right. He walked along, hardly looking around, heading up the hill. As we walked he identified the trees out loud.

"That's a hemlock. That's a pine. That there is a cedar. That's a spruce, but it's real little. That's another pine."

We cut back through the woods in a way that made me think my grandfather was following a trail, even though there was no sign of one here. My boots would have been just high enough to keep out the snow, but my grandfather was taking such small steps that he packed down the snow as he went. Then the land dipped ahead of us, and we were looking out over a small creek that had cut its way through the land as it made its way down to feed into the Kaydeross at Porter Corners.

"There's where the bridge was. I always used to drive the cows back 'cross from that pasture over there."

I looked where my grandfather was looking. Not only was there no sign of a bridge, it was clear to me that those trees where my grandfather said there was a pasture had to be really old—at least half a century. But I believed him, and I imagined him driving home that long-gone herd.

He turned to his left and walked back toward the road. We passed a small abandoned building, and then a view opened up in front of us as the road swept down, a vista that allowed us to see far to the east, past Schuylerville, where the big mountains of Vermont lifted high up in the bright December sky. The vista was made larger because of the lawn in front of the old house that was there on top of the hill. It was clear that no one was living in it. No one had plowed the driveway and the windows had a blank look, like eyes empty of dreaming.

My grandfather looked for a moment toward those mountains. He was smiling. Then he walked across the road and stood before the house, his hand touching one of two giant maple trees that stood in the front yard.

"Me and Jack planted these here maples when we was kids. They was thirteen of us."

I put my hand on my grandfather's tree. The bark was rough, as are all old maples, but I knew that beneath its rough exterior it still held the memory of the sweetness of many springs. My grandfather's eyes had tears in them, and mine did too. This was the house where he had been born, the house where his mother and father lived. Lewis Bowman, born near St. Francis in Canada in 1844. Alice Van Antwerp, born in 1855. Both of them buried in the Ballou Cemetery, only half a mile down the hill from where we stood. I had been there a time or two in the summers with my grandfather, to mow around their graves. There was a wild red rose growing near their headstone, and a little United States flag was planted in the earth of that grave by the Greenfield veterans every Decoration Day.

My grandfather never talked much about his parents or his brothers and sisters. But he had brought me here.

"Me and my brother Jack," Grampa said again. "Lord, it sure takes me back when I think of the wild things we did."

We stood there together for a long time. I thought about the times he must have had there, times that ended with his mother's death in 1909, after which his father had married her twin sister.

"Y'know," Grampa said, "when I left home *she* said to me I'd better not ever come back and ask them for no money. I didn't pay no mind to what *she* said, but I said to my father, 'If you ever need money, I'll give it to you.'"

The sun was almost behind the trees now, and he turned away from the maple tree.

"Let's find us a good one," he said. "There was always good trees up here."

My great-grandfather, Lewis Bowman

We searched all around the hill for a tree. But they were all too small or the wrong kind. At last, when it was getting dark, we walked back down to the car. I put the saw back onto the floor and got in. Grampa started the engine and turned us around, and we went back down the hill. We didn't stop when we got to our house, but kept going till we reached the parking lot in front of the old railroad station in Saratoga Springs. They were selling Christmas trees there, already cut, at two dollars a tree.

When we brought that spruce into the house, my grandmother held the door open for us.

"That's a very nice tree," she said. "Where did you get it?"

I looked at my grandfather. "It come from Cole Hill," he said.

And you know, he was telling the truth.

IN THE CREEK

I wasn't a child when I was first told the Seneca story of Skunny Wundy's skipping stone. But when I heard it, the little boy inside me smiled. It was a story that he already knew.

Skunny Wundy was a boy who loved to skip stones on the wide river that flowed near his village. He was the best of all at skipping stones. Though he was a great stone thrower, he never threw stones at the frogs or the turtles. When he found other children throwing stones at the frogs and turtles he would stop them. "Those little ones are my friends," Skunny Wundy would say.

One day he walked along the river to the north of his village. He had been told by his parents not to go to the north, because there was danger there. But he had not listened. As he walked, he skipped stones and shouted, "I am the greatest stone skipper of all!" Then he encountered a monster—a Genonsgwa, a Flint-Coat Giant.

The giant had been watching him skip stones and had heard his boast.

"You are not the greatest skipper of stones," said the Flint-Coat Giant, whose body was made of layers of flint. Then the giant picked up a huge stone and threw it. It skipped across the surface of the river, skipping many more times than Skunny Wundy's stone had skipped.

"Now I will eat you," the giant said.

"You are just afraid that I will beat you at skipping stones," said Skunny Wundy.

"I am afraid of nothing," said the Flint-Coat Giant. "Pick any stone. If you make it skip more times than my stone did, then perhaps I will not eat you."

Skunny Wundy looked around for a good stone. As he looked, one of the stones spoke to him.

"Choose me," it said.

Skunny Wundy bent down to look at the stone that had spoken. It was not a stone at all. It was a little turtle, with its head and legs pulled inside its shell.

"You protected us in the past many times," said the little turtle. "Now I will help you. Use me as a skipping stone."

Skunny Wundy picked up the little turtle, who looked just like a flat rock.

"I will throw this stone," Skunny Wundy said to the Flint-Coat Giant.

"Go ahead," said the giant, "but do it quickly. I am growing hungry."

Skunny Wundy held the little turtle close to his face. "My friend," he whispered, "do your best."

Skunny Wundy cocked his arm back, took a deep breath, and then threw the little turtle like a skipping stone. The turtle spun in the air and began to skip across the surface of the water. He skipped and skipped and skipped. Every time he started to slow down, he stuck out his legs and pushed so that he skipped more and more and more. The Flint-Coat Giant watched with its mouth open as the turtle skipped and skipped and skipped, and then finally sank beneath the surface. It had skipped many more times than the stone thrown by the Flint-Coat Giant.

"Wah-hah!" Skunny Wundy shouted at the giant. "I have

beaten you. You may eat me if you like, but you cannot beat me at skipping stones."

The Flint-Coat Giant had never been beaten before at anything. He became so angry that he started to shake all over with rage. He shook so hard that he crumbled into a pile of stones.

So it was that Skunny Wundy defeated the Flint-Coat Giant.

My world was bounded by roads, each with its own meaning and its own name. The State Road—Route 9N—as uncrossable a boundary as a wide, dangerous river, ran in front of the station. Middle Grove Road, like a smaller tributary, ran to our left. Behind us was Mill Road, which ran less than a mile before connecting to the State Road. We called it "the dirt road," and it was the only road I was allowed to cross.

Bell Brook ran along that road. One part of Bell Brook—just across the dirt road, right before the creek dove under the old stone bridge—was my special place. There were two big ledges of stone reaching down into the water like great steps. I could lay myself down on the lower one, where the water lapped over its edge. Then I could reach my arm down into the bone-chilling waters of the brook to feel under the ledge. Trout hid under there. If I moved slowly enough, gently enough, I could "tickle a trout," as my grandfather described it.

First the tips of my fingers would feel the slight vibration in the water of the trout's fins just in front of its gills. Those fins never stop moving as long as a trout is alive and underwater. Moving my hand closer and closer, slower than a stalking heron, I would feel the trout's smooth side. Then I could gently run my hand along it and under its belly. If I did this right, that trout would become mesmerized and would not move. I could bring it out from under the ledge and even lift it into the air, as it rested in the palm of my hand—although when I was very young, I always had to use two hands to do this, if the trout was more than a few inches long.

I could walk across the dirt road any time to play in the creek, making dams with the rocks or seeking out the many kinds of life I could find there if I was patient. Frogs were always there, sitting at the edge of the water on their favorite rocks, and each year I got to know some of them well enough to be able to feed them. I would hold out, at the end of a long straw pulled from my grandmother's broom, some bit of food I knew they would like—perhaps an insect that had been hit by a passing car and left fluttering in the dirt road. I would gently twitch the broom straw as I brought it slowly closer and closer, and then the frog's impossibly bulky, pale tongue would come shooting out and snare its prey, pulling it right off the end of the straw. The frog would swallow, its eyelids closing and its eyes disappearing as it forced the food down its throat.

Even when the frogs were not there, I could watch the movements of the caddis fly larvae on the bottom of the bed of the creek. You couldn't see them unless you looked long enough and knew where to look. An inch or so long, they would glue pieces of twigs around the outside of their bodies, leaving room only at the end for the head and a pair of legs to reach out and pull them along. They would sit motionless, blending in with the debris at the bottom. Not all of them used twigs; some preferred little stones and bits of sand. I would sometimes move these stone caddises over to the areas where there was debris on the bottom, to see what they would do. They always made their way back to the sandy part of the bottom. Not only did they know when to move and when not to move, they knew where they fit in.

I had to keep my eyes open when I was there in the creek. Though it was one of the places where I fit in, a place where I could be quiet and unnoticed, there was always a chance that one of the older boys in the neighborhood gang might come by. It was hardly a gang by today's standards, just a handful of five or six boys from the farming families around Splinterville Hill. The worst things they ever did amounted to acts of petty vandalism, the things that bored adolescent country boys will do when friends dare them to smoke a cigarette or throw a stone at a window or tip over a tombstone. My grandmother, though, had one word for all of them: BAD.

"You stay away from them, Sonny," she said.

By the time I was seven I was deathly afraid of those older boys. Years later some of them would be my friends, but childhood could be a pitiless time for a boy who was smaller, wore glasses, and was always afraid. They taunted me and called me yellow. They said I was a Grama's boy and afraid to fight. They were right. Whenever I heard the crunch of bicycle tires coming down Mill Road, I would scramble up the creek bank, and run as fast as I could on my little cowardly legs back across the field to the safety of my grandparents. Or, if they were too close when I first heard them, I would hunker down under the bridge or crawl into the bushes, breathing softly, hoping not to be seen or heard. Unless they were deliberately hunting me—as they sometimes did—they were usually too concerned with other things to notice and would pass me by, only stopping, perhaps, to throw rocks at my frogs or break a soda bottle on the exposed stones of the creek bed.

One day, as I sat under a tangle of grapevines near the stone bridge, watching one of my favorite frogs, I heard them drop their bikes and come clambering down the bank. I crawled back further under the vines and held my breath in terror, but they hadn't seen me. I caught a glimpse of their backs as they bent over my ledge, thirty feet away. Then I ducked my head down and closed my eyes. I had the irrational thought that if I couldn't see them, they couldn't see me. I'm like an ostrich sticking its head in the sand, I thought. And then I thought about how silly it was that people believed that ostriches stick their heads in the sand. Even then, at the age of seven, I had read enough to know that ostriches did not do this. But they sometimes would lower their heads close to the ground when they were trying not to be seen.

"But they never stick their heads in the sand," I said out loud without thinking, caught up in my internal dialogue. I said it just loud enough to be heard.

"You say something?" said another voice from the direction of my ledge.

I almost jumped up when I heard that voice. It was Ricky Hamstead. He was twelve years old, with long arms and a look on his face that seemed to say he was ready for anything. He was a head taller than me. He used to come to my grandparents' store, until the day I saw him putting candy into his pockets when my grandfather's back was turned. Ricky saw that I had seen him. He put his finger up to his lips in a gesture asking for silence. Then he winked at me.

"Grampa," I said, "he's stealing stuff."

My grandfather had looked down at Ricky who, tall as he was, was still shorter than my grandfather. Then my grandfather had held out his hand, not saying a word. Ricky's face had turned beet red, and he had reached into his pocket, pulled out the bubble gum and jujubes he had taken, and put them in my grandfather's hand. He looked like he was waiting to get hit, but my grandfather just stood there with a disappointed look. Ricky had turned and run out the door, gotten on his bike, and pedaled away. Now whenever he went by on his bike and I was sitting out front, he would stare at me stone-faced or lift up one hand from his handlebars and point at me, and keep pointing as he went around the corner. I knew what he meant—he was going to get me.

"I said, gimme the straw," another voice answered, from a bit farther away. I recognized that voice too. It was Pauly Roffmeir, and he was even worse than Ricky. He'd been out to get me ever since I had seen him smoking a cigarette under our apple tree by the Mill Road. I had gone and told my grandmother, and she had called his mother and told her. It was two days before Pauly was allowed out again on his bike to do things with his friends, and I noticed that when he rode his bike past the station he did it standing, because it hurt too much to sit down. Not only did he hate me, he had told me he would break my neck if he ever caught me out from under my Grama's apron strings.

"No," Ricky said, "I thought I heard someone else."

"Forget it," Pauly said. "I got a big one. Gimme that straw now."

So then it was quiet, except for the pounding of my heartbeat that I was certain had to be loud enough for them to hear. I put my hands over my chest, trying to cover the sound that only seemed to grow louder. But the two boys were too busy with what they were doing.

"Look at him," Ricky said, laughing.

"Shoulda brought the BB gun. Bet he'd pop if we shot him now."

"Let's go get it," Ricky said. Then I heard them going again up the small trail of flat stones placed to make steps from the road down to my ledge. Their bike chains clanked, pebbles rattled, and I knew they were gone.

I came out from my hiding place and what I saw took all the fear out of me. Small as I was, if Pauly and Ricky had still been there I would have tried to break their necks. There, floating on his back in the pool, was my frog. The soda straw that they had used to fill his intestines with air was still sticking out of his backside. I knelt down, and as I did so an eddy in the water spun him toward me, and one of his eyes seemed to look up into mine as he weakly moved his legs. He was still trying to turn over and dive for safety to the bottom. I knew just what stone he wanted to hide beneath.

I picked him up and ran up the bank, ran across the field so fast that I didn't remember myself running or opening the door of the house. I was crying and looking for my grandfather and trying to talk all at the same time. I couldn't see clearly. I had lost my glasses when I came out from under the grapevines. Suddenly my grandfather was there in front of me, kneeling down.

I held up my frog, its body as bloated as an overinflated balloon. I wasn't even sure that it was still alive.

"Grampa," I said, "it was Ricky and Pauly. Why did they do it?"

My grandfather took the frog out of my hands. "They don't need no reason. Boys are jes' cussed mean, sometimes," he said.

He was looking carefully at the frog. I had pulled the straw loose. But it hadn't helped.

My grandfather went over to my grandmother's sewing box. "Sometimes," he said, "they does grow out of it. But some jes' stays cussed."

I was no longer crying. I leaned closer to see what he was doing. He had taken a long sharp needle out of the sewing box, and he was looking at the frog. One of its front legs moved. It was still alive.

Carefully he pricked the frog's belly with the needle. A single small drop of blood welled up around the needle as he slowly pressed it further in. The frog's distended belly began to shrink down. My grandfather turned the frog over and put it on the rug. It blinked its eyes and then made one weak hop.

"Frogs is tough," my grandfather said. "We kin take him

back now." He looked over his shoulder to make sure my grandmother was not anywhere she could see him, and then wiped the needle on his pants and stuck it back into her pincushion.

As we walked back toward the creek I saw two boys on bicycles disappearing down Mill Road, one of them with a Daisy air rifle over his shoulder. When we reached my spot Grampa handed me the frog, and then walked down the small trail to the ledge. My glasses were there, but the frames were bent and the lenses shattered. Someone had stomped on them and I knew who it was. My grandfather picked them up and put them into his pocket.

"Guess we'll be seein' Doc Boyle," he said. Doc Boyle was the optometrist who had fitted me for my first pair of glasses. I was his most regular seven-year-old customer.

Grampa climbed back up the bank. "Better take him up the crick where they won't get him."

Together we walked along Bell Brook, crossing Middle Grove Road and walking into the field that went behind the house where Mr. and Mrs. Komada lived. I was never allowed to cross Middle Grove Road alone, but I could do anything with my grandfather. We walked for what seemed to be hours, but with my short legs and the tall grass it was probably only a few minutes. At last we reached a part of the creek I'd never seen before. An old stone wall was built along next to it, and I could see where there had once been a dam of some sort. The pool of water in front of us was even deeper than the one by my ledge—and that pool by my ledge was deep, so deep that when I waded into it, it almost came up to my waist.

"Ought to be safe here," Grampa said.

We placed my frog down gently on the bank. He sat there for a few deep breaths, his sides moving in and out. Then he made one big hop into the clear, safe water of Bell Brook and dove down, his strong hind legs driving him down to the bottom, where he found a new rock to hide under.

My grandfather went down onto one knee next to me.

"Sonny," he said, "there ain't no need to tell your Grama about this. It'll jes' make her upset."

"But what about Ricky and Pauly? Their mothers ought to know what they did. Can we just let them get away with it?"

My grandfather took me by the hand and we walked silently back to the house. He hadn't answered my question by saying anything. Instead, as he did so often, he spoke to me without words. And as we walked that long way through the field, so long that I had to lift up my arms and have him carry me the last part of the way, I kept thinking about why I shouldn't tell. I couldn't understand why, but I knew my grandfather's silence was telling me that I should be silent myself.

Though there would be other times when I would run to my grandmother and let her know about the things I had seen the bigger boys do, I said nothing to her that day. I didn't want to upset her. That made me feel good, like I was taking care of her. Somehow, too, knowing what I knew and not telling it made me feel stronger. That night as I got into bed, with the covers tucked in tightly so that I would be safe, I thought about our frog there in a place where he too would be safe. I held that thought in my mind as calm as the water in that deep, clear pool.

"Good night," I called to my grandparents. "Sweet dreams, I love you!"

And then I slept peacefully in my bed.

RETURNING THE DRUM

In the spring of 1994, at the Second Annual Abenaki Heritage Days in Swanton, Vermont, something happened. They brought back the drum to this community known to the Abenaki people as Missisquoi, *the Flint Place, the second of the two northern places of refuge. There, on a day bright with sun, in the center of the airport field, the first public Missisquoi drum in many decades was played. Abenaki voices sang songs in our language, and people danced to songs that had not been heard in this way for a hundred years. They sang and drummed and people danced, joined by singers and dancers from the Canadian town of Odanak. These visitors had come down to symbolically reunite the two communities, which were separated by the borders of nations newer than the songs shared that day. My son Jesse was one of those who played that drum and sang those songs. As I listened, I remembered.*

The Christmas when I was four, my grandmother and grandfather gave me a drum. I hadn't been allowed to have one before and I loved it. It wasn't an "Indian drum," but the kind of drum that I had seen carried in parades. It was so big that I could barely put my arms around it. It was blue and had red and white stars painted on it. I sat for hour after hour, beating it with a drumstick. I offered it to my grandfather. I knew that he loved music. I had heard him play the Jew's harp and the harmonica that he always had in his shirt pockets. He had shown me the fiddle that he kept in a worn black case in the wardrobe in their bedroom. My grandfather took the drum and tapped out two double beats: one-two, one-two.

"You kin do it like that," he said. Then he handed me back the drum.

I don't recall what happened to that drum. Did it disappear when I took it with me on one of those weekend drives I had to take with my mother and father and my younger sister? I was afraid of those drives and I may have taken the drum with me, thinking it would protect me. Or is my memory of a large person crushing that drum under his foot only something I have imagined? Did I just misplace the drum or break it myself? I can't remember for certain, but I will never forget it. My grandfather showed me that my heart-beat was in that drum.

I do remember crying because my drum was gone. And I remember my grandfather picking me up, placing me on their bed, and taking out his fiddle case. He didn't say anything about either my drum or his fiddle. He just opened the case, rosined up the bow, and began to play. I listened and I am still listening.

My grandfather was not one to brag about the things he could do. But if he said he could do something, he would do it. I remember the day when a group of men was in the store. They were men who worked the woods, and they were bragging about how good they were at logging.

"Why, I'll tell you what I can do," Lester Smith said. Lester was the kind of thoughtless, bigmouthed man that people called a blowhard. But since he was six feet tall with a chest like a barrel, few people ever made him back up his words. The muscles on his arms were so big they looked like balloons. "I can drop a tree right onto a stake and drive it into the ground. I'll bet you couldn't do that, you old nigger."

His words were addressed to my grandfather, and even though I was not more than eight years old, I felt the ripple of tension that went around the room when that last word was spoken. My dark-skinned grandfather didn't like to hear such things said—not to him or about anyone else.

Chairs scraped back on the linoleum floor and one or two people coughed nervously in the silence that filled the room.

My grandfather lifted up his head and stared at Lester Smith, who looked to be at least twice his size. Then Grampa spoke. "Ten dollars says I kin drive a stake with a tree before you kin."

"Well, that's a bet then!" said Lester Smith.

But my grandfather wasn't finished. "No saws," he said. "We cut them trees with an ax."

As Lester Smith went out to his truck to fetch his ax, my grandfather took his double-bitted ax out of the cellarway, where it hung next to the old two-man crosscut saw. By now my grandmother had caught on that something was in the wind, and she came out of the house where she had been fixing dinner. But she didn't say anything. She just stood there with her hands in her apron, watching. She nodded as my grandfather pulled down the lever on the cash register and, as the bell rang and the cash drawer slid out, pulled out a crisp ten-dollar bill.

"Be right back," he said, putting the ten-dollar bill into his pocket.

"I'll watch the station," she said.

Grampa went over to the grindstone and stepped on the treadle that made it spin. There was a Coke bottle filled with water hung above it, and he wet the stone good before touching the blade to it. Sparks flew as he moved the blade back and forth. But he only sharpened one side of the double-bitted ax. I understood that. He had explained it to me when I was very small.

"One side is fer cuttin', the other side is fer limbin'."

The wood lot, where Grampa had been thinning out some trees that we'd use for firewood, was behind the house. Grampa led the small circle of men, which had grown larger while he was sharpening his ax, back to the trees. He slapped his hand against first one tree and then another thirty paces away. Both were at the edge of the wood lot and could be felled into the field.

"Pick yer tree," he said to Lester Smith.

Lester Smith stepped back, eyeing one tree and then the other.

"This 'un'll do," he said.

"Set yer stake," Grampa said, holding out one of the three-foot lengths of one-by-twos that he had picked up from his shed as he started toward the field. But before Lester could turn away, my grandfather poked him in the chest with the second of those stakes. "Might as well set mine while yer at it."

Lester Smith eyed my grandfather much as he had eyed those trees, but he took the stake and walked off twenty paces with it, a little smile showing on the edge of his mouth.

My grandfather looked down at me and then nodded his chin toward Lester Smith, who was walking out into the field at an angle away from the tree my grandfather was to cut. I could see that the big man was going to set the stake away from the natural lean of the tree, making it harder to hit.

My grandfather reached into his pocket and handed the ten-dollar bill to Jim Rollins. "You want to hold this?" he said. "Be sure and get his ten too."

Jim Rollins took the money and then walked out to Lester

Smith, who was setting his own stake now, placing it right under the lean of the tree he had chosen. I couldn't hear what they said, but I saw Lester Smith wave his arms and shake his head twice before finally reaching into his pocket and pulling out his wallet.

When Lester Smith walked back to take his place by his tree, I looked closely at him and at my grandfather. Not only was he twice as big as my grandfather, he was less than half my grandfather's age. Where my grandfather's hair was gray, Lester Smith's was bright red. He wore the boots and the flannel shirt of a woodsman, and my grandfather had on a pair of comfortable old deerskin moccasins and a green short-sleeved shirt. You could see the bones in my grandfather's sinewy arms, while Lester Smith's were as packed with flesh as huge sausages.

"Say when," my grandfather said.

Lester Smith spat on his hands and took a grip. My grandfather waited, leaning on his ax. Lester Smith smiled and made as if he was about to turn away from the tree and pick something up. But as he leaned over, he suddenly shouted "When!" and swung his ax into the tree, trying to get a jump on my grandfather.

Whack! went Lester Smith's ax. Whack! Whack! Whack! He was swinging as fast as blue blazes, bringing every stroke up from his heels—until the fourth blow, when his ax wedged itself into the tree and he had to put his foot against the trunk to lever it free.

My grandfather, though, started slower. He looked the tree up and down, walked around it, and then stepped in front of it to cut out a wedge. Whump-whump, whump-whump, whump-whump, whump-whump. With an easy rhythm, hitting above, hitting below, he cut out a wedge at the front of the tree, angled just a bit to the left. It looked as smooth as a cut made by a saw. Then he stopped, squatted down, put a small straight stick into that wedge, and sighted along it toward the stake. Meanwhile Lester Smith had gotten his ax stuck for the second time. I noticed it because the sound of his puffing breath was replaced by language which could only be described as colorful.

Now my grandfather was cutting at the back of the tree. Whump-whump, whump-whump. Those double strokes had a rhythm to them, a music that I felt in my blood. Remembering them now I realize they were like the deep, slow beats of a big drum. The tree began to quiver, like a horse standing in its traces and ready to go at the command of "Giddyap!"

But Lester Smith had almost cut through his tree now, despite the fact that he had gotten his ax stuck half a dozen times. He swung one last hard stroke that went clear through the tree, which pulled Lester's Smith's ax right out of his hand as it hopped off the stump, balanced for a moment, and began to fall, twisting as it toppled.

My grandfather's tree fell at the same time. It went down with the same swift ease of his ax striking into the trunk. It fell as if it had been asked to fall and was showing its agreement. The wedge in its trunk caused it to swing hard to the left as it went down, and it fell straight onto the stake, driving it straight into the earth.

I looked over toward Lester Smith. He was staring at the tree he had cut. Then he kicked it hard, and immediately began to hop on one foot because he had broken his big toe. His tree had fallen a good twenty feet to the left of the stake he'd set.

With a broad smile on his face, Jim Rollins walked over to hand my grandfather the twenty dollars.

When the Catholics took the drum away from the Abenaki people at Odanak, the Abenakis took up the rattle in its place. They kept the old songs and the dances, but they sang them more softly and they danced to the rattle's rhythm. The sound of a rattle would not carry far in the night when people gathered to do the Snake Dance or the Friendship Dance. And you could conceal a rattle in your clothing when you were on your way to a dance. It was hard to hide the shape or the sound of the drum.

Among the Missisquoi Abenakis at Swanton, the fiddle played an important role. Some said that the fiddle took the place of the drum, but it wasn't exactly that way. The drum wasn't lost at Swanton, it was just kept hidden. Two generations ago, if the Abenakis at Swanton got out a drum and played it at night, the neighbors would hear it and call the state police. But by the time the state police arrived, all they would find would be a fiddle player and a bunch of people square dancing. The fiddle helped them hide the drum, it helped them hide what they knew and who they were from a world that was hostile to the heartbeat rhythm connecting the generations to the earth and to the old ones.

I remember the last time my grandfather played his fiddle. It was when I was seventeen, the year after my grandmother died. I walked into my grandfather's bedroom and sat on their bed.

"Grampa," I said, "I can't remember when I last heard you play your fiddle."

He didn't say anything. He just bent down and picked up the case. He placed it on the bed and took the fiddle out. The bow was already rosined and, though he plucked the strings to check, it was in perfect tune. He held the fiddle up to his chin and then tapped the strings with the bow four times, making them sing a double beat— plong-plong, plong-plong. *Then, before that harmonic echo died away, he swung down the bow and began to play. His right arm moved with an ease that I've seen in few fiddle players other than Lawrence Older, our neighbor in the nearby town of Middle Grove, whose songs are still sung by Pete Seeger. The sound of "She'll Be*

Comin' Round the Mountain" flowed into "Turkey in the Straw," and then became a song I couldn't recognize. Its tempo was different, and I would not hear it again for another thirty-four years, not until a bright spring day when people gathered in a circle in an airfield in Vermont.

Then, as quickly as he had started, my grandfather stopped. He took the fiddle out from under his chin, nodded once, and returned it to its case, leaving me another memory.

ASH

My grandfather's parents pounded ash. Black ash, the basket tree. A ten-foot or twelve-foot length, the base log of a hundred-year-old tree, would be stripped of bark and laid down on the ground. Then, using the flat-headed side of a splitting maul, my great-grandfather Lewis Bowman would go along the tree, striking it to loosen the seasonal rings, to lift up the ashwood splints that would be split and thinned and trimmed and then woven into baskets.

I have dreamed of my great-grandfather, seen him looking much as he does in the picture on my wall, a straight old man with a bushy white mustache, wearing an old suit coat and standing next to a big stone. In my dream he holds the maul and strikes the log— bum-bum-a-bum. Two blows forward and then one back, so that the rings lift up evenly. A music that fills the woods and echoes off the hills. He does it without great force, swinging the maul so that its weight and its momentum do most of the work. Letting his tools work with him. Just as his sons learned to do.

"You can't force yer hoe to do nothin'," my grandfather said to me as we worked in his garden, showing me how to chop weeds so that my small hands wouldn't blister. "Jes' hold it tight enough, not too tight. Don't make it work, let it work with you."

*And though I never saw my grandfather pound ash—for the
making of baskets was an Indian thing, best left behind—I have
seen other Abenaki men doing it, and I have recognized my grandfather's easy, economical motions in their actions. Maurice Dennis.
Fred Watso. Never moving with violence, always with care. With respect, coaxing the tree to give up its splints to be made into baskets.*

*The Abenaki people of Maine, the people known as the Penob-
scot and the Passamaquoddy, long ago made an agreement with the
Commonwealth of Massachusetts. No matter who owned the land,
they had the right to the ash trees. And that was as it should be.*

It is said that the technique for making splint baskets was intro-
duced to the Abenaki by the Europeans sometime more than a
hundred years ago. But other kinds of baskets were always
made: baskets of birch bark, folded and sewn with spruce root,
baskets of woven basswood bark. Baskets that were used to
carry those things that carried a culture, baskets that carried the
culture itself. Baskets like those my grandparents had on
shelves in the house and on our porch, baskets so tough that
they were still pliable and strong half a century after their
making.

Splinterville Hill, where the tall house of my grandparents
stood, was given its name not just for the plank road that ran
past it. It was also said that the name came from the splint factory that once stood on Mill Road just behind my grandparents'
house. The factory, owned by my grandmother's parents, was
long gone by the time I was born. There baskets were made,
mostly by women, made in the way which had been popular-
ized by the Mohawk and Abenaki people who came each summer to camp in Congress Park in Saratoga Springs. That factory
could sell baskets cheaper than those that were Indian-crafted.
The women who made those baskets, their hands moving
swiftly even when the sharp edges of ash splints cut their fin-

gers, were paid per basket and paid only pennies for their work. Most of those women were not Indian, or if they were they would have denied it.

Across the street from my grandfather's general store was another gas station and general store. Rocky Rayburn ran it, and he and his wife Tootsie were my grandparents' business rivals. Rocky was also a mechanic—unlike my grandfather, who limited his automotive work to fixing flats and changing the oil. Although Grampa always said with a smile, "As long as it kin be fixed with a hammer, Rocky's the man to do it."

Just up the hill from Rayburns' was an open field. That field had once held my great-grandfather's cider mill—before Bill Mayer burned it down. And before the cider mill was there, there had been a little house in the early 1800's owned by a man named Sam Hill.

Sam was Abenaki, a basket maker who was well over six feet tall and weighed close to three hundred pounds. Once a week in the summer he would take the baskets he'd made, tie them together, and fasten them onto himself, so that he became a giant walking mound of baskets. He'd walk the three miles to Saratoga and then go down Broadway, stopping at each of the great hotels, hotels such as the Grand Union or Congress Hall, where the well-off tourists sat on the open verandahs looking out over the street. They were the customers for his baskets and they'd look for Sam Hill to show up, regular as clockwork, each Saturday morning. Sam wore an old suit someone had given him that had more patches on it than regular cloth, and he was truly a sight to behold. When local folks said "You look like Sam Hill" to describe someone's rough, disheveled look, or "Where the Sam Hill is he?" they had our Sam Hill in mind.

Sam's cabin was burned down after he died, leaving ashes where once ash baskets had been made. And another building was built on its site, which would itself one day return to ash.

Ash trees grew all around my grandparents' home. I remember watching the seeds of the ash spinning down from those tall trees, whirring through the air like detached airplane propellers. Sometimes they would land next to the foundation of the house and stick in the soft earth, which was gray and gritty, sparkling with green pieces of melted glass from the heat of the fire set to kill my great-grandparents. To this day I can still dig into the earth there and find melted white and green and blue pieces of glass from the windows and the bottles, the vases and the cut-glass pitchers that stood in the windows on that side of a home that became an inferno.

Bill Mayer was a man who let no one stand in his way. My great-uncle Jack Bowman, Jesse's younger brother, told me about Bill Mayer. From the tone of his voice, that memory of events fifty years gone was still as fresh and painful as if it were only yesterday.

Mayer was a railroad detective and carried two pearl-handled revolvers. He was a thief, and a bold one. One time he pulled his wagon up to the coal car of a train, pulled out those revolvers, and ordered the workers to fill his wagon with coal. When they were done, he holstered the guns and drove the wagon off to dump the coal in his own yard and sell it. In the Prohibition years of the twenties a man like Mayer could make a good bit of money at various trades—including rum-running for the likes of Dutch Schultz, who spent more than one summer at Saratoga. Yet even as a rumrunner Bill Mayer was a thief, kicking off barrels of whiskey to be picked up by his brothers as he came down from Canada. Not many people would want to go up against a man who could steal from Dutch Schultz and never be called to question.

My grandmother's parents, Edward and Flora Marion Dunham, were well-off. They had a farm, an apple orchard and a cider mill, wood lots and a sawmill. My grandfather Jesse and his brother Jack worked for them. One or the other could usually be seen driving their wagon—which had painted on its side the words DUNHAM'S SLABS AND CIDER, LOGS AND LUMBER.

It was the early 1920's. My grandmother's parents had long ago given up on breaking up the romance that had developed

My great-grandparents, Ed and Flora Dunham,
with my mother, Marion Flora Dunham, at age eleven

between their semiliterate, swarthy hired hand and their daughter, Marion Edna, a graduate of the Skidmore School of Arts and the Albany Law School. Sending her to Virginia to stay with her brother, who worked running a hotel in Warm Springs, had not been a success. Jesse had followed her there and taken a job as a stevedore—was hired, in fact, by her brother—and when my grandmother had returned home to Greenfield she had brought him with her.

My grandmother's determination was legendary. Even the fact that my grandfather had already been married didn't stand in her way. In a sense, that marriage hadn't been a real one. According to one family story, Jesse had married his younger brother's girlfriend because she was "in the family way." Jack was too young to get married, and that way the child would have the Bowman name. My grandmother used her knowledge of law and had the marriage annulled, so that she and Jesse could be wed. The Dunhams were known to be stubborn in general. Stubbornness had to run in a family that could claim descent from the *Mayflower* when the only recorded Dunham aboard that sainted ship was an unmarried man—with no children—who died on the voyage before reaching America.

It was the Dunham stubbornness that led to the problem with Bill Mayer. One day he bought a load of cider from Ed Dunham, even though the cider had gone hard and Ed was about to dump it. When Ed told his wife, as he was giving her the money—something Ed did every night—she gave him a hard look. It was the look of a staunch member of the Woman's Christian Temperance Union.

"Edward," she said, "you know what that man is going to do with that hard cider."

Ed knew, even though he didn't want to say it.

"He is going to use it to make bootleg liquor," Flora Marion Dunham said. "You know what you must do."

Ed knew, but just to make sure that he did, my great-grandmother told him.

"You are going straight to the sheriff to tell him about this."

"Yes, Mother," Ed said, and he went to the sheriff.

It was one of the two times in his life when Bill Mayer found himself called into court with a man who dared to testify against him. The fine that Bill Mayer paid was a small one, but that was of little importance to him. He threatened my great-grandfather. No one was going to be allowed to get away with squealing on Bill Mayer.

The December day after that fine was paid, the collie dogs disappeared from the backyard of my great-grandparents' house. My grandfather found them in the creek, frozen into the ice. The strychnine in the meat that had been tossed to them had made them crazy with thirst, and they had broken through the ice to get water. One of the dogs, King, was dead, and the other would have died had my grandfather not broken up half-burnt pieces of wood from the stove and forced them down Lady's throat. The charcoal absorbed the poison and Lady lived another six years, though she lay close to death next to the woodstove in the little henhouse out back for many days.

And then more things began to happen. As my great-grandparents readied themselves for bed one night, Ed Dunham heard a familiar clicking sound, the sound of a hammer being drawn back on a rifle outside. He pulled Flora Marion down to the floor, and the bullet that shattered their bedroom window passed over their heads and buried itself in the wall. The following spring, the Volunteer Fire Department was too late to save their sawmill when it burned to the ground, so soaked with gasoline that nothing could save it. The cider mill was burned down too.

In the summer of 1923, their fences were cut and every one of their cows was shot dead in the pasture. One morning in August, my grandfather went out to hitch up Starbaby Lee, my grandmother's favorite horse. She was gone. He found her a day later, out in the field with her throat cut.

They spoke to the sheriff and to the state police. Everyone in Greenfield knew that it was the work of the Mayer boys, but vengeance on this scale was so staggering that no one—not even the men in the uniforms of the law—wanted to take it on themselves to make an accusation. And there was no evidence and no witnesses. Jesse and Jack Bowman kept watch over the house day and night now, and for a time nothing happened. Perhaps the Mayer boys felt that the score had been evened.

But then one night when Jack was away, Jesse woke up just before dawn and smelled smoke. There was no time to do anything except to pull the women of the house out of bed and hurry them downstairs, out across the porch and into the road to safety. Jesse and Ed threw a few things out of the windows to save them. My mother still owns a green glass pitcher that has a crack in its handle from being thrown out onto the lawn. Few things were saved, and the house was burned to the ground.

The neighbors took in my great-grandparents and my grandmother. My grandfather disappeared into the night. Someone told me that he was holding the old .303 deer rifle that he kept in the barn, and that they saw him heading up Middle Grove toward Grange Road and the Mayer farm. There was a grim look on his face.

"Your grandfather never liked to kill anything," my mother once said to me. "He wouldn't even chop the head off a chicken. Your grandmother had to do that."

And this was so. My grandfather was a man known for his gentleness, a gentleness that showed itself the most with children and animals, with all living things smaller and weaker than he was. But in that gentleness was a streak of real fierceness when it came to defending those weaker ones and those he loved.

Bill Mayer had meant to kill my great-grandparents; he meant to do nothing less than that. He had killed other men who had crossed him before, though their bodies had not been found and, as always, no charges had been filed. One of those men had been a younger brother of my grandfather. He had seen Bill Mayer with a load of stolen furniture and made the mistake of telling the police.

It was, as my uncle Jack told me years later, certain sure that Mayer wanted all the Dunhams dead. Yet after that fire that failed to take their lives, there were no more attacks. They were impoverished, and dependent now upon a man they had once deemed too low for their daughter to marry, but Ed and Flora Dunham were never bothered for the remaining years of their lives.

And though I cannot say that I know for sure, I have seen it in my dreams more than once. I have seen it as I've held a handful of those ashes from the old house and looked at the strong new house my grandfather built on the old one's foundation. In that dream my grandfather stands as tall and as straight as an ash tree on the lawn in front of the Mayer house. He holds that deer rifle in his hands, a shell jacked into the chamber. Then he calls the name.

"Bill Mayer!"

He calls it only once and his voice is soft, but the house in front of him trembles at his words.

Bill Mayer comes out of his front door. The sneer on his face melts away when he sees the look my grandfather gives him.

"You've done all yer going to do," my grandfather says.

Bill Mayer starts to talk, but it is as if his mouth is frozen shut. He is like the men in the old Abenaki stories who are confronted by a m'teowlin, a man of power. The m'teowlin speaks one word and they are turned into stone.

"Yer family is done on this land," my grandfather says in my dream, and then he turns and walks back into the night.

For that was how it was. Bill Mayer and his brothers died bitter deaths, leaving no children to carry their name. Their two sisters were left alone in that house, gray old maids in a gray building, until at last they sold their farm and lived out their few remaining days in the Home of the Good Shepherd.

The last of the Mayer family, Anthony Mayer, ran the family fuel business in Saratoga Springs, living like a hermit in a little shack near the piles of coal and the oil tanks until the day he was murdered by two young men. They thought he had money hidden everywhere. They tortured and killed him for it, but they found no money. And the Mayer name was blown away, the way a wind that sways the branches of a tall ash tree scatters the ashes from a fire.

GOING SOUTH

My son Jim and my sister Marge told me a story about their journey by canoe to return the remains of the Abenaki old ones to their ancestral home. One of those old ones appeared to have been a shaman. A tall man, he wore wrapped around his waist the long skeleton of a snake. And though he had gone into the ground thousands of years ago, the leather medicine pouch that was hung about his neck held the skeletons of three more snakes of different kinds.

Those on that hundred-mile journey took to calling him Snake Man. Those who rode in the canoe that carried him knew he was there. He made his presence known to them and at times, my sister said, she felt as if he were probing each of them, testing them to see if they were up to the task, almost like a man saddling up a horse to carry him on a journey home.

The old ones are like that.

Though he sometimes showed his emotions—especially to those he loved—more clearly than any other man I ever knew, my grandfather was also a person of strength. And like Pudgie, his fox terrier, his defense of his home and those he cared for could be fierce. If someone tried to push him around or to take advantage of someone smaller, my grandfather would never take a backward step; and when someone hit the ground, it seemed that person was never Jess Bowman.

"I jes' had to take ahold of him," my grandfather would say, in eloquently simple explanation.

He was the right kind of man to live with a strong woman. I cannot remember him ever telling my grandmother "no." Whatever she chose to do, he was always there behind her. His deference to her intelligence sometimes made people wonder why a woman with so much education and so much promise had chosen to saddle herself with a man like him. Some, who never saw the two of them alone together as I did, even thought my grandmother was simply using him, or that their marriage had only been the result of some other thwarted romance and that she had chosen him on the rebound. But that was not true at all.

Even as an old man, my grandfather was beautiful in that way which some men who are close to the land and share its integrity can be beautiful. Women were always attracted to him. He had the rough, strong grace of a well cared for work-horse. His features were clean, and his eyes always shone with a brightness and a sort of mischief that let anyone know there would never be any dullness when you were around Jess Bowman. In the one picture I saw of him as a broad-shouldered young man in his twenties, his hair was raven black and his dark good looks were like those of a movie star, a backwoods Valentino. He was five feet nine inches tall and two hundred pounds in weight. I imagine him working as a hired man for my grandmother's parents and I see my grandmother watching him, watching the ripple of muscles on his sweaty back as he loads a wagon or splits wood, watching him as he handles a horse with that certainty he never lost, even in his eighties.

One day when I was eight, he and I went together to the

My grandparents with my mother in 1923

Ballston County Fair. Going to fairs was something we all loved and there was a whole round of them that we visited every late summer and early fall, from Schaghticoke to Schuylerville. It was the smells of hot dogs, cotton candy, candied apples, and popcorn from the midway, and the sounds of music and creaking metal from the Ferris wheel and the Tilt-A-Whirl that attracted me the most. That mixture of allure and nausea makes me taste those fairs in my mouth and feel them in my stomach.

What my grandfather liked best, though, were the animals. Not just looking at them either. He would call them up to the fences, lean over and pat them, feel their coats, let them nuzzle his face. Whether it was goats or cows, pigs or sheep or horses, my grandfather related to them more as long-lost friends than creatures on exhibit. Especially the horses.

That one day we were walking by the corral for a horse show, in which horses were being judged. A girl in her teens was leading a big red stallion. She was doing just fine until something spooked it. The stallion whickered and then reared up, pulling her off her feet. Its front hooves pawed the air like a fighter getting ready to throw a haymaker. People in the crowd yelled. They could see the girl was going to get badly hurt by the big, scared horse.

Instead of yelling, my grandfather went through the fence as quick as a weasel into a henhouse. Moving faster than I'd ever seen anyone move before, he reached the girl and her horse in two shakes of a lamb's tail. He leaped up, grabbed the bridle, and pulled that horse back down onto its four feet. Somehow he had gotten his face right next to its ear and his arm around its nose, and he was talking to it. You could see the tension go out of the horse's body. Slowly my grandfather let go of his hold and began to stroke the horse's neck.

Then, without saying a word to her, he handed back the reins to the girl and left the arena.

People were shouting and some were applauding, but my grandfather ignored them as he came right over to my side. I waited for him to say something, but he didn't. He just took my hand and turned around to watch the rest of the show.

"How did you and Grama get together?" I said to my grandfather one day.

The smile that came over his face was so broad that it seemed as if his whole body was going to break into laughter, and it took a while for him to speak.

"I was working fer them," he said at last, "and she jes' set her mind on it."

Then he did laugh. "But they didn't like it none."

And indeed the Dunhams did not. They liked it so little that they thought of firing my grandfather. But finding another hired man as good as Jesse Bowman was hard to imagine. So they sent my grandmother off instead. In those days, a young woman in her early twenties generally could be counted on to do what her parents told her, and so my grandmother went.

Of course she was sent off to family, the most distant family they could find. My grandmother's older brother Orvis had a good job in Virginia, working as a sort of manager at the Homestead Hotel in Warm Springs. That was where she went, a dutiful daughter. But before she left, she spoke to my grandfather.

"Tole me she expected me to meet her there," he said.

So, only a few days after my grandmother came to Warm Springs, Virginia, my grandfather arrived there too. He ended up being hired to work at the hotel. Too light-skinned and too unsophisticated to join the staff of African-American hotel waiters, too dark-skinned and too uneducated to work out front where he might be seen, he was given work down back as a teamster and as one of the men who loaded and unloaded the supplies for the kitchen.

"There was this Eye-talian, Mr. DiMaria, who was in charge of the crew," my grandfather said. "He was a good old man, and he always called me his Jess."

When they unloaded the wagons, the things for the kitchen, which was two stories up, were placed in a small elevator, just big enough to carry a few hundred pounds. You had to lean into it to load it up, and then close the gate and press the button to make it go. It was in the early days of elevators and that one was always malfunctioning. Sometimes it would work and sometimes it wouldn't, and when it did go it took off with a jerk.

One day my grandfather carried a whole pig over, to drop it onto the bed of the elevator. For some reason the safety switch didn't work and the elevator took off with a jerk, catching my grandfather just as he had bent over with his heavy load, so that his arms were trapped under the dead weight of the pig. To the horror of the men in the yard, the elevator lifted my grandfather out of sight, half on and half off the platform, scraped up between walls that allowed a clearance of no more than eight inches between the elevator and the shaft.

"My Jess," Mr. DiMaria shouted. "Dey kill my Jess!" He went up the stairs three at a time, reaching the first floor before the elevator reached it. My grandfather's bloody shoulders and back rose into view, his shirt nearly torn off. Mr. DiMaria grabbed him and pulled him free as the elevator continued to rise up toward the next floor, where the shaft narrowed further still and my grandfather would surely have been killed.

"It jes' about did kill me," my grandfather told me many years later. "My ribs was stove in and my legs was bad hurt. They wasn't sure I was even goin' to keep on breathin'."

But he did keep breathing, and though for days he swam in and out of dark realms of half-consciousness and pain, and it was weeks until he could walk again, he recovered. And during

Uncle Orvis's Warm Springs Inn, Virginia, in 1949

that time of convalescence my grandmother was always there by his bedside whenever he woke from his fever. It was in those weeks, I believe, that what might have only been infatuation, at first, grew into the kind of a love that the years never diminished.

It might be an exaggeration to say that her brother Orvis was in cahoots with my grandmother to thwart their parents' attempt to save the family name. It might be more accurate to say that he knew her well enough to know that when she set her mind to something, it would take hell and high water for anything to change it. I noticed something years later, when we would make our annual spring trip south to visit Warm Springs, and spend a few days as Orvis's guest in the little inn he owned and ran for decades after leaving the big hotel. On those trips—which invariably led through the Delaware Water Gap and the Gettysburg Battlefield, Washington, D.C., and the Blue Ridge Parkway—my grandfather seldom came along. He had to stay and watch the station, he said. That was all.

But what I had noticed those few springs when my grandfather did travel with us to Virginia, was that when Grampa Jesse was along, Uncle Orvis always lodged us in the basement room next to the boiler.

TO MAKE ENDS MEET

Carol and I were driving down a back road a few miles below Ballston Spa. It was late June. We both saw the hand-lettered sign that read BERRIES. We pulled over into a farmhouse driveway where a table in a small shed was covered with boxes of ripe strawberries. No one was around. We waited a while, but no one came out of the farmhouse. There was a note, though, obviously written by the same hand that had lettered the sign by the road. It was tacked to the table with the strawberries, next to an open cash box. Inside the box was a small stack of one-dollar bills.

BERRIES ARE $2 A BOX, read the note.

Carol and I looked at each other and smiled.

"It used to be like this everywhere," I said. "My grandmother always used to say that trusting might not make so much money, but you slept better at night."

We placed six dollars in the box, but we took only two boxes of berries. An extra two dollars might help them make ends meet.

It was not easy to make ends meet when you ran a general store the way my grandparents did. Years later I would look through the neat books kept by my grandmother in the late

1940's and early 1950's. On one side in each black-covered book with two columns for income and expenses, she would itemize the daily expenses for things such as gasoline from Congress Gas and Oil, candy from Finkel's, bread delivery from Freihofer's, milk from Hall's Dairy, and soda pop from the Coca-Cola man—who (as I would learn years later) was Howard Bowman, the son of my grandfather's brother Jack. On the other side she would list the day's income, usually a bit more than the outgo, but not by much. It was only when I looked into the other book, the one in which they kept the charge accounts, that I saw where the profits were kept—or lost.

There were never fewer than thirty people with running accounts for gas and groceries. "Gas—$6," it would read, or "Groceries—$4.50." Sometimes it would just list an amount and not indicate any purchase. In those cases it meant that someone had come by the station with no money at all, so my grandparents had loaned them a few dollars. Perhaps half the people with charge accounts paid their bills monthly. Another quarter of them, people who worked the woods or farmed, those whose incomes were not regular, would settle up when they could—sometimes only two or three times a year. The remaining quarter were the deadbeats, those who could be trusted to pay at most only a few dollars now and then and who never cleared their accounts. My grandparents knew just who those people were. I often heard them talking about them.

"That Smiley, he jes' ain't ever going to pay up," my grandfather might say.

"I believe you are right," my grandmother would agree.

But the next time Smiley showed up, my grandfather would just trust him again.

When I was old enough to watch the station, Grama would sometimes tell me, "Now if this particular person comes and wants to get gas or groceries, you tell him it has to be cash."

I would nod my agreement, knowing just what her words meant. They meant that if that particular person showed up when she was not around, either shopping or working in her garden in the lower yard, I was to get to him before my grandfather did. If Grampa were to wait on him it would be as it was with everyone as far as Grampa was concerned. No questions asked, and pay when you can.

So Grampa went out to work again for the county. He worked the road crews, and in those days—when the men on the job did "by guess and by gosh" much of the work that an engineer would outline on a blueprint today—my grandfather was a valued man. He could lay out a road so that it had a perfect slope from its center on down to either side, was banked just right on a curve, and had perfect drainage. And if there were trees to cut along the way, it was Jesse who handled the ax or was in charge of the crosscut saw.

One afternoon my grandfather came home early. I heard the side door that led into the kitchen past the cellar stairs open and close, as I sat back in my room reading one of the *Smiling Pool* books. My grandmother had just picked me up at school.

I was in third grade and had been switched for that year to School One. It was ten blocks away from School Two, where my head had been cracked open a year before on the school wall. I didn't know why I had been transferred. Such things just didn't happen in those days. When you started in one grade school you went there from kindergarten to eighth grade, unless your parents moved out of town. It was only a long time later that I learned about the visit my grandmother paid to the principal of School Two, and then later to the entire school board, the day after I had been beaten up. I no longer even rode the school bus. Each morning either Grampa or Grama would drive me in. Each afternoon their old blue Plymouth would be waiting at the curb in front of the buses, my grandmother behind the wheel.

My grandmother was in the kitchen cooking, so I didn't get up to greet my grandfather right away. I had come to a part in the book where my favorite character, Little Joe Otter, was teasing Reddy Fox. But I dropped the book when I heard Grama's voice.

"Oh my Lord, Jesse!" she said. "What have you gone and done?"

Something in the tone of her voice frightened me more than her words. I froze for a moment, unable to move. I held the book tight in my left hand, nervously tore off the bottom corner of one of the pages, and stuck it in my mouth. Somehow I had developed a taste for books in more ways than one. All my favorite books had the bottom corners torn off every page, though I was careful to take only the part of the page that was well below the last line of print. Then I dropped the book and scrambled off the bed.

The first thing I saw as I rounded the corner to the kitchen was the open cellar door, and the trail of blood that led up the steps into the kitchen and onto the floor. Then I saw my grandfather. He was sitting in the middle of the kitchen on one of the old wooden chairs, his back to the sink where my grandmother was running hot water into a pan. His face was calm, even a little amused, but a handkerchief soaked crimson lay on the linoleum next to his feet, and he was holding a towel to the right side of his head just above his ear. Pudgie was sitting on his lap and licking his hand as my grandfather absentmindedly petted her.

My grandmother turned from the sink and looked at me. She looked very unhappy, but it was the kind of unhappiness that reassured me. It was not a look of fear. It was the look she got when someone did something she didn't approve of—the "Someone is going to hear about this!" look.

"Sonny," she said, her voice clipped, "go and get some of those old towels from the bathroom, the ones under the sink."

I ran to do as she said. There was no downstairs bathroom in our house in those days, and you had to go upstairs to use the toilet or take a bath. Since we took in tourists in the summer, mostly the same people every year who came for the racing season at the Saratoga track, we had to have a bathroom upstairs. But because it was for the guests, Grama and Grampa seldom used it. My grandparents kept a chamber pot in the corner of their bedroom for those "nighttime calls" that couldn't wait. After I'd turned seven, it was my unpleasant job to carry that sloshing chamber pot out each morning and dump it in the men's room toilet. (It was only after my grandmother's death in my sixteenth year that I realized that I had been the second generation to have the onerous and odorous task of "emptying the pee pot." The day after my grandmother died, my mother walked into their bedroom with a set look on her grieving face, picked up the chamber pot, and carried it down to the woods, where she smashed it into a hundred pieces.)

Even during the day my grandparents would go out to the men's room and the women's room of the station, rather than going upstairs. It wasn't as much of a climb to go out to use the toilet in the station for my grandmother, whose weight made the steep stairs hard for her. My grandfather just plain preferred the men's room. Out there he could sneak a cigarette—for my grandmother had forbidden him ever to smoke them. Grampa was allowed to have his briar pipe, but Grama restricted the use of it to the outdoors. Although we sold cigarettes in the station, my grandmother was convinced that they were unhealthy and considered our selling them somewhat morally suspect. However, the fact that we never sold beer—despite the many people who came asking for it—helped restore the moral equilibrium that the selling of smokes slightly unbalanced.

Grampa also liked that men's room because he could open the door a crack as he sat there and look down the road. He'd do that on the coldest winter days. I would look out the window and see a white cloud of breath—maybe thickened whiter by a bit of smoke from a Lucky Strike—coming through the slightly opened door, and know that Grampa was out there. He'd been raised in the country, and after decades of using an outhouse, he didn't like the thought of using a bathroom with no outside view and no fresh air.

And so, as my grandfather sat bleeding in the kitchen, I ran up the stairs to the bathroom in such a hurry that I stumbled twice. I grabbed as many towels as I could carry and went down the stairs two steps at a time, holding on to the wooden rail to keep from falling, and leaving a trail of towels behind me as I skidded into the kitchen. My grandfather was still sitting there, still smiling that little smile and holding the towel, but the blood had soaked through it already in the short time I was gone.

My grandmother took one of the towels from my trembling hands, pried the bloody one from Grampa's grasp, and dropped it into the pan in the sink. I could see the six-inch-long gash, like a red second mouth, opened up high on the side of his head above his ear. Then my grandmother pressed the towel to it, took my grandfather's hand, and placed it up there to hold it in place.

"I had to take ahold of him, Marion," he said.

"I know you did, Jesse," my grandmother answered.

"Is Grampa going to be all right?" I said. There must have been something more frightened in my voice than I had intended, for they looked at me with the same look they gave me those nights when I was a very small child and cried in my sleep, and woke to find them both standing over my bed.

"Wull, I'm all right, Sonny," said my grandfather. His smile grew broader then, and he actually chuckled. "You jes' ought to see the other fella."

"Jesse!" Grama poked him in his shoulder, but she did so in a way that had a kind of fondness to it. Even then, as a child, I could see that.

"It's a bad enough cut. . . ." my grandmother said.

"Tried to scalp me with that shovel," Grampa broke in, laughing out loud as he said it.

My grandmother poked him harder, and he shut up.

"It's going to need stitches," Grama continued. "I've called Doc Magovern. He'll be right out."

Doc Magovern was our family doctor. He had delivered me, and the sight of him entering our door with his black bag that smelled of leather and antiseptic alcohol was always one of the reassuring moments of my childhood. It was a moment in which we always thought, "Everything is going to be all right now. Doc Magovern is here." His big gentle hands had brought so many into the world and cared for so many along the way, and he had been welcomed into the homes and hearts of so many families, that to our community he seemed more like a holy man than a medical practitioner. He was a tall man, broad-shouldered, with a big angular face and intelligent quizzical eyes arched over by thick dark brows. His voice was deep, calm, and caring.

Sometimes there was a note of gentle irony in that voice, but when Doc Magovern said a word of praise, it was something you never forgot. One of my proudest moments had been when my grandmother took me into his office on Broadway in Saratoga to have the stitches put in my head. I knew that I was little and I knew that I was afraid, afraid of the bigger boys, afraid of the stern principal of School Two, afraid of getting hit by the cars that went whizzing down Route 9N, afraid that my grandparents would die and leave me unprotected from my biggest fear of all, from that tall, angry shape with huge hands that came to me in my nightmares. But Doc Magovern made me feel brave—for the first time in my life.

"Look at how . . . *humh* . . . still he's sitting . . . *humh* . . . while I put these stitches in," he said, as his needle moved swiftly, making quick little pricking sensations in the skin at the back of my head. They felt like bee stings, but as soon as he said those words, the bees and the pain seemed much smaller. "You're a . . . *humh* . . . brave boy, Sonny."

He pulled the last bit of surgical thread through, making the skin at the back of my head feel tight and stretched. Then he tied it off and clipped it.

"Is that all?" I said.

"You see what I mean, Marion?" Doc Magovern said. Then he opened a big glass jar and pulled out a green lollipop that he handed to me. "I wish I had a hundred patients like you, Sonny."

When Doc Magovern arrived, I was sitting on the steps waiting. His big white Buick pulled up into the outside drive, and he was out the door almost before the engine stopped. Doc Magovern was one of those men who moved with a lanky ease that was deceptively quick. One minute his car door was opening, and the next he was standing there with his right hand on my shoulder and his bag in his left hand.

"You're taking care of your grandparents, aren't you, Sonny?" he said, going through the door as he spoke.

"I am, Doc," I said, holding his hand as we walked together into the kitchen. "I sure am."

The wound on my grandfather's head took fourteen

stitches. Each time he put in a stitch, Doc Magovern made that little sound, *humh*, as if to say the stitch was a good one and it would hold.

"Good thing . . . *humh* . . . you have a hard . . . *humh* . . . head here, Jess," Doc Magovern said in his dry voice.

"That fella's shovel bounced off like a dull ax off a rock maple," Grampa said.

"Jesse!" said my grandmother, and my grandfather clammed up again. Doc Magovern, though, was laughing.

"That other man . . . *humh* . . . you had . . . *humh* . . . this little . . . *humh* . . . squabble with, Jesse, he's . . . *humh* . . . down to the . . . *humh* . . . hospital now. You'll . . . *humh* . . . be happy . . . *humh* . . . to know . . . *humh* . . . he finally did . . . *humh* . . . wake up . . . *humh* . . . even though . . . *humh* . . . he doesn't . . . *humh* . . . have a job anymore."

Doc Magovern tied the last stitch in, snipped it off, and stepped back to look at his work. "*Humh*," he said, one final time. "Now, Jesse," he said, "after he hit you with that shovel, just what did you hit him with?"

My grandfather looked up at my grandmother. The little smile was back at the corner of his face. He knew she was going to poke him again, but he went ahead anyway.

"Nothin' much, Doc," he said, holding up his fists so that Doc Magovern could see his skinned knuckles.

I listened through the open door between our bedrooms that night to hear the story. The man on the road who had attacked my grandfather was the one he called Mack. I had heard my grandfather say, only the week before, that Mack was one of those fellas who had a mouth that was bigger than his brain. It was a rare thing when Grampa didn't get along with someone, and so I knew that Mack had to be a mean-spirited person at the very least.

One of those who worked next to my grandfather was a black man named Skinny. I call him a black man, even though I remember that his skin was no darker than my grandfather's. In those days, Skinny was not called "black" or "African-American." He was called "colored" or a "Negro" by those who were being friendly to him. There were a lot of other names that Skinny was called by those—like Mack—who were not. The only African-American on the crew, Skinny always came to work with a lunch bag that held one peanut-butter sandwich. Grampa had taken to having my grandmother make at least one extra sandwich to put in his lunch pail each day, so that he could say to Skinny as they sat together during the midday break, "Wull, I guess this one is goin' to go to waste. You want to take care of it for me?"

Grampa took to sharing his coffee with Skinny too, both of them drinking out of the thermos cap that screwed off to become a cup. Mack took exception to it. Grampa ignored the things Mack said to the other men. They looked embarrassed when Mack leaned over, pointed to my grandfather and whispered, "Now which of them two is the darkie?" But that one day, when Mack began to physically bully Skinny, my grandfather stepped in.

"Find someone yer own size to pick on," my grandfather said.

"I don't see nobody that big around here," Mack answered, puffing his chest out.

"Nope," my grandfather said, "that's right. Yer the only hot-air balloon around here."

Then he turned his back on the big man and began to walk away.

Someone yelled my grandfather's name and he turned, ducking as he did so. But he didn't duck far enough to avoid getting grazed by the sharp end of the shovel that Mack had swung at him from behind.

Mack didn't get a chance to take a second swing. My grandfather stepped into him and leveled him with one punch. When Mack struggled to his feet, my grandfather leveled him again.

"He must of got up seven times," my grandfather said. "I'll give him credit for that. Last time, though, he stayed down, by thunder!"

When Mack woke up in the Saratoga Hospital with a broken nose and three missing front teeth, he found his notice from the foreman waiting for him. My grandfather, even though he was told he could take off a sick day, was back at work the next morning.

"We need that money," he said. "We got to make ends meet."

GOING FOR A RIDE

It was not until I was in my late thirties that I would encounter a term that rang in my head like one of those movie alarm clocks which fill the screen when someone is supposed to wake up. Two bells are balanced on top of its round face, and a metal hammer whips back and forth between them so swiftly that it is only a blur of motion as a sleeper is jolted suddenly out of a dream. That ringing term was "in denial."

All through my childhood, my parents never explained to me about why we didn't live together. It was just the way it was. People were always saying to my parents, "I didn't know you had a son." Whenever I heard that remark it sent a chill down my back. I'd be off with my parents and my little sister on those weekend drives that I anticipated with dread. I knew what was going to happen next.

"Is that your son? I thought you only had a daughter."

My father or mother would always respond in the same way to that kind of statement by some out-of-town acquaintance or customer of my father's.

"Sure we have a son," they would answer.

And that would be that. But that would not be the end of it. My father's shoulders would tense up, the way I had seen a lion's shoulders grow tense when it was about to charge after an

At the Catskill Game Farm around 1948

unsuspecting gazelle in one of the Disney movies my grandparents took me to see. Except that in the Disney movies the gazelle always got away from the onrushing lion. I knew I was not that gazelle.

When I was in third grade I loved nature movies. I loved the way they would begin with an artist's paintbrush making a landscape that flowed into life on the screen, becoming prairie or desert or jungle. For some reason, anything that had to do with animals or people who lived with animals attracted me. By my eighth year I had already amassed a considerable library of my own books. I was never much interested in the Hardy Boys—there were no animals in their stories, and they never really lived in Africa or India or South America like Tarzan or

Mowgli, like Bomba the Jungle Boy or Tom Steele in the Amazon rain forest. I imagined being like the Swiss Family Robinson, marooned on an island—with my grandfather and grandmother, of course, and all kinds of strange animals for our friends and pets.

And then there were the books of Ernest Thompson Seton, telling the stories of the wild animals of North America—although any story that ended with an animal being shot was one I would never read again. Other boys my age might have said that they wanted to grow up to be a fireman or a policeman or a soldier. I had other aspirations. I was going to be a naturalist.

It was because of that that I would agree to go on those Saturday or Sunday car rides with my parents and my little sister Mary Ann.

"Now, you don't have to go if you don't want to, Sonny," my grandmother would say.

But I would usually reply—even though I knew it was at least partially a lie—"I don't mind, Grama. It'll be all right."

After all, there was a chance that we might be going again to Frontier Town—where a kind-faced Pueblo Indian man and his wife had their little house set up by the archery range, near an enclosure that held four huge black bears. That Pueblo man's face was as brown and gentle as my grandfather's. His name was Swift Eagle, and he held my hand as he pointed out the different bears to me. He told me stories once about the bears, how each bear had its own personality—until my father grabbed me hard by my shoulder, growled, "Get back with us," and shoved me onto the path that led on into the miniature Western town. Perhaps if we went there again I would be allowed to spend my time with the bears and the Indians, and not be dragged off to visit Fort Custer and go on the stagecoach ride—where cap-gun-toting kids could fight off an attack of slightly bored bandits in bandannas, who were wearing the same clothes as the men who had demonstrated how to throw a lasso an hour earlier.

There was a chance too that we might be going to Animal Land in Lake George. Mr. Lukaris, the owner of Animal Land, was a customer and friend of my father's. He displayed animals from Dad's taxidermy business in the souvenir shop that we had to walk through to get to the pens and cages filled with animals from around the world. Still, Mr. Lukaris really seemed to understand my attraction to everything that was living and breathing and covered with fur or scales.

"Someday I give you job here?" he would whisper.

I would nod my head, not wanting my parents to hear. They usually had sarcastic things to say about the places we visited on the weekend rides.

"That lion looked half-dead," my father would say, when we were all in the car again and he was pulling out of the parking lot. "I could make it look a lot more alive than that."

"That's right, Daddy," my little sister would say quickly. "If you mounted it, it'd really look good!"

"Did you smell those alligators?" my mother would say. "I don't know how anyone can stand that."

My only response was to be silent, to lean against the door of the car on "my side," right behind my father's broad, intimidating back, and close my eyes and wish that I was back in my own, safe bedroom. I was certain what was going to happen next.

Or we might be going to the Enchanted Forest again. It was located in Old Forge, New York, deep in the mountains. Theme parks had sprung up all over America, especially in such vacation areas as the Adirondacks. There were rides and people dressed up like fairy-tale characters in all those places: Storytown, U.S.A.; the Magic Forest; the Enchanted Forest; the Land of Makebelieve; Santa's Workshop. We went to them all. Some of them had Indian villages and, whenever I was able to escape from my parents' control, that was where I went. In the Enchanted Forest there was a reconstruction of a whole Abenaki village that had been built by a stocky, muscular man named Chief Dennis. He was teaching me how to throw a hatchet at a target when my mother finally grabbed me. In the Magic Forest in Lake George there was a Mohawk family headed by Ray Fadden, whose Indian name was Aren Akweks, which means "High Eagle," though he never said he was a chief. I was about to shoot his bow and arrow, holding it just the way he had showed me to hold it, when I felt my father's fingers digging hard into my right shoulder.

Even though my parents would travel up to a hundred and fifty miles from Greenfield Center to visit tourist attractions, this was always more for business than pleasure. My father usually sold things, whether it was mounted heads or leather jackets or moccasins or deerskin gloves, to their gift shops. More often than not, we got in without paying, because my father was given free passes.

"Don't ever do anything if it can't make you money," he would say, in the rare moments when he felt it appropriate to offer me advice.

Every vehicle he owned was green.

"The color of money," he would say.

Unlike Grampa Jesse, who never had more than five dollars on him, my father always carried a huge wad of cash in his pants pocket. With a thick rubber band around it, the wad was rolled so that the big bills were on the outside. He carried it so that he could buy things, as he put it, "in cash." Whether it was shotgun shells or a new Chevy pickup truck, my father would always pay for it in cash, first asking what the price would be if he paid in cash and then whipping that wad "big enough to choke a horse" out of his pocket and peeling off the bills. "Never get anything on credit," he'd say.

It was not until decades later that I would understand that an edge of pain and desperation had always been in his words, a legacy of the pain that so many people of my father's generation had felt in the world of the 1930's. It was a world in which even the banks went out of business, and your life savings went with them. It was a grim world in which there were no jobs, and the real chance of starvation faced many families, especially if the parents spoke English with a foreign accent.

By the time the day of sight-seeing was over and we were in the car, my parents would have that strained look on their faces I knew all too well.

My father would look back over his shoulder at my sister and me.

"Now you stay on your own sides back there. Don't make me stop this car."

"Yes, Daddy," my sister would say in a bright voice.

"Yessir," I would mutter.

Sometimes I would just nod. It really didn't matter what I said. I knew what was bound to happen.

We'd get underway and then, when we were on the road, my mother would say something to my father. It didn't matter what, because he would respond in a loud, quick voice.

"Yes, sir!" he would say to her.

"Don't shout at me!" my mother would shout back.

It might continue on from there, or both of them might become silent. I didn't like that silence any better than the shouting. It reminded me of the eye of a hurricane, where the wind doesn't blow and it seems as if the danger is over. But the worst is yet to come, because you are still right in the center of the storm.

"I want to stop and get those rolls I like," my sister might say.

"That restaurant is fifty miles from here, honey," my father would answer, looking back over his shoulder. "We'll stop some-place else."

"But I want those rolls."

"Listen to your father," my mother would snap at her.

"She just asked a question," my father would growl back.

"Don't you shout at me!"

It was usually about then that my mother would suggest we count cows. I was supposed to count the cows I saw out from my side of the car; my sister would count those she saw out of her side. The idea was to see who could count the most. Somehow this always ended up in an argument over whose cows were being counted. Then one of us would get kicked, and that person would kick back, and soon I'd see my father's angry eyes staring straight into mine in the rearview mirror. And then the car would fill with the sound of my sister crying.

"Daddy," she would wail, her eyes brimming with tears, "Sonny kicked me."

My father would turn the wheel suddenly and we would all be thrown sideways and then forward, as the car swerved onto the dirt shoulder and squealed to a stop.

Even before it stopped, my father would have risen up and leaned over the back seat, his roaring voice telling me that the eye of the storm had indeed passed over. I was about to feel the force of the hurricane.

"Goddamn, what the hell is wrong with you?" he would shout.

I would lift up my hands, knowing what was coming. My father's hands were quicker. His reflexes were like a cat's, and he could grab a fly out of the air in midflight. His huge palm would come toward my face, in slow motion now, as I waited— unable to move, like a bug stuck on a piece of flypaper. I would hear his hand striking the side of my face, and then feel a wave of heat wash over my cheek before the arrival of the sharp, stinging pain. The blow would throw me back against the door, my head hitting the window so hard that a lump would rise there, the red outline of my father's fingers still printed on my throbbing face.

It was at that moment that my sister would suddenly become my defender.

"Daddy," she would scream, "stop it!" And she would push herself between my cowering shape and my father's still upraised hand.

"Joe!" my mother would say. And then my father would stop.

"I didn't want to do that," he would say to me. "We were having a good time, and you had to spoil it. Now, you behave."

Then he would settle back into his seat, put the car into gear, and we would be on the highway again. He would not take us to a restaurant or make any stops, even to let us use a bathroom. We would head straight to Greenfield, where my father would pull up next to the outside gas pumps and I would open the door as fast as I could, to scramble out and run for my grandparents.

They would always be standing there, standing, it seemed, in the same place they had stood when my father's car had pulled out that morning, carrying me away as I pressed my face against the window and waved good-bye to them. In my dreams I still sometimes see my grandparents standing and waiting all day long, their eyes turned toward the road, waiting as patient and still as statues for my return, waiting because they knew how much a small, frightened boy would need them.

My father would pull out before I reached my grandparents, his rear wheels spinning up gravel as he turned onto Middle Grove Road. Neither he nor my mother would look at the old man and the old woman who stood there, although Mary Ann would roll down the window to wave and shout, "Bye-bye, Grama and Grampa!"

Then I would press my burning face against my grandmother's side and feel my grandfather's hands carefully rubbing my bruised shoulders. And as my grandmother whispered, "It's all right, you're home now, Sonny," I would cry and cry and cry.

SPRING PAINT

There is a story that is told all over the Northeast. I've heard it from the Mohawks and from the Abenakis, from the Algonquin people and the Anishinabe. I don't know who told it first, and so I think it is a story as old as the winter and the spring.

A fierce old man sat in his lodge in the woods. He was alone there, for everyone was afraid of him. His hair was thick and white and as pale as frost. His nose was as sharp as an icicle. His eyes were as white as sleet. His lodge was a wigwam made of sheets of ice, and whoever came too close would freeze. In the center of his lodge was a cold fire made of white ice that flickered with a chilly light. Whenever he came out of his lodge, the birds and animals would hide because his breath would turn the waters of the streams and lakes into stone; and wherever he stepped, the ground became covered by a thick white blanket. His only friend was the Great White Bear, that storm wind which came down from the Always Winter Land.

One cold day the old man heard someone scratching on the outside of his lodge near the door.

"Go away!" the old man shouted in a harsh voice. "Go away from my lodge."

But now a voice spoke. That voice was as soft as the old man's was hard. It was sweet as the songs of the birds.

"Old Man," the sweet voice said, "you must let me into your lodge."

"Come in, then," said the old man. He smiled a hard smile, knowing that whoever came into his lodge would freeze.

Then a young man entered the wigwam. His face was painted with red lines and circles that looked like the sun. There was a warm smile on his face; and as he sat down on the other side of the fire, the old man felt the young man's warm breath. The old man began to sweat. He felt himself growing weaker.

"Go away," said the old man.

"No," said the young man, his voice as gentle as the sound of a summer breeze. "It is you who must leave now. Your season has ended."

As the young man spoke those words the walls of the old man's lodge fell away. All around the lodge the snow was almost gone, and you could see the dark earth and the green of grass. The old man felt himself shrinking away, smaller and smaller.

"Go with your friend, the Great White Bear," said the young man. "Go back to the Always Winter Land, and do not return until my season has ended."

Then the Great White Bear, who is the North Wind, swept down in one last cold blast. He picked up Old Man Winter and carried him off to the cold land they shared together. Now all the land around the young man came alive with the songs of birds, and the leaves began to appear on the trees. There on the ground before him, where Winter's cold fire had been, was a circle of flowers—the first white flowers of the spring, the bloodroots. They are the sign each year of the victory of that young man, whose Abenaki name, Sigan, means "Spring."

Just below my grandparents' house on Splinterville Hill is a small stretch of woods. Never more than fifty yards deep, it ends at the stone wall that was the boundary, when I was a child, between our property and the property of Mrs. Williams. Mrs. Williams was a retired schoolteacher who lived there in a big old house with her mother. I used to walk through the woods and climb over that stone wall, bags of groceries in my arms, to make deliveries to her from our store.

Following the line of the stone wall, the woods stretch from Route 9N on the east to Mill Road on the west, where they are bordered by Bell Brook. There I first followed the tracks of animals in the snow—the exclamation-mark paw prints of rabbits, the round, delicate tracks of red fox, the tiny marks of field mice that would end at a circle in the snow where their hidden runs dove out of sight. Although it seems small today, that little forest seemed very large to me when I was young. I always called it the Woods; and when I went outside after school or on the weekends or in the long summer days, I only had to say to my grandparents, "I'm going to the Woods," and they'd know where to find me.

It was my grandfather who first walked with me in the Woods, holding my tiny hand and reassuring me that this was a place where I could be safe—as long as I understood what was around me. It was not that I couldn't get hurt there. You could get hurt anywhere, Grampa said—and I surely understood that. But knowing what could hurt you, that could help you keep away from it. He showed me the nettles that would sting my skin, and the thorns on the raspberry bushes. He pointed out the places where the wire of the old fences that had been buried over the decades stuck up and might trip me. We were always pulling out those old wire-mesh fences, which had once been part of the pens for the wolves that Mr. Otis, who owned the house before Mrs. Williams, bred as pets. An ancestor of his had invented the elevator, and keeping eagles and wolves in his backyard had been his pastime. Knowing the story about those eagles and wolves who had lived here, caged but still wild, always made me feel as if their spirits were watching over me when I was alone in the woods.

For everything in the woods that might harm me, my grandfather pointed out a dozen things that gave me delight. He showed me the different kinds of trees, from the smooth-limbed maple to the rough-barked elm. He showed me the three big old apples, ancient gnarled trees that were covered with sweet-scented flowers each spring. Although the fruit that came on them each late summer was small and marked by insects, no apples in the world ever tasted as good as theirs, and my grandfather said we'd maybe build a tree house in the biggest apple tree one day when I was big enough.

He showed me how I could swing on the grapevines and how I could make places to hide under the honeysuckle bushes, just like a rabbit does. He showed me the different rocks, how some of them were soft sandstone that you could break pieces off with your hand, while others were hard and had quartz in them that sparkled brighter than diamonds. He showed me how some rocks were alive once. "Though maybe they still is alive, in a way of saying," he added. They had fossils in them, like the ancient blue cryptozoan stones that made up the stone retaining wall right behind our house, a wall my grandfather had built. More than anything else, though, I remember how he showed me the flowers. And more than any other flower, I remember the first one of them all, the bloodroot.

It was in the Woods that I first saw bloodroot in bloom, that delicate white flower which is the first spring blossom in our Adirondack foothills. Rising up on a smooth stalk, its center is as golden as a tiny sun, surrounded by white rays of light.

"Soon as you see the bloodroot," my grandfather said, "you know winter is goin' fer sure."

SPRING PAINT

When the last mounds of April snow were shrinking down in the huge dirty white piles that the town crews had plowed up below our driveway, Grampa and I would put on our green rubber boots. Mine were exactly the same as his, but so much smaller that I could put on my boots and then pull his on over mine. Then I would go galumphing along next to him, giggling while he said to my grandmother, "Wull, Sonny's got his boots on, but now I can't find mine."

"Grampa!" I would finally say. "Look! I got your boots on."

He was always surprised at how silly he had been, not to be able to see that.

Then we would go down into the Woods to look for the bloodroots. There would still be little patches of snow here and there at the bases of trees, and the ground was alternately hard as rock or so soft that our feet would sink in, and we could only pull them out with a sucking sound, as if the earth wanted to swallow us. Soon, though, we'd find the first patch of blood-root. They would be clustered together in a circle, the green palmate leaves surrounding the base of the white flowers that thrust up toward the sun. My grandfather would always pick one of those first bloodroot flowers we saw. Then he would take its stem, which dripped orange sap like ink from a broken pen, and make marks on my face as I looked up at him.

"This here's yer spring paint," he said. "Helps keep them bugs away."

The lines and circles he painted on my forehead and cheeks would dry there, and I would forget that I had them—until I looked in the mirror later in the day, or saw how a customer stared at my face as I stood on an empty Coca-Cola box to clean the windshield while Grampa pumped the gas.

Sanguinaria canadensis is the Latin name for the bloodroot. I looked it up when I was eight years old and wrote it down in one of the notebooks I kept then, listing every bird or flower or animal I had seen. I learned, as I read my field guides, that it is a member of the poppy family. Found in the humus-rich woodlands and along streams, its range is across Canada and south from Nova Scotia to New England. Fragile and brief as the first days of spring when it blooms, its flowers open to the sun and close at night—like small white hands, trying to hold in that first warmth. Its Latin name, *sanguinaria*, means "bleeding." The orange juice that comes from its stems was used by the Abenaki people and the Mohawks as an insect repellent, as a dye for clothing and baskets, and as an ingredient in face paint.

And so, once again, without saying or perhaps even knowing, my grandfather handed down to me a part of my heritage that was as ancient as the story of the coming of spring.

14

DOWN MIDDLE GROVE ROAD

Grama Bruchac, my Slovak grandmother, told the story to us when my wife Carol and I were visiting her in her home shortly after our wedding in 1964. At the reception, Grama Bruchac had been drinking champagne. When Carol's aunt Trix asked her why it was that I was not raised by my parents, my father's mother had told her the story. Trix had told it to us, and now we wanted to hear it from my grandmother herself.

"Grama," I said, "we heard a story from Carol's aunt Trix about why I was raised by Grama and Grampa Bowman."

Grama Bruchac took a deep breath before she spoke, breaking that long silence which always shrouds family secrets. She wrung her apron with her hands and sighed.

"It vas awful," she said. "Your vater, he go over dere to get you—and Mr. Bowman, he get out his shotgun!"

As she said those words a memory came to me, something so long ago that it was as hazy as a dream. In that dream my father's face is huge and violent. He is reaching for me with his big hands. In that dream my grandmother pushes me behind her and tells me, more firmly than I can ever remember her speaking before, "Go into your room." In that dream my mother stands behind my father. My

mother seems stunned by it all, and her eyes go back and forth be-
tween her husband and her parents. She is holding my wide-eyed,
two-year-old little sister in her arms, and Mary Ann is crying. There
is a mark on her face as if someone has struck her, and her eyes are
so full of sorrow that they make me want to cry with her. In that
dream my grandfather is holding something in his hands and even
though he is much smaller than my father, he is standing very
straight. Although his voice is not loud and angry like my father's,
everyone hears his voice when he speaks, and everything becomes
very quiet.

In his hands, on that night of violence, pain, and division that
would mark all our lives in the years to come, my grandfather held
his shotgun. He slipped a shell into the breech, his thumb pressed
down the release for the pump, and he jacked the shell into the bar-
rel. His finger flipped off the safety. Then my grandfather stepped
back from my father, lifted up the shotgun, and held it to his own
head.

"Take him," my grandfather said, "and ye'll never see me alive
again."

"And vot could your vater do?" Grama Bruchac said, tears still
in her eyes more than a quarter-century after those events had
happened.

And what, I thought, could my grandfather do? But when Carol
and I went back home that night, I ran a wire cable around the
gunrack and my grandfather's shotgun and fastened the ends of the
wire cable with a padlock.

By the time I was eight my grandparents thought I was old
enough to ride my bicycle on Middle Grove Road. It was a blue
Schwinn, and I thought it was the most beautiful thing I had
ever seen when it appeared under the Christmas tree. All that
winter I would balance myself on it, halfway between the living

room and the dining room, holding on to the doorway, imagining myself riding it down the roads with the wind in my face. Learning to stay up on it once the snow was gone proved to be a harder matter. My grandfather held on to the back, and my grandmother stood in front.

"Now, pedal," Grampa said.

I pushed down on the pedals as hard as I could, and fell over.

When my grandfather had untangled me and helped me find my glasses, he put me back on the bike.

"You push down one pedal at a time, Sonny."

"Oh," I said. Then, before he had a hold on me, I did just that and went careening forward so fast that I ran straight into my grandmother, and all three of us—my bike, my grandmother, and me—ended up in a heap under the blue spruces.

Within a few days, though, I was able to ride on my own, and I was soon going back and forth up and down Middle Grove Road. I wasn't allowed to go any farther than up to the lane of my parents' house, a quarter of a mile up the road. And I didn't go down the lane to their house, just turned around at the end of their driveway. I know they must have seen me, for I waved at Mary Ann standing in front of their house, a hundred yards down that long lane, the first day I made the turn around.

An hour later, my father pulled out of the lane in his station wagon, my seven-year-old sister in the seat next to him. I could see she had been crying as they went by me. Her face was still all red from the crying, and I could see how her scar, where her bangs were pushed aside, stood out paler on her flushed forehead. But when they came back up the road again I was still riding, and I could see a smile on Mary Ann's face. In the back of the station wagon was a brand-new pink bicycle. It was just like mine except that Mary Ann's bike had a basket on the front, a rack on the back, tassels dangling from the handlebars, and a fancy chain guard.

When I reached the end of the driveway again, my father was walking next to Mary Ann, holding her up on the bicycle as her legs tried to reach the pedals. I turned around and headed back down toward the station, glad that my father hadn't spoken to me. When he did it was usually to yell at me. And I was still afraid that he was going to carry through on his threat to send me to reform school, even though my grandmother had been telling me for a year now that she and Grampa would never allow that to happen. Late at night I would wake up and remember the anger twisting his face as he shouted those words at me the day I threw the stone.

The day it happened we had been playing in the field. Mary Ann had come over, as she often did, to play with me. Sometimes when we played together it was fun, and I was glad to see her because she was the only person anywhere near my age that I ever had to play with. I was always too little, too much of an egghead, too scared, too much of a Grama's boy, for the few other kids who lived within a mile of us to want to play with me. Saratoga Springs, where I went to school, was three miles away, and I hadn't been allowed to ride the school bus since second grade because my grandmother was afraid that I would get beaten up again and have my glasses broken. So, when I was in school, my only friends were the books and the teachers. When the other kids went out to recess, I went into the library. When my grandfather picked me up at school and brought me home in the afternoon, I went into the Woods. Except when Mary Ann came over to play.

That day we were playing hit-the-bat. The way hit-the-bat worked was pretty simple. The batter would hit the ball, and the pitcher would try to catch it. If you caught it, you got to bat. If it got past you, you had to go get the ball. Then you were allowed to run with the ball back toward the hitter until he or she dropped the bat. You had to stop where you were as soon as that bat hit the ground. Then you had to throw or roll the ball to try to hit the bat. If you hit it, you got to be the batter. If not, you had to keep pitching.

When I played the game with my grandfather, we were always even. I was at bat half the time, and he was at bat the other half. Each of us would let the other get within twenty or thirty feet before we'd drop the bat. But Grampa couldn't play very long before his legs got tired, and he had to keep watching the station. So I was always glad at first when Mary Ann came over to play. But she mostly wanted to bat, and when I finally got tired of always pitching and demanded my turn, she would often go home, taking the ball with her.

I don't remember being angry at her the day I threw the stone. I only remember that we were both out in the field looking for a lost ball. I found a rock, hefted it in my hand, and threw it up to see how high I could throw it in the air. It went up and up and then began to come down, faster than it had risen. Mary Ann was standing there, looking up as if she was hypnotized, watching the stone as it fell.

Thinking back on that day, I believe I remember shouting as I threw it, "Watch how high I can throw this stone!" But the stone dove down like a kingfisher heading for the water and struck my sister in the forehead, knocking her to the ground.

I didn't run to her to see how she was. I was certain of the worst. I turned and ran toward the house, toward my grandparents. I was sobbing and shouting, they told me. The words I was shouting were, "I've killed Mary Ann!" Only a few paces behind me, though, Mary Ann was also running toward the house. Blood was streaming down her forehead. She was crying and shouting too, shouting, "I'm not killed!"

We reached my grandparents' house at almost the same

time, and the relief I felt as I saw my still-living sister coming up the lawn behind me vanished when I saw two things. I saw the blood on her forehead and I saw the face of my father. There, standing behind the house, were not only my grandmother and grandfather, but Mom and Dad. Mom screamed and Dad grabbed at me. I ducked aside and my grandparents put their arms around me, shielding me from him.

"I didn't mean to do it, I didn't mean to do it," I kept sobbing.

My father grabbed my sister's arm as my mother tried to press a handkerchief to her bleeding forehead.

"Look at her!" my father shouted. "She's scarred for life. Scarred for life! I'm going to send that goddamn boy to reform school. You hear me? He's going to reform school for this. He tried to kill his sister. He tried to kill her. And he's damn well going to get sent off to reform school."

My grandfather stood up and put his body between me and my father. Although Mary Ann was the one who was injured, somehow all the attention had become focused on me, and it was almost as if Mary Ann had been forgotten. There was a lost, despairing look in her eyes. My mother held a crimson handkerchief to her daughter's forehead, but she too was staring at me.

"Yer not sending him nowhere," my grandfather said.

My father opened his mouth and then he closed it. He turned and looked down at Mary Ann as if seeing her for the first time. Then he grabbed her up and carried her to where the car was parked on Middle Grove Road, my mother following him. My mother got in, and my father threw Mary Ann onto my mother's lap. As she stared out that window, for a moment my sister's eyes met mine. I think, at that moment, there was an unspoken understanding between us. We were two little children caught in a tidal wave of confused emotion and love and pain that was larger than either of our lives. But that moment ended quickly. The car screeched off down Middle Grove Road and turned south onto 9N toward Saratoga Springs and Doc Magovern's office. There the wound in her scalp would be stitched, but it would turn into a scar—a scar that, for my father, was forever marked on my own head as well.

HEN HAWK

In the spring of 1986, after my father's death from a second major heart attack, I was helping my mother clean up their old house. In the last ten years of his life I had grown closer to my father. He had often talked to me about the things he felt, the things he worried about, the things he cared about. Although his life had been spent with dead animals and he had killed them by the hundreds in his lifetime—at least one deer for each of the seventy-four years he lived—there was a love for the woods and a respect for the animals within it that had grown deeper in him every year. That love and respect was reflected in an article I found in his desk drawer. I remembered when he had shown it to me.

It was a day when I came over to help him move some boxes. I found him sitting at his desk with tears in his eyes.

"What's wrong?" I asked.

He didn't answer. Instead, he handed me that article. It told of a whole herd of migrating caribou being drowned, when it crossed a river just as Hydro-Quebec released a great flow of water from one of their dams in the James Bay Project.

"This should never have happened," he said, and I knew he was referring to all of it. He had been to that part of Quebec as a *young man, and a Cree guide had taken him along those rivers that were now drowned under dams built for useless human power. So much had been lost with James Bay, and as the flooding waters released the natural mercury in the soil, even the fish had become poisonous for the Native people there to eat.*

I put my hand on his shoulder, something I'd never done before. He let my hand stay and he put his head down. And then both of us stood there, crying for the land and the people and the animals.

I had grown closer to my mother too, in that decade before my father's death, and I found myself helping her as she limped through a house that was frighteningly empty to her, living in a life with too many empty rooms. That day in 1986 she was trying to find something. But it eluded her. My father, who had saved everything— every single one of the six buildings that made their home and business was piled high with the things he had saved, including forty-year-old boxes of moldering order forms for his taxidermy business and every issue of every hunting magazine he had gotten since 1933—could find things, much of the time. But it was his system, not my mother's.

"Maybe upstairs," she said. "Would you go and look?"

The upstairs of their old house had never been finished. There was half a wall up there that had boxes piled in front of it. I moved the boxes aside and looked behind them. There in that dark, narrow, unfinished room I saw the red-tailed hawk. It was mounted with its wings spread wide on an artificial base that looked like a tree with moss on it. Its glass eyes did not hold life, but its feathers, even though they were dusty, glistened and vibrated as I breathed on them.

Those wide-winged birds have always circled our lives and our stories. Stephen Laurent, whose father was a chief at Odanak, had talked to me about the way the Abenaki people see the hawks. I sat

*in his little shop in the midst of the White Mountains of New
Hampshire and thought about the many hawks I had seen circling
overhead as I came close to his home. In his eighties, a keeper of our
traditions and a great linguist, Stephen nodded as I mentioned the
hawks. Then he spoke in gentle, precise tones.*

*"We honor those birds of prey by carrying their feathers. I have
heard it said that they are a sort of spirit guide. One would never
wantonly kill a hawk."*

*I thought about their fierce, knowing eyes and of the ways they
have visited my dreams. Whenever I travel I always keep an eye
open for hawks. To see one perched on a tree as I pass—or to look
up and find that there is a hawk above my car, keeping pace with
me as I drive—has always been a sign for me that my travels will be
safe, my road blessed. For a time, because they were hunted in
many areas almost to extinction, and because of pesticides that had
entered the food chain, I saw few hawks. But in the last two decades
they have begun again to become more common, to grace the wind
with their flight. And of all the hawks, perhaps none are so lovely to
watch in flight as* Buteo jamaicensis, *the red-tails.*

My father called them "hen hawks." When my grandfather
mentioned over the party line—in a call to someone else—seeing a red-tailed hawk circling over the back field, my father
showed up unbidden half an hour later, with his shotgun. He
walked out back, crouched down in the chicken-house door,
and watched. In those days, in the summer of 1952, birds of
prey were not protected by law nor regarded as especially use-
ful by most of the country people, who saw them as nuisance
birds. The rule then was to kill anything which might eat the
same things that people ate. Some places, still, even paid bounties on predators. Kill the wolf, kill the mountain lion, kill the
eagle, kill the owl, kill the fox, kill the hawk. And then, ironi-
cally, their slaughter would be called "predator control."

HEN HAWK

I was nine years old. Aldo Leopold's *A Sand County Almanac* had already been published by then, and there were other books I had read that talked about the web of life, the potentially balancing and beneficial relationship of predator and prey. I'd read about the deer herd on the isolated Kaibab Plateau in Arizona. When all the wolves and mountain lions were killed, when all the predators that culled out the sick and the weak animals were eliminated, that deer herd grew larger and larger until most of the animals in it were sick and weak and starving for lack of food.

So I watched my father, watched from the safety of an upstairs window. The hawk appeared over the distant elms, so far away that it was a thin double-curved line, like the decoration on a birch-bark basket.

I knew my father had seen it too. His eyes were always good at seeing things to shoot. In the yard in front of him the Rhode Island Red rooster, the one that had put a run in my grandmother's stockings yesterday with its claws, strutted back and forth. I had a scratched wrist from when it flew up at me as I'd entered the chicken yard to collect the eggs that morning. I would have been happy to see a hen hawk take that rooster. But I knew what was about to happen.

The red-tail circled overhead now, a wide, sunwise gyre. The crimson of the sun caught in its wide-fanned tail, and I saw it moving its head back and forth as it looked down on the ground. It was seeing something, readying itself to dive and strike. I knew that red-tails ate mostly rabbits and rodents. A big red-tail might take a baby chick, but there were no baby chicks in our hen yard that day. That hawk had other prey in mind. There were rats that had been eating the chicken feed, and one was making its furtive way across from the woods' edge toward the back of the chicken house. That was what the hawk had its eye on.

With my father in 1945

HEN HAWK

As I watched from the upstairs window I felt myself to be at the same height as the hawk. For a moment I thought I could close my eyes and lift up with it, feel a thermal lifting me, and see the land spread wide and green below. The hawk circled lower, and I felt its wings tensing as it readied itself to stoop. But I had forgotten my father. He stood up suddenly and raised the shotgun toward the sky, as if he was ready to shoot the heart out of the sun. My shout blended with the *thwump!* of the shotgun. As if struck by a great angry fist, the hawk jerked in midair and then plummeted, wings loose, feathers fluttering like broken fingers. It landed with a small thump only a few feet away from the place where the rat, which now had found safety under the hen house, had been.

I do not think my father heard me or saw me. He put his shotgun down and walked over to the hawk. He picked it up by its wings, extending his arms to spread them out. He had used fine bird shot and, aside from killing it, he had not harmed it. I could imagine him thinking that, and I knew that he was seeing it as a fine specimen to mount. Holding that dead, beautiful bird, he picked up his shotgun and walked back to his truck.

In those last years of my father's life we came to an understanding and an appreciation of each other. He told me, and no one else, of the place where he had gone—and of those who spoke to him there—when his heart stopped after his first major heart attack at the age of seventy. He told me of seeing himself, looking down on his own body lying on the table in the hospital, and deciding to come back because there were things he still needed to do. And he tried his best to do them.

It was because of such moments of closeness that I found myself, as a grown man with sons of my own, finally being the son that my father had lost, the son who was within sight but never to be touched in a gentle way. It was because of such moments that I was able to walk in my father's taxidermy studio and no longer feel that sickness in my heart and my stomach, that feeling of the meaningless in the loss of their lives, as I looked at perfectly mounted birds and animals.

And so I could hold that red-tailed hawk he had shot and feel no repulsion. This work of death had been his life, and yet a part of him had always been close to Native people. From slaughter he created an appearance of vitality, a memorial to the life and beauty that crumpled to the earth at the sound of a gunshot. It was, I saw, like the prayers I had heard Native elders speak after the death of an animal that gave its life to be their food.

I brought the hawk downstairs to show it to my mother.

"Oh, don't let anyone see that," my mother said. "Your father hid all his hawks and owls. The state was fining taxidermists who couldn't prove they'd mounted them before it was illegal." My mother leaned to look closer at the red-tail. "This one here he must have mounted thirty years ago."

"Just about," I said, gently stroking the bird's feathers from its head down toward its tail. "Can I take this, Mom?"

"You'd be better off digging a hole and burying it. But you can have it. Just don't let anyone see it."

No one saw me take that hawk from my father's house. I carried it into the woods where I knew a pair of red-tails were now nesting. Descendants, perhaps, of this old one whose flight ended on a summer day long ago. At the base of a tall straight maple, I freed its feet from the artificial perch and then smudged its body with the smoke of burning sweet grass. I thanked it for its life and its flight and for the gifts which it and its people had given my ancestors and me. As I held it, its tail came free in my hand, loosened perhaps by the decades, though I felt as if it were another gift.

Three months later, a package came to Stephen Laurent at his home in New Hampshire. When he opened it he found a beaded fan, made of the wide, beautiful tail of that red-tailed hawk.

LADY

Among the Abenaki, this story is told. After you die you travel along the Milky Way, the spirit trail that leads into the sky. But as you travel you will come to a place where there is a break in the trail. There is a log across that deep chasm, and you can walk over that log. But it is held firmly in place by all the dogs that you have owned on the earth. They hold the log with their teeth. If they hold it firmly, then you will be able to get across.

Those dogs look at you as you step onto that log. They remember how you treated them when they lived with you. If you did not treat them well, if you beat them or starved them, they will not hold the log steady. You will fall, and you will continue to fall.

When I was a child, I could not imagine what life would be like without a dog. There were always dogs in our house. The first was Pudgie, who lived to be almost sixteen years of age. Until the day in my seventh year when my grandmother took Pudgie to the vet's to be put to sleep because she could no longer walk and her every breath was racked with pain, she was always with my grandfather, my grandmother, and me. She rode with us in the car. She perched on our laps as we sat outside the station waiting for customers. When my grandfather walked in the Woods with me, Pudgie would be by his side. She had a special kind of dignity and control, and even though a squirrel might run right in front of her she would not chase it unless she heard the word from my grandfather.

"All right, Pudgie—go to!"

Only then, her legs churning like a propeller, dead leaves flying in all directions, would she charge yapping after the squirrel. She was fast and very well might have caught a squirrel, but I noticed that my grandfather never gave her that command of "Go to!" until the squirrel was close enough to a tree to make its getaway.

I was seven when I discovered the dog novels of Albert Payson Terhune. They were stories that were at least loosely autobiographical, and they focused on Terhune and his wife and their life with their dogs. *Lad: A Dog, Lad of Sunnybank*—I read all those books, which were always about collies. My grandmother's family had always had collies—even before those two dogs that were poisoned by the Mayer boys. And as soon as Pudgie, who wouldn't tolerate another dog in our house, was gone, my grandmother wanted us to have a collie again.

"Sonny needs a dog," she said to my grandfather.

So we drove over to the farm of Truman Middlebrooks. Truman's farm was only three miles from the station. To get there we went down Middle Grove Road and then turned left at the corner where North Greenfield Road began. The road went down into a little dip to cross over Dunham Brook—which was named after my great-grandparents—and there was the Middlebrooks farm on the right-hand side.

There was a big white farmhouse right next to the road, with fields stretching off behind it. Back a little farther, behind the house and to the left, was a long low barn. Truman

LADY

Middlebrooks came out of the barn. I remember him as a big man with long arms and a loose-limbed way of walking. He had a florid face and a ready smile and was always teasing me.

He was a special friend of mine and always talked to me when he came to our station. I had a wooden gun that he had made for me when I was only five. It had a crank handle on the side. When I turned the handle, the teeth of a wooden gear would lift up the end of a stiff piece of lath just enough so that it would pop down against the next tooth. When you turned the handle fast, it sounded like the tommy gun it was meant to imitate.

I loved that tommy gun, though at the time it was given to me I knew nothing about the fact that only two miles south of Splinterville Hill people had once used *real* tommy guns. From the bootlegging Prohibition years to the 1940's, Saratoga Springs was a town associated not only with the legal gambling at its two racetracks, but with illegal gambling. Years later, in my teens, I would hear the story about one man who tried to horn in on the territory of the local family that controlled gambling in the area. He went out to dinner with a group of men he thought had switched their allegiance to him. They got him roaring drunk and then, instead of driving him home in their black roadster, dropped him off on the steps of the Saratoga Hospital. As he stood there, swaying back and forth and wondering why he wasn't at his own house, another black roadster came roaring up. Two men with tommy guns leaned out and—just like in the movies—"filled him full of holes" right there, saving him the trip to the hospital.

I am certain that Truman Middlebrooks never had anything to do with gangsters, but everyone of his generation knew about them. So there might have been a little irony in his gift of a tommy gun to me. But I loved that gun. I still have it, more than four decades after Truman Middlebrooks handed it to me on a quiet summer afternoon (which lost all semblance of quiet after that gun was in my hands).

Grampa really liked that gun too. After I'd been playing with it for an hour or so, he asked if he might have a turn for the same time as me. Since Grampa and I always shared just about everything, I agreed that it was fair. Grampa took out his pocket watch, which was fastened to his belt at the end of a long chain. We looked together at its big face.

"I'll play with it fer an hour, then you kin have it the next hour. See, when this arm gets to here and this one gets to here."

I nodded. I was good at telling time, and it had become my responsibility at certain times to remind my grandmother—who was awfully forgetful, it seemed—that it was time to start cooking dinner, or time to turn on the radio because *Straight Arrow* or *The Lone Ranger* was going to be on.

"It's five o'clock, Grama," I'd say. "See where the hands are on the clock? That's time to start dinner."

"Sonny," she'd say, "I don't know how we ever got on without you."

So I was able to read my grandfather's watch well enough to be able to tell him for certain sure when his hour of playing with my tommy gun was up.

"You sure the hour's done?" he said. For some reason he wanted to play with it longer, though I wasn't certain why. During that whole hour he'd had it he hadn't even made a sound with it, but had just held it in his lap while he sat in front of the station.

That day, when we went to Truman Middlebrooks's farm, we were going to get something even more exciting than a tommy gun. Truman Middlebrooks raised collies, and we were going to get one. Back then, some forty-five years ago, the collie was a different dog than it is now, even though the breeding of the dog was already tending toward the kind of collie we have today. Albert Payson Terhune even mentioned it in his books, bemoaning the fact that the way a collie looked on the outside was more important to owners of show dogs than the heart it had on the inside. Today a collie has such an unnaturally elongated head that there's hardly any room for brains in there. There's a vacant look in the eyes of many of them. But the collies that Truman Middlebrooks bred were the old kind. They had broad foreheads, and the looks in their eyes would range from laughter to concern to real sorrow.

Truman took me by the hand and we walked out to the barn.

"Be real quiet," Truman said. "She's nervous about her puppies."

I nodded. Mother animals got worried when people were around. At the fox farm, just half a mile above our house on the other side of the railroad tracks, the mother foxes in their pens had even been known to kill their young ones when people made too much noise around them.

It was dark in the barn, and it smelled of cows and hay like the big barn up at Hall's dairy farm, where we went to get our milk for the station. But, as we stood there waiting a bit till our eyes got used to the dark, I could smell something different. It was a warm, milk-sweet, furry scent unlike any other, the smell of puppies. And as I listened I could hear them whimpering as they nuzzled up to their mother inside the horse stall.

Truman opened the door of the stall and we looked in.

"It's okay," he said, speaking both to us and to the mother dog who gazed alertly at our faces.

We stepped in and knelt down. Princess, the mother of the puppies, looked at us. Her dark liquid eyes were full of concern. Truman put his hand on her head.

"It's all right, honey," he said. "These nice folks are going to adopt one of your babies. Now you come with me."

Princess stood up at his command and gingerly walked around her babies, who crawled after her as she moved. They were old enough that their eyes had opened. I knew that puppies and kittens are born with their eyes closed, blind and totally reliant on their mothers—not like baby deer, which can run only a few hours after their birth. But, although their eyes were open, these puppies were still too little to be without their mother for long. We were only choosing one today, and we'd come back and pick it up to take home in two weeks.

"Which one will we pick, Grampa?" I whispered as the puppies came toward me, little bundles of fur on unsteady legs. I wanted to lie down and bury my face in them, but I tried to control myself. I knew that I had to help Grampa make the right decision.

"Jes' watch 'em for a while."

I watched. I began to notice that each of them seemed to have its own personality. Of the seven puppies there was one that kept on whimpering. I petted her gently.

"Not this one," I said.

"That's right," Grampa said. "She's too skeered."

I kept watching. I saw there was one puppy in particular that seemed always to be on top as they played with each other.

"Snap yer fingers," Grampa said.

I snapped my fingers. The puppy that was on top of all the others immediately turned its head toward the sound.

"Hears good," Grampa said.

I picked the puppy up and looked at its tummy.

"She's a girl, isn't she?"

"Ay-yup."

The puppy began licking my face as I held her. Her tongue was hot and her breath was sweet.

LADY

"We should choose her," I said.

"Ay-yup," Grampa said.

We had Lady for three years. She followed my grandfather everywhere, just as I did—but since I was now in school during the days, she took my place. But whenever Grampa came to pick me up at the end of the school day, Lady was in the car with him. Her tongue licking my face was my first greeting when I opened the door to get in.

When I walked in the Woods, Lady would come with me. I felt safer with her, and when she was by my side none of the bigger boys ever tried to bother me—as they did when I was alone. There was only one time I was confronted by several of the neighborhood boys on the back road when Lady was with me.

I heard the sound of their bikes coming as I sat by the creek. Lady was just below me, out of sight from the road.

"Four-eyes," a familiar voice said, "we're goin' to break your neck."

I stood and looked up the bank to see Pauly Roffmeir staring down at me, a satisfied look on his face and a stick in his hand. Then I snapped my fingers, and Lady jumped up and came to my side. As the two of us walked up the bank together, the three boys backed up. The ruff on Lady's neck was standing up. She had heard the tone of Pauly's voice.

"We're not afraid of your dog," Pauly said, in a voice that told me just the opposite.

Then Lady started growling and took a couple of slow steps toward them. Those three boys were on their bikes and down Mill Road faster than you could whistle "Dixie."

From then on, whenever I was with Lady, they gave me wide berth.

As a puppy, Lady would eat my shoes—until she discovered

the wonder of rubber bones—and she wet the rug more than once before she learned to go on the newspapers and then to go outside. But I remember her most as she was when she was full grown and dignified. She was a big quiet dog with a thick golden coat, a white ruff around her neck, and delicate white feet. I remember her weighing over fifty pounds, too heavy for me to lift after she turned ten months of age.

We never taught her any tricks. My grandfather just liked a dog to be a dog. To come when you called her, and to lie down next to my grandmother's or my grandfather's chair—that was all we expected of her. That, and to keep us company. And anyone who has ever owned a dog knows how good, how very good, a dog is at keeping you company. I remember how she would come over to me with her rubber bone in her mouth and make a little growling sound. That meant she wanted me to grab the end of it so we could play tug-of-war.

Those three years she lived with us went almost as fast as this quick summary of her life. They ended just as abruptly on the day when she walked out into 9N and was hit by a truck. The driver stopped and got out. He wasn't one of the kids who tore around our corner every day—like twenty-year-old Jimmy Peekpod with his hopped-up Ford. The truck driver was a middle-aged man who'd been obeying the speed limit. He had children of his own and his face was almost as grief-stricken as ours were. He reached into his pocket and took out his wallet.

"I want to pay for your dog," he said in a hesitant voice, standing over my grandfather as he carefully ran his hands along Lady's body, finding the bones that were broken in her neck, and knowing for sure that she was gone.

My grandfather waved off the twenty-dollar bill.

"She walked out in front of you all on her own," my grandfather said. "It weren't yer fault."

Then he bent over and picked Lady's limp body up from the

road. Even though she weighed almost as much as I did, he picked her up with almost no effort, the muscles tight in his thin brown arms.

We buried Lady in the backyard at the edge of the Woods. I put her favorite rubber bone next to her, and then my grandfather filled in the hole.

I cried until I got the hiccups and couldn't stop, even though my grandparents tried to comfort me. I was still crying when I went to bed, but I could hear them talking in their room.

"Jesse," my grandmother said, "I can never have a collie again."

I understood because I felt the same way. We didn't want another collie to share or confuse the memories we now would carry with us of Lady.

My grandfather was silent for a long time. I found myself wondering if he understood. Then, as always, he said just the right words.

"Tomorrow," my grandfather said, "we'll go and get Sonny another dog."

17
I BE A
DANGEROUS MAN

In 1993 I was in Mexico, visiting the Lacandon Mayan people. There I learned that some of their beliefs about dogs are much the same as those of the Abenaki people. Hunting was always of great importance to those people of the jungle, just as it was to my ancestors in our northeastern forests. A good dog was more than a man's best friend; a good dog was often the difference between life and death. And a dog's loyalty goes beyond life.

"They will greet you after you leave this earth," old Chan K'in said to me.

Among the Mayan people they tell the story this way. When a man's soul leaves the body after death and travels to the underworld, that soul comes to a wide river. There he is met by his dog.

"What do you see here, master?" the dog asks him.

"I see water that is very deep," the man answers. "There is a strong current and giant alligators. I cannot cross it."

"Master," says the dog, "you always treated me well. I will help you. Lie on my back and hold onto my ears, and I will carry you over the water."

Soon another man's soul comes to that wide water. He too is met by his dog. He also sees that the water is wide and that the current is swift and that there are great alligators waiting to pull him down. He says this to his dog, and his dog answers him.

"Master," the dog says, "you cut off my tail and my ears; you drove me away from you. So I have no ears for you to grab hold of and no tail for you to grasp. I will not help you. You must cross this river alone."

So Chan K'in Viejo, who was over a hundred then and would live for three more years, told the story.

One morning, when I woke up in his village of Naha, hearing the sound of the jungle birds calling from the tall trees, I told Chan K'in about a dream I'd just had.

"I dreamt," I said, "that someone sold my little dog."

Chan K'in was silent for a while. I was surprised. Chan K'in always liked to hear people's dreams and interpret them. His usual morning greeting included the question, "Did you dream?"

Then I realized why he did not say Neh tsoi, *which means, "that is good," when I finished telling him about my dream. My friend Robert Bruce, who has lived in Mexico for four decades among the Lacandones and was acting as my guide and interpreter, also looked concerned. Among the Lacandon Maya it is not a fortunate thing to dream of a dog. In their interpretation of the symbolism of dreams, a dog means that disease is coming to you. Finally Chan K'in shook his head and smiled. He spoke a few quick words in Mayan to Robert. Robert nodded and laughed.*

"Chan K'in says that, though dreaming of a dog may mean illness, then again perhaps in this case it is only that someone actually has just sold your little dog."

But it was not. The sand-fly bites that I received on my ankles that morning as I went to the stream to bathe carried leishmaniasis. The wound on my left ankle grew larger and larger until, two months later, it was the size of a fist. It would take a year and six rounds of antibiotics before that wound would finally heal. The scar, which will be with me for the rest of my life, is brown, and its shape is almost that of a small sitting dog.

But here, in the land where my Abenaki ancestors hunted with their dogs for thousands of years, to dream of your dog does not mean that illness will come to you. It has only meant, for me, a reassurance that I will see again those dogs that I loved. It means only that I, like so many other human beings whose lives are brief, have dared to care for creatures whose years on this earth will always be fewer than our own.

Scotty was his name. He was a little, black, short-legged mongrel who, according to the man at the animal shelter, was mostly Scotch terrier. While the other dogs hung back or yelped hysterically, he came right up to the fence and stuck his nose against the back of my hand as I held it out to him. Then he sat back on his haunches and lifted up his front paws. There was so much weight on his backside that he looked like the four-foot-tall Joe Palooka punching bag that I'd had when I was three—it was weighted at the bottom, and when you hit it, it just swung right back up to a standing position.

I laughed. Then the little black dog looked up at me and barked. As soon as he barked he fell over on his back, and I laughed harder.

I looked over to my grandfather. He was already counting out the three dollars into the hand of the animal shelter man.

"Yup," Grampa said, "he says he wants us to take him home."

Scotty was perhaps three years old when I got him, but his exuberance was always that of a puppy.

"That there is a dog with more personality than brains," said Dan Atwell, one of the loggers who often stopped by our store, as he watched me walking around the lawn while Scotty hung onto my pants leg with his teeth and growled softly.

I didn't answer that. At the age of ten I had learned there was no good answer to such remarks, whether they were about dogs or people. I just stopped walking and said, "Sit." As soon as I did that, Scotty let go of my pants leg and swung up into his sitting position, his little front legs bent, his mouth open and his tongue hanging out.

Dan started laughing. "Well, he minds good, I'll give you that," he said.

"You don't want to try to take ahold of me with that dog around," my grandfather said. "He'll come right after you."

That was what my grandfather always said about every dog we ever owned. The strange thing was that it was true. Though I never saw Grampa do a single thing to make any of our dogs come to his defense, and I never heard him say "Sic 'em," all anyone had to do was make a threatening gesture toward my grandfather to find out that his words were not just bluff.

"Quit kiddin', you old rooster," Dan Atwell said. He reached out a hand as if about to take my grandfather by the arm. My grandfather didn't move, but Scotty did. In two shakes of a lamb's tail he had jumped in between Dan and my grandfather. Front legs spread wide, teeth bared, he growled at Dan Atwell with such ferocity that Dan, even though he was six feet tall, jumped back.

"Jeezum!" Dan said.

"Tole yuh," said my grandfather.

Although Scotty became a part of our lives, his time with us was even shorter than Lady's. I was walking down Middle Grove Road with him only a year later, when I heard the screech of tires behind me. I turned to see a hopped-up Ford swerving as it squealed around the corner in our direction. The car almost hit me as it went past.

Scotty, who had jumped between me and that car, was not as lucky. I picked him up. There was blood in his mouth and his eyes were open. I carried him across the driveway toward my grandparents. Both my grandmother and my grandfather had stood up from their chairs in front of the station and were coming toward me, but Grampa's eyes were not on me; they were looking down Middle Grove Road.

I heard tires squealing and the roar of a four-barrel engine growing louder; then the same Ford that had struck my dog screeched to a stop in the driveway behind me. The driver jumped out and slammed his door. It was Jimmy Peekpod.

"What did you—" my grandmother started to say, but Jimmy Peekpod didn't let her finish.

"Your goddamn dog got right out in the road," Jimmy Peekpod shouted, his face reddening more as he yelled. "I could of had an accident. Look at my fender there. Who's gonna pay for that?"

My grandmother's face became as pale as one of her china plates. She took a deep breath. "How can you say that? You just killed Sonny's dog."

"Hell!" Jimmy Peekpod said, stepping closer to my grandmother and poking a finger at her. "You keep that kid out of the road or I'll goddamn run him over too."

My eyes filled with tears, I put Scotty's body down on the driveway. I couldn't believe what this tall, mean-voiced man was saying. I couldn't believe the way he was treating my grandmother, a woman that everyone treated with respect. She had been town clerk for a term and she had just been elected to the school board. But Jimmy Peekpod didn't know or care about any of that.

"You hear me, you fat ol' bitch?"

I was looking for something to hit him with, but I didn't have to. My grandfather's voice spoke from behind Jimmy Peekpod.

"Don't you never talk that way to my wife," he said.

Jimmy Peekpod whirled around and lifted a big fist.

"You ol' red nigger," he said, "I'm going to—"

He never finished that threat. My grandfather's right hand came up so fast that all I saw was a blur of motion. That open palm struck Jimmy Peekpod on his left ear with a loud hollow *whop!* And even though he was a head taller, forty pounds heavier, and more than forty years younger than my grandfather, Jimmy Peekpod went down like a poleaxed ox.

"Come on," Grampa said. "Get up." He spoke in a voice I'd never heard before, cool and violent all at once. It was not a voice any man would want to hear directed at him. My grandfather stood there with his left foot forward and his right foot back, in the easy stance of a man who'd fought so many times that it came as natural to him as breathing. His hands were at his waist and balled up into fists. Out of the corner of my eye I could see Grampa's friend Jim Rollins running across the road toward us from his car. He'd seen what was happening and was coming to help my grandfather. But Grampa didn't need help.

Jimmy Peekpod scuttled away on the ground like a crab. My grandfather didn't follow him. Jimmy Peekpod pulled himself up the side of his car and held his hand to his ear, where blood was pouring out.

"You broke my ear!" he said in a high, hysterical voice. "I'm gonna get the law on you."

"Come on," my grandfather said again.

But Jimmy Peekpod was not about to come on. He fumbled open the door of his car, started the engine, and drove off up Route 9N toward Greenfield Center.

"You all right, Jess?" Jim Rollins said.

"I expect his eardrum *is* broken," my grandfather said. Then he turned to my grandmother. And although they were never ones to make a public show of affection—which my grandmother said was undignified—he put his arms around her that day in sight of all the world that was going by, and she let him hold her.

We were coming back up the lawn from burying Scotty, me carrying the shovel, when the sheriff's car pulled in. My grandmother was already talking to the deputy when Grampa and I arrived. Jim Rollins, who had stayed around to see what would happen and to take care of any customers that might come, remained seated in one of the chairs in front of the station. He knew better than to get in my grandmother's way when she had her dander up.

"You've got no call to get out of that car, Bobby," my grandmother said. "That boy threatened me and my husband and said he'd run over Sonny."

"I can't help it, Mrs. Bowman," said the sheriff's deputy, Bobby Bentson. "He has swore out a complaint. I got to take Jess in."

"Let him out of the car, Marion," my grandfather said.

My grandmother stood back from the door of the police car, and as the deputy climbed out, Grampa held out his hands.

"I'll go with you, all right. But I'm not going to take a step unless you put them handcuffs on me. I be a dangerous old man."

"That's right," said my grandmother.

Bobby Bentson shook his head, but he knew my grandparents. He took the handcuffs off his belt and fastened them onto my grandfather's wrists.

"Now turn on that siren," Grampa said. "Yer bringing in a dangerous old man."

Bobby shook his head again, but he did as my grandfather said. Siren wailing, the police car went up 9N.

"Sonny," my grandmother said, "you stay and watch the station. Mr. Rollins will help you out."

"I surely will," Jim Rollins said. "You give 'em heck now, Mrs. Bowman."

My grandmother got into the blue Plymouth and went up 9N in the wake of the siren, which could still be heard wailing faintly in the distance.

"Don't worry about them two, Sonny," Jim Rollins said to me. "That snotass Peekpod kid still don't know what hit him."

An hour later they were back. Grampa had been brought before Town Justice Charles Cedric Weirman, still wearing those handcuffs. Deputy Bobby Bentson never got a chance to explain that my grandfather had insisted on being handcuffed. Instead he had to fumble for his keys and get those cuffs off as quickly as he could, while Justice Weirman went up one side of him and down the other about treating an old man like a common criminal.

Jimmy Peekpod, who had sworn out the complaint to bring my grandfather in, was either too angry or too stupid to see which way the wind was already blowing. When asked what had happened he stepped forward, holding a handkerchief to his ear.

"His damn dog ran out in the road, and when I stopped my damn car that old bastard hit me with a hammer," he said. "And . . ."

His testimony was interrupted by the crack of the Judge's gavel. "There will be no swearing in my court. I hereby fine you five dollars."

"What the hell?"

The gavel cracked a second time. "That is ten dollars. Would you like to try for fifteen, young man?"

"Better shut your yap, kid," said someone from the crowd that had assembled in the town hall. The ripple of laughter that went around the room subsided as Justice Weirman looked out at the audience.

Then, as Jimmy Peekpod stood there speechless, Justice Weirman turned toward my grandfather.

"Where's that hammer, Jess?" he said.

My grandfather held up his open right hand. "Right here, yer Honor," he said.

Even Justice Weirman joined in the laughter that followed my grandfather's words.

"Now, why did they bring you here in handcuffs, Jess? Did you resist arrest?"

"No sir, I reckon they figgered I was a dangerous old man for picking on that little boy there."

Justice Weirman looked over his glasses at Jimmy Peekpod. "A great lunk like you, twice the size of Mr. Bowman here, and you accuse him of assault? Is that right?"

Jimmy Peekpod thought a minute and then nodded his head.

"Then you're an even bigger fool than you appear to be, young man. Charges are dismissed." The gavel cracked down again.

Jimmy Peekpod turned away, but before he could reach the door the deputy sheriff stopped him at a signal from Justice Weirman.

"Young man," said Justice Weirman, as my grandparents left the courtroom, "have you forgotten the matter of ten dollars which you owe to the town of Greenfield?"

TO BE HUNTERS

"We were born to be hunters." That is how Maurice Dennis explained it to me one day almost two decades ago. "It is the way the Creator made us."

I had heard those words before and I would hear them spoken again by other Abenaki elders. Each time I heard them I would think of my grandfather.

When Ktsi Nwaskw, the Great Mystery, made all the beings that walk and fly and crawl and swim, they were made in such a way as to give them special powers and a special place to live. They were given instructions on how to live. Those instructions were put into their hearts and in the shapes of their bodies. So it is that the fish people were given the ability to live beneath the waters and the bird people the ability to fly high above the land. And the animal people were given the ability to walk on two legs or four legs or to crawl upon the earth.

So that they would not be lonely, Ktsi Nwaskw made it so that all beings would have children to care for, and their children would have children, and it would always continue on in that way. But Ktsi Nwaskw saw that if this were so, if every being continued to have children forever, there would no longer be room to live upon this earth. And if every being lived forever, they might not value the great gift of life. So Ktsi Nwaskw made it that all beings would eventually die. To keep them alert and strong, Ktsi Nwaskw made it that some beings would hunt the others, and some would be the hunted. That is how it remains to this day.

Maurice Dennis was a smallish man, as firm and blocky as a log cut from a cedar tree. Although he was a wood-carver, his hands were broad and his fingers were short. His large round eyes looked straight at me as he spoke, and I saw the bear within him.

"Our instructions on how to live are written in our eyes," he said. His small hands, with index fingers extended, reached up to touch the cheekbones on each side of his face. "If you look at the deer and the rabbit," he continued, "you'll see that their eyes are on the sides of their heads. That is so they can see in all directions around them because they were meant to be the ones who are hunted." His hands moved back to the front of his face and then he brought those two fingers forward in a graceful gesture. "But the eyes of the fox and the wolf, the bear and the mountain lion, are in the front of their heads. That is because they are supposed to be the hunters; that's how the Creator made them. That's how we were made."

I was born in October, the moon when the leaves are falling. My grandparents always told me that made October my own very special time. Then, when the frost had come and painted the woodlands with crimson red and bright yellow, we would go hunting in the woods behind Chet Barton's house.

When my grandmother was a girl, those woods across Route 9N were part of the property owned by her parents. There was no such thing as fire insurance in those days—or if there were, it wasn't something that people in Greenfield Center had. So, after the fires that destroyed their mills and their houses, my great-grandparents had to sell off most of the land they owned in Greenfield to make ends meet.

Even though those woods belonged on paper to Chet, my

grandmother and grandfather still continued to go into them freely, and Chet would not have dreamed of complaining about it or trying to stop them. After all, he brought down his cow Sonaska to stake her in the field behind our house where the grass was better. When I was ten years old, one of my jobs—when I carried the slops out to our hogs in their pigpen on the back side of the Little House—was to check Sonaska and make sure that she hadn't pulled her stake loose. As placid as she seemed when she was grazing, Sonaska had a mind of her own and would take off, dragging her stake and her rope behind her.

When we went hunting in Barton's Woods, my grandfather and I, we never carried guns or weapons of any kind—though Grampa would bring his jackknife, for no man ever went anywhere without one when I was young. We were hunting for autumn leaves.

My grandfather would use his pocketknife, and I would pull down the end of a beautiful maple branch so that he could carefully cut off a spray of leaves patterned with shades of orange and red and green that always differed, one leaf from another. Those small bright branches were placed in vases all around the living room and on the dining-room table.

The best maple leaves—the ones with the most unusual patterns on them, the ones that were most perfectly shaped—I would save. I'd take a bar of paraffin, the wax that my grandmother used to seal the tops of canning jars, and melt it in a pan. Then, holding a leaf by the very tip of its stem, I would dip it into the wax. Once waxed, the leaves would never dry up or lose their color, and from the time I was six I kept a scrapbook filled with years of leaves.

I kept that scrapbook till I took it to my fifth-grade class and, following my teacher's instructions, left it over the weekend on display on the bookshelf at the back of the classroom. When I came in Monday morning, the scrapbook was gone. I didn't want to cry. I knew that the bigger boys wanted to see me cry. But I cried when I got home. It had been a bad day in more ways than one.

"It's not just my leaf book. They all hate me at school," I said to my grandmother. "They call me a brain and 'four-eyes,' and they pick on me because I'm little and I have glasses and I know more than they do." I reached my hand up to rub the scar on the back of my head where Doc Magovern had sewn in those stitches. There was a little bald spot the size of a dime where the hair never grew back.

"It's all right, Sonny," my grandmother said, reaching over to pat me on my back. My grandfather didn't say anything, but I felt him sitting behind me and I felt safer in the circle of their caring. But I had to tell my grandmother the worst thing of all.

"My teacher isn't like Miss McTygue at all," I said, referring to my fourth-grade teacher, whose gentle ways and quick mind had endeared her to me forever. "She makes mistakes! Today in class we were doing questions and answers in social studies. You know I always get the answers. Then it would be my turn to ask the questions and I had some really good ones. So when Molly Wingman asked the first question, I-got-my-hand-up-before-anyone-and-I-stood-up-to-answer-the-question."

I was talking faster now, my mouth rushing to keep up with everything in my mind. I could feel my grandmother stroking my head, but it didn't calm me down. I pushed my glasses back up my nose as I talked. They kept falling down because they were taped together at the bridge. They had been broken, yet again, when someone had thrown a basketball at me on the playground and I hadn't been able to get my hands up in time.

I took a breath and told my grandmother about it. Molly Wingman had asked this question: "What natural resource is black and comes out of the ground in Texas?"

Of course I knew that one. I smiled as I said, "The answer is petroleum." I was about to explain how petroleum is refined into gasoline and motor oil, but I never got to do that.

"No, it is not," Molly Wingman said. "The answer is *oil*."

I had turned to look at the teacher, amused that Molly Wingman didn't know that petroleum is, as I had read in the dictionary that I kept by my bed, "an oily flammable bituminous liquid that occurs in many places in the upper strata of the earth or in reservoir formations where it is obtained by drilling." Oil, on the other hand, I knew to be "any of a number of substances that are typically unctuous, viscous, flammable liquids." But there was no look of understanding on the face of Mrs. Jay.

Instead, Mrs. Jay had looked at the notes in her hand, nodded, and said to Molly, "Good, you can ask another question. Joseph, *sit down*."

"Grama," I said, "I don't think Mrs. Jay knew that petroleum is oil or that oil isn't always petroleum. Oil is *not* always a bituminous liquid that occurs in the upper strata of the earth or in reservoir formations! I thought teachers had to know everything."

My grandmother let me talk. With her arms around me, she was rocking me back and forth now, and I was hiccupping as I cried. I hated it when I cried, but there were still times when I couldn't stop it. Finally, when I was quiet, my grandmother spoke to me.

"Sonny," she said, "Grampa and I love you. Someday you are going to grow up and be bigger and stronger than all those boys who pick on you now."

My grandfather put his hand on my back. "Jes' wait, Sonny," he said. "Time to come, them boys will all want to be your friends."

"What about Mrs. Jay?" I said. Then my grandmother said

something that took me half a lifetime to understand—even though I knew, without understanding why, that there was truth in what she was saying.

"She's stopped looking," my grandmother said. "But you're always going to be looking. That's the way you were made."

19 TWO DEER

In my dream my father holds the heads of two deer in his hands. They are young deer, not fawns, but no older than their second year, for their antlers are thumb-long stubs. I'm a teenager in this dream, and I've been asked to come over and help my father at his taxidermy shop, half a mile up Middle Grove Road from the station.

"The thing about these deer," my father said, "is the way they grew together."

He holds up the two heads, and I can see that they are joined forehead to forehead by a thin piece of bone. Their eyes have that dry, milky glaze of the dead animal, their tongues are loose in their mouths.

"Man who brought 'em in wants 'em mounted this way."

He hands me the deer heads and I am alone with them in the room. They are heavy in my hands—the weight of flesh still in them, unlike the much-lighter, already-mounted heads. Those heads are no more than tanned skin stretched over a papier-mâché form with the antlers fastened on the top, held in place by screws driven through the small triangular piece of frontal bone where the horns are connected, sawed from the deer's skull. Tanned skin and antlers, glass eyes to imitate life: the head bolted to a flat wooden plaque so that it can be hung on the wall.

*And I remember how I felt about taxidermy in those years. I re-
member the feeling of being suffocated when I stood in my father's
showroom, surrounded by hundreds of beautifully lifelike animals
and birds and fish hung from all the walls. All of them caught in a
still-life pose, frozen like a single frame in a movie, none of them
holding the breath of life. It always saddened and frightened and
fascinated me. Had I not been afraid of my father's anger, I would
have placed my hands on each one of those creatures, trying to feel
what it was like when a heart still beat and the wild flood of life
still coursed through its blood.*

*So, in my dream, as I held those two heads I knew what I had
to do. I carried them to the hide room at the back of my father's
shop. The hide room was a long low barn with a concrete floor.
There, covered with salt, were the flat skins of hundreds of deer,
waiting to be loaded into the green pickup and taken to the Karg
Brothers' tannery in Johnstown. Still holding the linked deer heads,
I picked up the skins that had been theirs and walked with them to
Bell Brook, where I washed away the salt.*

*My father will be so angry, I thought. But I did not stop. I
placed the skins on the autumn earth of the field near the creek,
where the yarrow plants were green and the timothy had turned
brown from the first frost.*

*Then I separated the heads from each other, breaking the thin
link of cartilage between their foreheads. I placed each head by the
skin that had covered its body in life, and I began to sing. And as I
sang, the earth rose beneath them and filled them with life, and two
young deer stood there before me. They danced in the wind that
grew stronger as their feet touched the earth. Then each of them
bowed their head to me and leaped; and they were gone, disappearing back into the forest.*

*And when I woke the next morning and walked outside I found,
in the new snow, the tracks of two deer close to our house.*

My father was a taxidermist. He began what would be his life's work when he was a very young man. It was the time of the Depression, and jobs and money were equally scarce. His father, who had learned the trade of masonry in his native Czechoslovakia, was often away from home, looking for work. As the oldest child my father must have felt that weight of responsibility grow heavier on his shoulders every day.

So my father turned to the woods. My Slovak grandfather had always loved the woods. He told my younger sister Margaret once that it was because of the woods that he seldom went to church. "Dey are Catolics," he said, referring to all the rest of his family. "I follow de old religion." It was in the forest that my Slovak grandfather, Joseph Bruchac, went to pray. And though I grew up knowing little of that side of my family, I still remember that my Slovak grandfather's eyes were always as large and as bright, as alert with life, as the beautiful eyes of a deer. It was from his father that my father gained his first knowledge of woodcraft, of hunting and trapping. And during the Depression it was my father's traplines, set mostly for muskrat whose pelts would be sold for a quarter each, that fed his mother and his four younger brothers and sisters.

He began to learn taxidermy then. He learned it from books and from an uncle who had been a taxidermist. He studied and he taught himself by trial and error. His mother hated it. She called him lazy and a bum. She shouted insults at him in Slovak and in broken English. She told him he was afraid of real work. With real work you get a salary every week, you put in regular hours. My father heard her words and, I now understand, those words hurt him. They fed the anger and frustration that would come out years later in words he would shout at his wife and his children. But he did not give up taxidermy, just as his mother never gave up urging him to do real work. Even when

My father in his taxidermy studio, 1957

he had become successful at his business and was a man in middle age, he would say that his mother still thought he had to be doing something illegal if he was making a living as a taxidermist.

Because they were so poor, their clothes were different. My father would never forget the tattered fur coat he had to wear, winter after winter, to keep out the cold on winter mornings. When my father and his brothers and sisters walked the three miles to the one-room school on Locust Grove Road, a mile from the store my maternal grandparents ran, other kids would make fun of them, taunt them, tell them they were wood-chucks. There were more Slovaks every year in Greenfield Center. Some came from the New York City area, while others were recent immigrants from the little towns near Bratislava in Slo-vakia. They built a Sokol Hall in Greenfield, where they did gymnastics together and put on plays in Slovak. But the Slovak kids were always outnumbered.

"They called us brown-heads," my father said. And his only friend when he was in grade school was another child as mis-placed as he was, an African-American boy named Ed.

The only answer to it all, my father thought, would be to make money. With money he'd be respected. If you had money and if people thought you had money—that was the way.

Because I grew up with my grandparents I did not see a great deal of my parents when I was a child. Mary Ann would spend Saturday night with us sometimes when my parents went out together, but it was never the other way around. I never spent the night at my parents' house. When I was eleven years old they built a new house, fifty yards from the old one that Grampa and Grama had given to them, on the eighty acres of property that we always called "The Farm." In that house there was a bedroom for me. They called it "Sonny's room." It was always empty.

There were only two regular times I spent with my parents. One was when we went for those rides that ended so often in disaster. The other was when my father's brothers came up from Flushing and Norwalk with their families, and there would be a big dinner at Grama and Grampa Bruchac's house. I was always taken along to those dinners.

Sometimes I sat at the smaller table set up for the kids in the front room. But when I became eleven, as the oldest of the male grandchildren, I was seated with the grown-ups at the big table. I wished then that I was back at the kids' table. I was un-certain of what to say or do. The adults spoke in English and in Slovak, a language that I never knew. My mother didn't know it either. I remember one time when my mother looked at me across the wide oak table with a sort of sympathy that surprised me, during a long discussion in Slovak between my aunt Rose and Grama Bruchac.

At those Bruchac family gatherings everyone knew each other in ways that I never could know them. Mary Ann was best friends with our cousin Pam and was invited to spend a week with her and Uncle Milt and Aunt Ethel. Mary Ann was happiest, it seemed to me, when she was sitting at that table with all the Bruchacs.

I knew that I would never get such invitations to visit. I liked my younger cousins Bruce, Uncle Milt's son, and Chip, Al's son. But I knew that I would neither be invited nor allowed to visit them. Long Island and Connecticut were as far away as the moon. I knew, too, that people were always talking about me. I saw how they all stared at me when they thought I was not looking. And there would be times when I would walk into the kitchen and find Grama Bruchac with tears in her eyes, saying something to one of my aunts or uncles about that boy who, God knows, should be with his parents. I would walk out quickly then, go past them out the back door through the woodshed, to sit on the concrete steps near my grandmother's chicken coop. It was soothing to listen to the *pock-pock-po-ock* of the Rhode Island Reds as they strutted back and forth and scratched for food. I could put my hands through the chicken wire and they would peck softly at my fingers.

I was always glad when their conversation shifted to other subjects. It might be my father's business or Al's liquor store or, sometimes, Aunt Margaret. Margaret had been my father's favorite. When World War II came, it was Margaret and Al who served. My father's bad eyes and the fractured skull he'd gotten in a motorcycle accident kept him out of the army. But Al saw all the worst fighting, from Sicily to the South Pacific. And Margaret, who had been a nurse in the Philippines, became ill there. When she was shipped home, she was dying. My father met the plane and carried her to the car.

I could always tell when he was speaking about that, even if he spoke in Slovak. My father acted very differently in his mother's house. His voice was no longer so loud, and his face didn't seem to get as clouded with anger as it was almost every other time when I saw him. In his mother's house, his face became gentler, more vulnerable, especially when he spoke of Margaret. His large, dark eyes would fill with tears, and he would take off his glasses to wipe his eyes with the back of his hand.

The Bruchacs. *Back row, left to right:* My mother, holding Mary Ann; my father; his brother Milton. *Front row, left to right:* Grama and Grampa Bruchac; my father's brother Albert and his wife, Patricia. *Seated:* My Aunt Margaret, and Uncle Milton's children, Pamela and Cynthia

"My little sister," he would say, "she weighed almost nothing."

She died in an army hospital in 1945, and the trunk full of her clothes and uniforms sat in the attic in Grama Bruchac's house. No one was allowed to touch it. Years later that trunk would be given to my sister Margaret, who was born nine years after Mary Ann and given the most sacred name.

At times, after midday dinner when they were all talking, I would look into the living room. My father had bought his mother a television, and if it was the right time on a Sunday afternoon the religious shows—Bishop Fulton J. Sheen and the others—would be over. Then, if it was a holiday weekend, a cartoon might come on. I was always amazed when I could see parts of Mickey Mouse in *Fantasia* or a Bugs Bunny cartoon from the 1940's. But if a football game was coming on television, there would be no room for me.

"Hey, a football game," Uncle Milt might say to me. He was my favorite uncle. "Sonny, you going to play football when you get bigger?"

Before I could say anything, my father would answer. "He's not interested in sports. He's afraid to get hurt."

I would go to the front porch where my coat hung, put it on, and go quietly down the big steps that led to the lawn. During the summer that lawn was edged with long beds of flowers, almost as many as Grama Bowman had planted in her gardens all around the station. I could sit under the tall hibiscus and foxgloves and delphiniums. I could smell the scents and let the hours go by until I would hear my mother call me and know that they were going to take me back home, take me the three miles south down South Greenfield Road and east along Middle Grove, home to my place of refuge, my grandparents' house on Splinterville Hill.

BLACK SHEEP

 *The people who some call the Ojibway call themselves* Anishinabe, *or "Human Beings." The Abenaki call themselves* Alnoba, *which means the same. We say they are our cousins. Long ago, it is said, we all lived together, until our cousins left us and traveled far in the direction of the setting sun. But our languages and our traditions remind us that we are relatives and that we should never forget who our relatives are.*

The Anishinabe tell this story about the one they call Manabozho. *Long ago, they say, Manabozho was out walking around. He was very hungry. When at last he did get some food, he immediately made a fire and began to cook it. He was so hungry that he could hardly wait. As soon as that food was ready he grabbed it with both hands.*

"This food is mine," said his right hand.

"No," said his left hand, "I grabbed it first. It is mine."

Then his two hands began to argue, getting angrier and angrier as they did so. They forgot that they were relatives. They forgot that both of them were taking the food to the same mouth to feed the same stomach.

"It is mine."

"No, it is mine!"

His hands pulled the food first in one direction and then the other. Finally, his hands became so angry that each one took a knife and attacked the other.

The scars from that fight can still be seen to this day. They are the lines that all people have on their palms.

My grandmother had three brothers. Wyllis, the oldest, was the town lawyer in the town of Corinth (pronounced Kuh-RINTH by locals and KOH-rinth by those new to our area) twenty miles up 9N. He came down once a week to engage in serious games of cutthroat canasta with my grandmother. I would set up the card table for them in the living room, just a few feet away from the front door. My grandmother would sit herself down in her chair, which always faced the door, waiting for her brother to arrive at two o'clock sharp. We'd hear his car pull up, and then we would see him through the thick-glassed window that filled the top half of the front door. He would come right in, a tall, stooped, elderly man with a deep voice, a high forehead, and a beaky nose. He'd hang his coat on a hook and sit down in his chair. Sometimes I would sit and watch them. My grandfather always made himself scarce and would usually go out to either sit in the station or in one of the chairs in front under the station's overhang, depending on the weather and the season.

Wyllis and my grandmother talked about their card game, and little if anything else was ever mentioned. My grandmother always kept score. They would play for two or three hours. Then Wyllis would stand up, put on his coat, and walk back out the door. If he'd been winning, he might say, "I'll see you next week, Marion." But if he'd been losing he'd not say anything at all. While my grandmother put away the cards in the special drawer in the cabinet, I would fold up the card table.

Orvis, the next oldest brother, seldom came to visit. He was shorter than Wyllis, and balder, and his voice was higher and less pleasant. But he still had the Dunham nose. Orvis came north only once every two or three years. Usually he stayed with his little hotel down in Warm Springs, which was not far from the Natural Bridge of Virginia, a giant arch of stone that we always visited whenever we made our spring migration south. Orvis had once owned a house that his parents gave him on Grange Road, only half a mile away, but he had sold it long ago. Orvis had a bit of a reputation for being tight with his money, and although my grandmother wrote to him, it was clear he wasn't her favorite brother.

Then there was Harry. Harry had been the baby of the family, and my grandmother told stories about what it was like when they were all children. One time, Wyllis and Orvis got together enough money to buy an air rifle. They shot at cans with it for a while, but before long they got bored. Then Harry came up to them.

"Kin I have a turn?" he said.

"Yer only eight years old. That is too young to shoot an air rifle," Wyllis said.

"Wait a minute," said Orvis, "I've got an idea. We'll let you shoot if you'll do something."

"Okay," Harry said. "Tell me what to do."

"You jes' run as fast as you can and we'll try to shoot you. We'll jes' shoot you in the pants and it won't hurt much a-tall."

Wyllis agreed that this was fair, and seeing as how Orvis was holding the gun, he was allowed to shoot first. Harry took off running. Orvis pulled up that air rifle, pumped it a few times, and then, pop! He hit Harry right in the seat of the pants.

"*Yow!*" Harry yelled. He fell down on the ground and commenced to roll around, holding the seat of his pants and bawling, "I'm kilt, I'm kilt."

Orvis and Wyllis went and stood over Harry.

Orvis thought it was pretty funny, but Wyllis looked worried.

"He ain't nowhere near kilt," Orvis said. "He's just bawlin'."

"I know that," Wyllis said, "but what if Mother hears him?"

As soon as Wyllis said that, Harry jumped to his feet.

"I'm a-going to tell Mother what you done to me," he bawled. Then he started across the field toward the house.

Orvis laid hold of his arm. "Hold on, Harry, hold on. Don't tell Mother."

"You can't stop me," Harry said. "You done shot me and I'm tellin'."

Before long, both Wyllis and Orvis were begging Harry not to tell. By the time he'd stopped crying and agreed, Wyllis and Orvis had given him not only that air rifle, but also all the change in their pockets and a whole bag full of cat's-eye marbles.

"Harry," my grandmother said, "just about always ended up getting his way." But whereas Wyllis and Orvis and my grandmother went off to college, Harry was content to stay home. His parents gave him a little farm on Dunham Road, which ran between Petrified Gardens Road and South Greenfield Road, just two miles from the station to the southwest. Harry settled in on that farm and never left it. He traded horses and drank beer and, as my grandmother said, "Never had any ambitions to better himself." He did marry, though, and had a daughter and a son.

By the time I came along, that farm of Harry's had become pretty run-down and he was living there with his grown son, Bobby—whose wife had left him, just as his mother had left Uncle Harry. Harry was, as I overheard my grandmother say, the black sheep of the Dunham family. While I only suspect that he was my grandmother's favorite brother, I know for certain that he was my Grampa Jesse's favorite in-law.

The bridge that went across Dunham Brook, another half

mile beyond Uncle Harry's farm, had gone out in the early 1940's. There was so little traffic that the town never repaired it and that stretch of road became abandoned. So Dunham Road became, appropriately enough, a dead end at Uncle Harry's place.

The farm was one of my favorite destinations when I was eleven. It was a full mile and a half away, and being able to get there on my own had been a major victory for me.

"I'm in sixth grade," I told my grandmother. "Everybody else in sixth grade goes everywhere on their bikes."

My grandmother peered over at my grandfather with a suspicious look on her face. She knew that he was always the one to take my side and encourage me to do things I'd been afraid to do before. My grandfather did not look back at her. He busied himself with his pipe and a well-used pipe cleaner.

Finally, with a sigh, my grandmother agreed: Harry's was close enough. The dirt roads that led there were so little traveled that I could be allowed to ride there on my bike—even though I was still strictly forbidden to ever set foot or wheel on 9N, which my grandmother considered a Road of Death.

Her judgment was not so melodramatic, when I look back and consider that I saw on that road right in front of our house not only the demise of six of my cats and five of my dogs, but also at least one fatal car accident every year. The outside post of the station was knocked out twice a year, on average, by cars that failed to make the curve coming down from Greenfield or Corinth—and if you looked down the hill from a hundred yards above our place you could see why. The road headed right straight for our gas station, swinging down fast to the left just after the intersection of Middle Grove Road that came in there from the west.

Most accidents took place late on a Friday or Saturday night, usually after we'd gone to bed. We'd hear the sound of brakes locked and the long screech of a sliding car and then, just when we thought they might have made it, the crunch of glass and metal as they went through the guard rails and plowed either across our lawn into the stone wall, or—if they'd held the skid a bit longer—over the bank and into the woods where the trees would stop them soon enough. Then my grandfather and I would be up, finding the flashlights and putting on our shoes, while my grandmother called the state police and the ambulance, whose numbers she had memorized.

So when I headed off on my bike to visit Uncle Harry's it was never, never, *not ever* by way of Route 9N. I was to use only the back roads. And I carried with me a note from my grandmother saying that she had given me her okay.

The first time I had gone to Harry's on my own three years earlier had been without permission. I had gotten into hot water. Uncle Harry knew his sister well enough to know that he had better call her if he knew what was good for him, as soon as he saw his eight-year-old great-nephew come teetering into his yard on a new bike, trying to ride and wave and look at Uncle Harry's cows all at the same time, and ending up going off the road into a tangle of grapevines.

While Cousin Bobby got me up and brushed me off, Harry rang up Central and asked her to connect him to one-one-eight.

When my grandmother arrived to get me, Bobby and I were standing by the fence looking at the pigs. Bobby was laughing, and as she came up to me with a set look on her face, Bobby spoke to her.

"Aunt Marion," he said, still laughing, "Sonny's disappointed. He didn't see what he came here to see."

"What is that?" my grandmother said, her curiosity piqued.

"The black sheep," I said. "I heard you telling Grampa there was black sheep here, but all they got is cows and pigs and some chickens."

For one of the few times in her life my grandmother was speechless. She carefully took me by the arm and led me to the car. We drove in silence all the way back home, and when we got there she stopped the car and didn't get out.

"Sonny," she said at last.

"Yes, Grama," I answered. And thinking to get my apology in first and make things a little easier for myself, I quickly added, "I'm really, really sorry I rode over there without asking."

"That's all right," she said. "You're only a little boy. You make mistakes sometimes." Then she was quiet again. I waited, running my hand back and forth on the chrome door handle. That handle was so big it took me two hands and all my strength to open the door. Grama took a deep breath.

"You can go to visit your uncle Harry and your cousin Bobby any time you want from now on—just as long as you ask. You hear me?"

"I hear you, Grama." I reached my other hand toward the door handle. I was ready to go around and pull my bike out of the trunk, but my grandmother put her hand on my leg and stopped me.

"But there is one thing, Sonny," she said in a very soft, kind of sad voice.

"Yes, Grama?"

"You must never, never, *not ever* talk about black sheep around Uncle Harry or Cousin Bobby again."

"Yes, Grama."

MY GRANDMOTHER'S GARDEN

The Little People are the ones whose job it is to care for the gardens. They are called Mikumwesu *by the Abenaki and* Djo-geh-oh *or "Jungies" by the Mohawk. They look like very small, perfectly formed human beings—when you see them. Few people are allowed to see them, though. They come into the gardens at night and use cups made of leaves to water the plants. The dew that you see early in the morning is the water that spilled from their cups.*

Sometimes, when you are working in a garden, caring for the plants, you can feel them watching you. The Little People have special respect for human beings who are gardeners. If you see them, it is supposed to be a special blessing, a blessing that will inspire you to song or help you to understand things that others do not understand. It is possible, I have heard, that those blessed by the Mikumwesu can do such things as make themselves invisible or see things far away. But if you see the Little People, you are never supposed to tell anyone about it, or that blessing they have given you may vanish.

Although I knew very little about how to deal with other kids of my age, especially girls, I did understand about the natural world. I understood how baby animals were born and how it was that mother animals and father animals got together to have babies. Those things were never shown in Disney's nature movies, but they were in the books I borrowed from the library. And I knew about gardens.

My grandmother's garden was out front, right along the State Road where the world could see it. She had carefully planned her plantings so that something was in bloom in every season, from the first crocus and tulips and daffodils through the iris and columbine and lilies to the dahlias and mums and gladiolas of late summer. I remember the trips we used to make every spring and summer around Greenfield Center, until the year she became sick. We would drive along every back road, keeping our eyes out for gardens that had flowers in bloom that we didn't have.

Sometimes we'd travel with a cardboard box of Grama's own flowers, dug up carefully from her garden to thin out a place where there were too many iris or an overabundance of lilies. Those flowers of hers were gifts for other women whose gardens were lacking in that particular bloom. We would pull into a driveway and as a woman came out, wiping her hands on an apron much like the one my grandmother wore, my grandmother would climb out and meet her and ask if she could have some of a particular flower in that woman's garden. I don't recall anyone ever saying no to her. Meanwhile, I would wander among the blossoms, smelling their intoxicating scent, carefully touching the elegant petals.

I think my grandmother would have been shocked if I had told her what I knew—that gardens were places filled with sex. The pistils of the flowers were the female parts, while the stamens bursting with pollen were the male parts. The scents and the colors were lures to draw in bees, involving them in a wonderful kind of interspecies mating ritual, as the legs of the bees while they drew out the nectar would carry pollen from one flower to another, insuring the vigor of the species by cross-pollination.

Perhaps, though, Grama knew this too. After all, she had chosen to marry my grandfather.

Reading so much about plants and animals did give me some advantages. I remember the one time before my high school days when I did the unforgivable. Billy Wilson, one of the boys in my sixth-grade class, had actually asked me to come down to his house after school. I'd helped Billy get the right answer when he was called on in class and then I had shared some of my wild cherry cough drops with him at lunch. Because of my grandparents' store, I always had more candy in my lunch box (and more cavities in my teeth) than any other kid in School Two. That day, though, after eating three entire boxes of wild cherry cough drops, I had had enough (enough so that I find it hard to this day to think of a wild cherry cough drop or those two bearded men on the boxes without feeling slightly nauseous). I gave the rest of the box to Billy, who was surprisingly friendly after that.

"You're okay, Bruchac," he said. "Wanta come to my house after school?"

I was uncertain. I knew that my grandmother would be busy that afternoon. She was planning a baby shower for my mother, whose pregnancy was known to everyone, it seemed, except Mary Ann. For some reason, my parents thought she was too young to be told directly what was going to happen. All that they said was, "Around December, we're going to give you a little surprise." She gathered from the conversations she overheard about the surprise that it was something alive. Her assumption, therefore, was that they were finally going to give her a puppy of her own.

I'd had my own dogs since I was a baby, but Mary Ann had never been allowed to have one. My father was the only one who could have a dog—a bird dog for hunting. And that dog had to be treated as a hunting dog should. It was to be kept outdoors on a chain and never brought into the house. It wasn't that my father treated his hunting dogs badly; quite the contrary. He loved them dearly and they worshiped him. But he had learned to believe that a dog's place was not in the home, and he lived by that belief.

All that autumn, my sister remained convinced that she was going to be given a dog.

"I'm going to have a puppy of my own," she told me.

I wasn't quite certain how to tell her. "I'm not sure about that," I started to say.

"You're just jealous," she said in a tone of voice that told me it was dangerous to continue the conversation. I knew those warning signals well, and I backed off. From then on, until the day in December when Marge was born, I didn't say a word to her about the real reason why Mom was getting so overweight. Perhaps I should have continued trying. Certainly my parents should have told her the truth. If they had, then perhaps it would have prevented those feelings of betrayal and jealousy that must have flooded Mary Ann's heart when they brought home a new baby, a baby given the attention and love that she wanted so much for herself.

Because the shower was planned for that day, it seemed to me that there was no way I could get a ride to visit Billy, even though I desperately wanted to. No one had ever invited me to his house before!

"I can't get a ride," I said to him, in despair.

"Don't you have a bike?" he said. The way he said it made me know I couldn't possibly tell him that I was not allowed to take my bike on the road. It would make me sound like even more of a baby than I knew I was. After all, I was almost eleven years old. Billy lived in Saratoga Springs, two miles down Route 9N. The road was called Church Street there, but it was the same dreaded State Road that ran past the station.

I thought fast. If I went down Mill Road, which connected to the State Road further down, my grandmother wouldn't know where I was going. I could spend a couple of hours at Billy's—the days were still pretty long in September—and be back before anyone knew. The thought of deceiving my grandmother sent shivers down my back. Those shivers, I must admit, were an equal mixture of shame, fear, and exhilaration.

"Okay," I said.

"Good," said Billy. "We'll go and get Cokes at the soda fountain with Davey."

It was just as I had expected it would be at home. Everyone was busy with the shower.

"I'm going for a ride on my bike," I said, "then I'm going to work on a dam in the creek. I'll be back for supper."

My grandmother nodded and my grandfather smiled. My heart was pounding so loudly I was sure they could hear it, and my feet kept slipping off the pedals of the bike as I headed toward Mill Road, looked back, and then turned left and began to coast downhill.

It was downhill most of the way to Saratoga and it didn't take me long to get there. Billy was sitting on his front porch with his best friend, Davey Sher. Billy's mother was there with them.

"This is Sonny Bruchac, Mom," Billy said.

"Hello, Mrs. Wilson," I said. "I am very pleased to make your acquaintance."

I knew how to talk to adults. Billy's mother smiled while Billy rolled his eyes behind his mother's back.

"Hello, Sonny Bruchac," she said. "I'm pleased to meet you."

"We're going down to the soda fountain, Ma," Billy said. "Can I have a nickel?"

Mrs. Wilson reached into her purse. "Here's a quarter, Billy. You treat your friends."

We all got on our bikes. It was an awkward moment for me. I'd never ridden my bike with other guys and I wasn't sure if I should go ahead or behind or next to them. But I wasn't given time to think. They took off down Church Street and I had to pedal as hard as I could to keep up with them, Billy in the lead, Davey next, and myself bringing up the rear.

I'd never been to the soda fountain before. It was across from the Adirondack Trust Company Bank, a place I knew well because my grandmother drove there every evening, handed me the deposit bag, and had me carry it up from her car, all alone, to place it in the after-hours deposit slot on the front of the bank's marble wall.

Billy dropped his bike against the wall of the soda fountain and Davey did the same. I put down my kickstand to make sure my bike wouldn't fall over while I was inside.

"Come on!" Billy said.

I walked into the dark soda fountain feeling as if I was walking into the devil's own sitting room. I'd never actually been downtown all by myself before and I kept expecting someone to catch me, point at me, and shout, "That's Sonny Bruchac! His grandmother doesn't know he came down the State Road on his bike."

But no one said anything except the soda jerk, a high school kid in a white uniform with a little white cap.

"What'll it be, gents?" he said.

"Vanilla Coke," said Billy.

"Vanilla Coke," said Davey.

Vanilla Coke? I thought. I'd never heard of such a thing. I thought Coke only came in bottles. But I knew that I couldn't hesitate too long. "Vanilla Coke," I echoed.

The soda jerk filled three glasses with Coca-Cola from a spigot and then squirted a shot of vanilla syrup in each. I took a sip. It was the best thing I had ever tasted in my life. The three of us sipped until the Cokes were gone. Billy and Davey made slurping noises as they finished off the last of theirs. I'd always been told never to do that. But no one yelled at them. Somewhat belatedly, I made slurping noises with my straw too.

Billy paid for our Cokes and was given a dime in change. He tapped his hands on the marble counter in an approximation of a horse's hoofbeats.

"Hi-ho, Silver!" he said, and spun off his stool.

Davey spun after him and I followed. They were already on their bikes when I got outside, but I managed to keep them within sight. All the way back up Church Street they went until they pulled into the driveway of Billy's house. By the time I got there, they were sitting together on the front porch. Billy's mother was nowhere in sight. Her car was gone.

They motioned to me to join them.

"We decided—" Davey said.

"To give you a little quiz," said Billy.

"We want to see—" Davey continued.

"If you are country-wise or city-wise."

"Okay," I said. I was always good at quizzes, although I sensed this one was going to be a different challenge.

"Question Number One," Billy said. He made a fist with his right hand, turned it palm up, and stuck up his middle finger. "What does this mean?"

I found it hard to catch my breath. As far as I knew, that meant one. Maybe it meant I was supposed to look up. Or maybe it just meant that he was holding up his finger. I considered our situation. We were three boys alone with no parents around. This had to be something bad. Probably really bad. My mind raced.

Suddenly I remembered something. I had been coming down the road with my grandmother a week ago. As we went past the drive-in movie below our house I saw that someone, kids probably, had rearranged the letters on the sign that listed what was playing. They had spelled out a four-letter word that I'd never seen before. It began with F.

"What does that word mean, Grama?" I said.

She looked upset, but she answered me. "That is a bad word that bad boys use."

Hoping it would be bad enough, I said the F word.

Davey Sher whistled. He looked shocked.

Billy nodded with a smile. "You got it," he said. "I guess you are country-wise. But now let's see if you are city-wise. Question Number Two. How do people do it?"

I paused. How did people do it? I didn't have a clue. But I knew about flowers and animals. I began to talk about pistils and stamens. I talked about the mating rituals of hawks and about tigers and lions, wolves and dogs, and how they mated. I was both as technical and as graphic as one can be with a bright sixth grader's command of zoological language.

"And people," I concluded, "are pretty much the same."

Billy and Davey looked at me, their eyes slightly glazed from it all. "Wellll," Billy said. Davey waited, letting his friend take the lead. "I guess we can say that you are *town*-wise. We need to ask you one more question to see if you are really city-wise."

But that question was never answered. My back was to the

driveway, so I didn't see the car pull in. But I heard the crunch of tires on gravel and I saw the wide-eyed looks that came over the faces of the two boys in front of me. I pulled my head in like a turtle trying to hide in its shell and turned around to see what I had known and feared would be there. It was my grandmother's car, and my grandmother—with a look on her face so grim that it would have stunned Medusa—was climbing out. Someone had told her I was here. Perhaps it was Billy's mother; perhaps just someone who saw me downtown with Billy and, knowing my grandmother, figured they had better let her know. It really didn't matter to me, any more than knowing who is behind the wheel matters to a squirrel in the path of a car.

"Sonny, put your bicycle in the trunk," she said. She didn't say anything else.

I did it and then I got in. As she backed out of the driveway I looked back at Billy and Davey. The disgusted looks on their faces told me that whatever I had gained that day in terms of their esteem had just been lost. I was clearly a Grama's boy, a little baby. I slouched down in the seat, wanting to shrink until I could hide between the cracks in the floor.

"Sit up," my grandmother said.

I sat up.

"How could you betray my trust this way?" she said.

I began to cry and I told her I was sorry. I told her that I loved her, and I knew she was just trying to protect me. I asked her to forgive me. She didn't answer. I began to cry harder until I crossed over that point between weeping and hysteria. I felt as if she hated me and the whole world was ending around me because I was such a bad person. I couldn't stop crying now, and the sobs were racking my body.

I felt the car stop and then my grandmother's big arms were around me.

"Sonny," she said, "Sonny, you're not bad. You just worried me so much."

She rocked me back and forth, and finally my sobbing stopped. She wiped my face with her apron.

"Do you understand?"

"I understand, Grama," I said. I took a deep breath, then asked, "Did the shower go okay?"

"It went fine." She started the car. "You can help me in the garden when we get home."

"Okay, Grama."

"I know you're trying to grow up," she said, "but I have to protect you. You understand that, don't you?"

I did, just as clearly as I understood that as long as she kept protecting me in this way, it was going to be very hard for me to ever grow up.

TREES

Ktsi Nwaskw, the Great Mystery, decided to make human beings. So Ktsi Nwaskw fashioned giant people out of stone. Life was breathed into these stone beings and they stood and began to walk around. But, though they were able to breathe and walk, to hunt and eat, there were things that those first people could not do. They could not bend down to the earth and they could not feel sympathy or love, for their hearts were also made of stone. They killed more than they needed to eat, and they crushed things under their heavy feet.

Ktsi Nwaskw saw that these stone people were not good for the earth. So they were turned back into stone. That is why there are so many stones here in the Northeast. Sometimes when you turn over a stone you may see that it has a face on it, and you are supposed to remember what happened to those people who treated everything else in creation with contempt.

Now Ktsi Nwaskw looked for something else that could be used to make people. There were the ash trees. They danced in the wind and bent close to the earth. Ktsi Nwaskw fashioned new people from those trees. Those new people were rooted to the earth and were in balance with the life around them. They were our ancestors, the first Abenaki. We are the children of the trees.

TREES

When I was thirteen—one of the smallest boys in eighth grade—I knew more about poems and trees than I did about other kids or the typical games of childhood. I could recite Shakespeare sonnets by heart and identify every tree in the woods and tell how it was used. But I didn't know how to hit a baseball or catch a football, and when sides were chosen up at recess or gym for anything, I was always the last kid chosen.

Basketball was the worst. If they were playing basketball, I was never chosen at all. Even the girls were better at it than I was, which was not that surprising since most of them were almost a head taller than me. If someone, by some strange chance, should throw a basketball to me, I would never get my hands up in time.

"Here," Coach Benny Fasulo would say, eternally optimistic. "You can catch this one, Bruchac."

Then he would make a two-handed pass to me. As the basketball came lofting through the air toward me, I would put my hands up thinking, "This time, this time I'll get it." But it would end up bouncing off my chest and knocking me down, or hitting me in the face—breaking my glasses yet again—or giving me a bloody nose that would send me to the nurse's office in the basement of School Two. My glasses were always held together by tape on the bridge, and usually at least one lens was cracked. It is hard to remember any of the scenes from my adolescent years without seeing them through a spiderweb of cracked glass.

Unlike School One, which had a real playground with grass and trees, there was nothing green in the asphalt courtyard of School Two, only the stone walls of the school and the chain-link fence. I could look out the window of my eighth-grade classroom and see the tall, vase-shaped elm trees along Van Dam Street and the smaller spreading maples, but that was as close as I could get to them. It was different at home. As other kids were getting onto buses or walking to the West Side Rec field for Little League, I'd be climbing into my grandparents' blue Plymouth with only two things on my mind—books and trees. If there was time, my grandmother would take me to the library, where I had been the most regular visitor to the Children's Room for the last eight years. If not, then we'd head for home up Route 9N. But that was just as good. The trees were waiting for me.

There was the mountain ash tree right next to the house. It had low limbs that I could jump up and grab, and it was perfect for climbing. Or I could just hang from its lower branches and pretend to be an African monkey. I knew that was how African monkeys hung from trees. Only the monkeys of South America had prehensile tails. If I climbed higher (very high if my grandmother wasn't watching), I could sit in the top of the tree among its small green leaves, and pretend to be one of the cedar waxwings which would flock to it later in the summer when its flowers turned into tiny red berries. My grandfather had planted that mountain ash.

"You always want to have a mountain ash around," he said to me. It was not until twenty-two years later that I would learn from Maurice Dennis that the mountain ash is regarded by many Abenakis as a guardian tree, a tree with such a good spirit that it will keep away those who have evil thoughts.

Then there were the blue spruce trees, three of them, which were planted behind the station. My grandfather had put them in before I was born, and they were taller than the house. Sometimes I could pick little balls of sticky resin off the trunks. I knew about amber and always looked to see if any insects had been trapped in that sap, thinking how it could preserve them whole for millions of years. At times, in those awkward adolescent years, I found myself making a wish. I wished that my life with my grandparents could be preserved just as it was when I was a little child being protected by them. I wished that we could live forever in that time. I wished it could be my grandparents and me there, in a world as changeless and peaceful as one of those small clear globes of near immortality.

There were other times, though, when it didn't seem to me as if things could change fast enough. I was always imagining how things would be, and my thinking would get way ahead of my doing. It had always been that way with me. One of my very earliest memories is of nailing together boards onto a box, knowing that I was going to make an airplane that would actually fly. I would drive in a nail and close my eyes, expecting to open them and find myself in midflight. Instead, though, I would always look around to see myself in the middle of yet another failed project.

"Be patient, Sonny," my grandmother would say. "Your time will come."

It was a familiar refrain on her part. It was repeated whenever I was frustrated by my earthbound dreams of flight. It was as familiar as the words she said when I asked why all the other kids hated me, when I asked why I never had any friends.

"You just wait," she said, "they don't know who you really are."

"You mean I've got a secret identity, like Captain Marvel?"

"Something like that," she said. I was seven then, and took things very literally. I think my grandmother regretted having said those words when I came back in the house a few hours later. My glasses were broken, my face was scratched, my clothes were dirty, and I'd lost one shoe. The cape I had made out of a sheet was no longer tied around my neck and it was badly torn.

"It didn't work," I said. There were tears in my eyes. "I must have jumped off the roof of the chicken coop a hundred times. I said 'Shazam!' every time, but it didn't work. I really don't have a secret identity, Grama."

My grandmother didn't laugh, nor did my grandfather, who patted my back as she rocked me in her lap. She didn't say anything. But that night when I went to bed I found a copy of the autobiography of Theodore Roosevelt on the table near my bed. I read it and read it until I went to sleep with it open across my chest. Roosevelt had been a sick, weak little boy with glasses too. But he had turned himself into an outdoorsman and gotten big and strong.

Although that book taught me something, it still didn't cure me of impatience. I had more than an ample store built up in me when I was in eighth grade. And in the autumn of that year my impatience released itself most often when I got out of that blue Plymouth after school in a dash toward the big apple tree.

The big apple tree stood behind my grandfather's vegetable garden near the Little House. There were wildflowers planted all around its base, and walls of beautifully shaped rocks of all kinds. I had planted all of those flowers, digging them carefully out of the Woods to move them there. Purple and white and yellow violets, trillium and jack-in-the-pulpit, wild iris and tiger lily, even a few lady's slippers that I had rescued from the right-of-way that had been staked out to straighten Middle Grove Road half a mile to the west, past my parents' home. My grandparents had promised me for years that, when I was big enough, I could build a tree house in the big apple, which spread its branches out like the arms of an old man waiting to embrace his grandson. That year, when I entered eighth grade, I was told that I was old enough at last.

By the week before my thirteenth birthday, in October, I had built a platform twelve feet up between the main branches. That platform, made of pine planks, sat on six old two-by-fours, connected solidly with six-inch nails. I had pounded every one of them in myself—with a little help from my grandfather. I'd worried some about driving nails into the tree, but my grandfather had reassured me.

"An old tree like this don't mind a few nails," he said. "Long as it's for a good cause."

When I sat on that platform up in the apple tree and closed my eyes, I could feel the tree sway in the wind, and I swayed with it in perfect rhythm. I could hear the birds singing, not up in the trees, but right next to me. I knew that when the summer came I would sleep up there, and I imagined where I would make my bed. I didn't have walls or a roof yet, but I would have a window, right there where the bed would be. I could have a pulley hung from a branch and use it to pull a bucket to bring things up into the tree from the ground. Grama could put my dinner in that bucket, and I wouldn't have to climb down to eat.

There was only one problem. It was the branch that thrust out right into the middle of the place I imagined my wall rising up. If I cut it off I'd be able to build the wall and put on a roof. I knew that if I asked my grandfather, he'd help me take that branch out. Somehow, though, I felt as if the apple tree didn't want to give up that branch. So I waited. I pushed down my impatience and I closed my eyes to become part of the tree. I thought about how perfect my tree house would be when it was finished. I thought too about my birthday party the next week. When the kids came to it, I would show them the platform. I might even take some of them up into the tree. I knew they'd be impressed.

When Monday came, I went to school with a pocket full of invitations. I'd written the names of every kid I wanted to invite. None of them were really my friends—in fact, in eighth grade I didn't have any real friends. The last time I'd been invited to a birthday party was when I was in third grade. No one came to my house, and no one had invited me to his since that disastrous afternoon with Billy Wilson two years before. Part of it was because I lived so far out in the country, part of it because my grandmother was still so overly protective that I wasn't allowed to do things with other kids.

The biggest part of it, though, was that I didn't know how to act around kids. I laughed at the wrong times, a loud, nervous laugh that made people look at me and shake their heads. I talked too much and usually said the wrong things. Other boys could identify every new car, while all I knew were the names of the birds and the animals. They could talk about baseball and football, while I could talk about poems and novels. If someone got angry at me and said they were going to hit me, I would run away and tell the teacher or tell my grandmother when I got home. Then she would get on the phone or make a visit to the parents of the boy who had threatened me. Since she was on the school board, such a visit was no small thing. Quite logically, the other kids despised me.

I was more comfortable with elderly people than I was with children. My teachers loved me. I was always the first to raise my hand, often saying to the kid next to me, "Don't you know the answer?" I was the first to finish every test. From first grade on I always had the most gold stars next to my name, and in those days of grading on a scale with 100 at the top, I never had less than a 95 in anything. My only competition was my sister Mary Ann. Although she was two grades behind me, our report cards were always compared, and her average was almost always just a little higher than mine. And, unlike me, she always seemed to have friends.

After my party, I thought, it would be different. I would have friends too. I got into our classroom early that Monday, before any of the other kids. I went from row to row, putting

At a birthday party for my mother in 1955 at my grandparents' house

invitations on the desks. I invited girls and boys both. I hesitated a minute at Fonda's desk. She was the prettiest girl in the school, and I'd had a crush on her since I was in second grade. Then I got my courage back up. It wouldn't hurt to try. I put an envelope on her desk and then on the desks of Molly, Kathy, Jan, and Susie. I had crushes on all of them. Since none of them ever paid any attention to me, I figured it only made sense to spread my affections around.

As I sat in class later that morning, listening to Mrs. Hall in social studies, something flew past my face. It wasn't unusual for people to throw things in Mrs. Hall's class. She was the oldest teacher in the school and her eyesight, kids thought, wasn't the best. Some people said she was over ninety years old and the only reason they couldn't force her to resign was that she had something on the school board. She'd been my mother's teacher and had looked just the same then as she did now. Her fluffy mop of hair was as white as a cherry tree in blossom, and her nickname among the kids was "Flossie."

I thought she was a wonderful teacher. She still had her pilot's license and had grown up on a ranch in Montana. Her mind was much quicker than most of the kids realized. There was a dry kind of wit in her remarks that went over a lot of their heads; and she was the driving force behind the Sports and Travel Club, which took the whole eighth grade on outings every year—to New York, Lake Placid, Wilderness Lodge. She knew enough to turn a blind eye to some things in her class. She liked to see children enjoying themselves.

So, when that paper airplane flew past my head—thrown from the direction of Paul Morley's desk—it didn't surprise me. The second paper airplane, which came from the other side, where Andy Delmonico sat, did surprise me. It surprised me because it dove right into the inkwell hole in my desk. Like all the desks in School Two, mine was an old wooden one from the days when pens were used that had to be dipped into inkwells. I pulled the paper airplane out of the inkwell hole. I don't know if I had intended to throw it back or not, but when I had it in my hand and saw what it was, I froze. It was one of my invitations. Another one landed next to it. And then another. I crumpled them up, putting them into my pockets, but they kept coming. There was a noise at the front of the room. Mrs. Hall was clearing her throat, a sign that she was about to turn around and look at the class. The paper airplanes stopped.

By the time the final bell rang that day, every one of my invitations had been returned to me, one way or another. Some of them were given back to me politely. Fonda actually spoke to me, telling me that she was busy that day, as did a few of the other girls. But all of them had been refusals.

My grandfather was in the car.

"How was your day?" he asked.

I knew what I wanted to say, but I didn't say it. Something was going on inside me. I didn't want him or my grandmother to know. I looked out the window as we turned up Church

Street. My grandfather said nothing in answer to my silence. He was good at silence himself.

When I got home my grandmother was sitting out front.

"Did you remember to hand out the invitations?" she said.

I froze again. Then I shook my head. "I decided I don't want to have a party, Grama."

"But why would you do that?"

"I'm too busy. I want to spend the time working on my tree house. I'd rather read. You can just make me a cake. Just the three of us and Mary Ann. That'll be enough. Parties are for little kids, anyhow."

I was talking faster and faster, and I knew there were tears in my eyes. My grandmother started to reach out for me, but I stepped back. She looked at my grandfather and he shook his head.

"I want to go work on my tree house now," I said. I spun away from them and ran toward the backyard, stopping only to take a saw out of my grandfather's big wooden toolbox. I don't remember climbing up the ladder onto my platform in the old apple tree. All I remember is the saw in my hand and that branch, the branch that was in the way. I sawed at it, harder and harder. It kept sticking as I sawed, as if the branch didn't want to be cut, as if the tree was protesting. But I paid no attention. I kept working the saw free, and cutting.

The branch was as big around as my thigh and it took a long time, but I didn't stop even though my arms and my back ached. My arms had been given the gift of great strength from all those years of climbing trees, even though I had never tested that strength before. The branch creaked at the cut as I pulled the saw one last time. Then it broke free. But instead of falling, the butt of that branch swung out, for the top of it was tangled in the other branches above. It swung out hard and fast, striking me in the chest. My feet left the platform, and I found my-self flying up and back and then down.

There was a loud sound, the sound of my back hitting the ground under the tree. I could see the platform, higher above me than it had ever seemed before. The tree was leaning over me. With its widespread limbs it looked for a moment the way my grandfather had looked when he used to come and tuck me in when I was very small. I couldn't breathe. It seemed as if my body had become a part of the earth and didn't belong to me anymore. I wondered if I was still alive. And that was when it all came to me. I had no reason to feel sorry for myself. What had happened today was only because of the way I'd been for so long. I'd been impatient and angry and sorry for myself, and I had ended up hurting both the old apple tree and myself.

"I'm sorry," I thought, looking at the tree. And then I coughed. It hurt to cough, but it brought the wind back into my lungs and I could move. I turned my head to look to one side and then the other. I had fallen right between two of the big stones in my rock garden, but I hadn't hit either one of them. Instead, the soft earth had cushioned my fall.

I sat up slowly. I could tell that nothing was broken. I looked over toward the house and saw, with relief, that my grandparents hadn't seen me fall. It might have given them a heart attack. I walked over to the tree and leaned against it.

"I'm going to be thirteen," I said to the apple tree. I don't re-member if I said thank you to that tree for what it had taught me, but I do remember that there was thanks in my heart as I picked up the saw and walked back to my grandparents' house with a smile on my face.

FISHING SONG

Two men were walking through the woods long ago. As they walked, one of them noticed a hollow high in a tree.

"I'm going to climb up and see if anything is in there," he said.

"Better not," said the second man.

But the first man didn't listen. He climbed up and looked inside.

"There's something in here," he said. "Come up and see."

"I'm staying down here," the second man said.

"There's a little pool of water in this tree, and there's a big trout swimming around in it. I'm going to catch it and bring it down."

"I don't think that's a good idea," said the second man.

But the first man didn't listen. He caught the trout and brought it down with him. He made a fire and cooked the trout.

"Here," he said to his friend. "Have some of this. It's good."

"No," said the second man. "I don't want to eat any of that fish."

So the first man ate it all. He even ate the bones.

"Now I'm thirsty," the first man said. "I'm going to drink some water from that stream."

He went over to the stream and stretched out on the ground and began to drink. He put his whole head in the water and drank and drank. The second man was getting worried. Then the first man lifted his head back up.

"This water is really good," he said. His voice sounded strange because his head was now the head of a fish. He slid into the water and disappeared.

The second man waited, but his friend didn't come out. So he sat down by that stream and waited. He waited all through the night and finally fell asleep beside the stream. The next morning, he was wakened by splashing water. A big fish was there in the stream, looking at him.

"My friend," said the big fish, "do you know who I am?"

"I know who you are," said the second man, recognizing his friend in the fish.

"You were right when you told me not to climb that tree. I shouldn't have eaten that fish there in the hollow of the tree. When people catch fish they should do it the right way. They should fish only for food, and they should always say thanks to the fish people when they catch them. You tell that to all our people."

"I will do so," said the man. Then the fish that had been his friend dove under the water and was never seen again. This is the story a Mohawk friend told me.

My son Jesse has sent me a cassette tape. On it, he and his friend Lalania have taped more than forty songs of the Abenaki people, songs that come from the Western Abenaki, the Micmac, the Passamaquoddy, and the Penobscot. Jesse made the tape to share with any Abenaki people who want it, to give free to any who want to learn our songs. At the end of the tape he mentions the names of all those who taught him the songs, listing many who were my own teachers and then mentioning my name as well.

As I listen to their clear, strong young voices I find myself re-

membering things that I had forgotten I knew. It is that way with music, with the sound of the rattle and the drum echoing your heart and your breath, the thunder and the wind. Among those old songs are new ones, ones that Jesse has composed in Abenaki. Hearing one of them I begin to think of my grandfather. I look at the playlist and see the name of that old new song my son has written—"Fishing Song."

I remember the first fish I caught. My grandfather drove us up Ballou Road, past the cemetery where his father and mother were buried. There, just below the hill where stood the house in which he'd been born, the South Branch ran under the road. I could hear the gurgling voice of its water on the rocks as it came out of the throat of the stone culvert under the bridge. He handed me his old bamboo rod, a worm already placed on the hook. He knew I was big enough to catch a fish all by myself, even though I was only six.

"Jes' walk up slow, and don't look over into the water or the trout'll see you. Jes' whisper what I tole you and drop yer line in the water."

I did as he said. I crept quietly, as quietly as Straight Arrow could creep on his radio show, where he was an Indian who lived his life disguised as a white man until it was time for him to fight injustice. Inch by inch I stuck the pole out over the wooden rail. Then I whispered, "This is for you," and flipped the line into the water. The trout struck it as soon as it hit the surface, yanking my line. I pulled back and the trout came spiraling out of the water to land on the bridge. It was a ten-inch-long brook trout, and it seemed as if all of the colors of the rainbow were there in the spots on its sides.

My grandfather picked it up and carefully wiped off the gravel from the road that had stuck to its sides. He said something that I couldn't hear, and then, putting his thumb in its mouth and his index finger on the top of its head, he gave a little twist. A quiver ran down the body of the fish and it was still. He took the hook out and placed the trout in my hands.

That was the only trout we caught that day. We didn't try to catch any more fish. That one was enough. My grandmother cooked it for my supper that evening.

Try as I may, I can't recall my grandfather ever taking me trout fishing again. But I do recall the few times that my father took me trout fishing the summer before I went into high school. I had never owned a spinning rod, and that was all that my father fished with in those days. He had three spinning rods, one of which he said was mine, though the only time he ever let me hold it was when I was in the boat with him and Mary Ann. He would cast out his line with a lure—usually a daredevil, striped red and white like a barbershop pole—sparkling at its end, to plop gently into the water far from the boat. My sister Mary Ann would then lift up her rod. I had seen her practicing her spin-casting on my father's front lawn as I rode my bicycle past the long lane that led to my parents' home.

According to my grandparents, that lane had once been lined with apple trees and flowering bushes, and there had been beautiful stone walls next to the road and all along the driveway. Soon after they gave The Farm to my father and mother, those walls and trees and bushes disappeared. My father cut down everything in front of the house that was living—with the exception of two big elms and the large maple, whose broadest lower branch was always used to hang the bodies of the deer he shot. He bulldozed out the stone walls and buried them. To this day, my mother still talks about the great big stone that she loved so much that used to be right out there by the edge of the driveway.

"But your father," she said, "he buried it. He said it would get in the way of the snowplowing, and he wanted to be able to see if anyone was coming in the lane."

So, even from a hundred yards away out on the road, it was easy to see the small figure of my younger sister holding that spinning rod with practiced ease—a small hookless weight taking the place of a lure at the end of her line—flipping out one long perfect cast after another.

When we were on the boat together, my father would cast his line, then look toward Mary Ann. With a smile that crinkled the skin on her forehead where her bangs covered the scar, she would throw a perfect cast to her side of the boat, a cast that floated out as if gravity had no meaning, a cast that often went nearly as far as my father's.

Then they would both turn to look at me. My hands sweaty, my tongue between my teeth, I would lift up the rod, swing it too far back, and try to throw it the way I did the stiff old casting rod that my grandfather had gotten for me, a rod that was banished from fishing trips with my father because it "wasn't any good at all" for the kind of fishing he did. But the tip of the supple rod would whip forward from my rough handling and hit the water as the line shot straight up into the air, the lure jerking as crazily as a gut-shot pigeon before it fell—sometimes in the water behind me or even into the boat—while the translucent nylon line snarled itself horrifyingly into a bird's nest of a backlash. I sat there, hoping that a meteor would strike the boat or that a brontosaurus, like the one I had seen in the movies when my grandmother took me to *King Kong*, would lift its head up from Avery's Lake and snatch me out of the boat. I would have gone gladly down its gullet to escape what always happened next.

"Goddamn, can't you do anything right?" my father would say. He would grab the pole from my hand and begin to work on the backlash. Usually it would take him a long time, for if my sister got a trout on her line in the meantime, as she usually did, he would put down the pole with the command to me, "Don't you touch that!" and take out the net to help her bring in her catch. And when the line finally was untangled he would cast it out himself.

"You just reel it in," he would say. "I'll do all the casting for you from now on."

For some reason, my father never understood that it was impossible for me to learn how to use a spinning rod unless I actually had the opportunity to learn how to use it. I think he felt that I should have been like a bird who makes its nest on instinct or a spider who spins a perfect web without a minute of instruction. And the next time that I was taken fishing with them the whole scenario would be played out in the same way all over again. By the time the day of fishing was over, I would have brought in no more than one or two fish, ones that my father usually deemed too small and would throw back.

"Just let your sister catch the limit for all of us." And she usually would.

Whenever we came home from one of those trips, my father would pull into the driveway of the station and get out of the station wagon with a smile of accomplishment on his face. I tried to smile, but I didn't do it very well.

"Mary Ann caught all the fish again," he would say. "She caught her own limit and then she caught Sonny's too."

My grandmother would hand him some newspaper and he would start counting out trout into it for my grandmother, my grandfather, and me. The limit of fish then was ten trout per person. If the fish were biting, though, my father wouldn't pay much heed to the limit. "We get more, we can give 'em away," he would say.

As he selected the fish, he might pull out the smallest one

first. "Now, this is the one Sonny caught," he'd say, placing it on the newspaper.

"The small ones always taste the best," my grandmother would say. And I would stand and watch, feeling a sorrow that I couldn't define.

We really did need those fish to eat. Anytime we could get a meal without paying for it was a blessing. I knew that my grandparents were poor. They argued about how they would be able to pay the bills for the gas. The past summer—explaining to me why they had to do it and asking me to forgive them—they had cashed out my savings account, which had four hundred whole dollars in it. I had been putting money into that account ever since I earned my first ten dollars by raising a calf and then selling it. It was supposed to help pay for college someday. But I understood.

They'd had to return the movie projector they'd bought me for my birthday after only four months, because they couldn't keep up the time payments on it. I had an inexpensive home-movie camera and had needed that projector to show the things I'd made movies of—a woodchuck up in a tree, a chipmunk on our stone wall, a hawk flying so far up in the sky that it looked like a floating eyelash, my cat, my dog, my grandmother watering the flowers out front in her beautiful garden, my grandfather sitting in his chair in front of the station with a fly swatter in his hand. But they had not had the money to keep up the payments at Starbucks, and so the projector had gone back.

"We can always borrow Mary Ann's projector," my grandmother said. The day after I had been given my movie projector for my birthday, Mary Ann had been given one almost like it. But Dad had bought hers in cash. He never bought anything on time.

I was understanding about it, as far as a thirteen-year-old boy can be understanding. Even though we didn't have money to buy me books, I could always go to the library in Saratoga Springs. I didn't have the money to buy clothes, but at least I wasn't going to school wearing shirts made out of chicken feed sacks as I had when I was in the first and second grade. Those sacks were made of patterned cloth so that farm wives could use them to make aprons, just like the aprons my grandmother always wore. I can't recall whether it was because they stopped making such sacks or whether it had sunk into my grandparents by third grade that I was being teased by kids who would walk past me going "*pock-pock-po-ock*" like a chicken.

It was that summer when I was thirteen that I began to go fishing on my own.

"Y'know," my grandfather said, as we were sitting at the table eating some of the trout that Mary Ann had caught, "yer cousin Bobby used to catch a mess of trout right here in Bell Brook."

"That's right," my grandmother chimed in. "Why, they still stock all these streams around here in Greenfield. And there's not many who fish them, except from the bridges. Trout are always running up into these little streams from the Kaydeross."

The next day I went with my grandfather down to the coupon store. In those days, trading stamps were given to you whenever you bought groceries, and you would paste them into a booklet, then save up booklets to redeem for merchandise. My grandmother gave me three entire booklets filled with stamps.

"The coupon store," she explained, "just doesn't have anything I really need this time, so you might as well use these."

It was just enough to get a green nylon fly rod. When I got home, I assembled the pieces of the pole, fastened my grandfather's old fly reel to the rod, and ran the line through the eyes. I had only three Number 6 Eagle Claw hooks, but I figured they would be enough. I took an empty Prince Albert tobacco can and went out into the garden with the spading fork. In half an hour I'd filled the can with worms.

"Now I'm going fishing," I said to my grandparents.

When I came back five hours later, I was wet from head to toe. My shoes were full of mud, and one lens of my glasses was cracked yet again where a branch had swung back and hit me. I'd lost all my hooks but one as I fished the length of Bell Brook, from Middle Grove Road all the way up to the State Road and back again. But I had caught my limit of trout. I had ten fish, none of them shorter than the six-inch minimum size, some of them as long as nine inches. I had cleaned them all out myself as I caught them, careful to leave the entrails and the heads of the fish by the side of the stream where the raccoons could find them.

Neither of my grandparents said anything about my glasses, my clothes, or the scratches on my face.

"That's as fine a mess of trout as I've ever seen," my grandfather said.

"Just the right size for eating," said my grandmother.

From then on, throughout every fishing season until I went off to college, I went fishing in the streams of Greenfield at least once a week. I always caught my limit. And we needed every fish I caught.

GIVING

Each year I go to the Onondaga Indian Reservation in the center of New York State, the place where the hearth fire of the League of Peace is kept. There I do poetry and storytelling workshops with the children of the Onondaga Nation School. And in 1980 I was given an Onondaga name.

On that particular day, I had finished class for the morning and was about to go to lunch.

"Dewasentah wants to see you at her house," I was told.

I walked outside and saw Dewasentah coming toward me from her house, which is just down the road from the school. I had first met Dewasentah when I was a student at Syracuse University in 1965 and used to ride my Harley-Davidson motorcycle out to the reservation. One of my dearest friends at Onondaga, she is one of the elders of their nation and the Clan Mother of the Eel Clan. She held something in her hands.

"You've been coming here for such a long time," she said. "And the way you use words, it has to be a gift from the Creator. So it is about time you had an Onondaga name."

She handed me what she was holding—a small lacrosse stick and an envelope with a name written on it: Gah-neh-go-he-yoh. Inside the envelope was an eagle feather.

GIVING

"That name," she said, "Gah-neh-go-he-yoh, means 'The Good Mind.' You know we believe that everyone has within them both a good mind and a mind that isn't good. This name will remind you that you always have to try to use your gift of words in a good way."

Saratoga Springs was an unusual town when I was growing up. Although it was in the southern Adirondack Mountains of New York, every summer the horse-racing season transformed it into a miniature New York City. Everyone in Saratoga changed gears then. Teenagers got jobs parking cars at the racetrack or working at the state park in the mineral baths. Schoolteachers became bartenders and waiters, or found work at the track. One of the high-school social studies teachers published his own racing tip sheet on a printing press he kept in his basement; he could be seen selling it by the stoplight where people turned off the main highway to go to the track.

The mineral springs also drew people from all over the world every summer. The springs were sacred to the Mohawk people, especially the Medicine Spring of Raweneyio, the Holder-Up of the Heavens, which flowed from a mineral cone in High Rock Park. For thousands of years people had come to Saratoga to bathe in the mineral-saturated water and grow well. It was said that there was no warfare in the area around the medicine spring because it was such a blessed, sacred place. That healing spring was a gift that the Great Spirit had given to all people, and in return they were expected to live together in peace.

Many of those who came to Saratoga in my teenage years were survivors of the German concentration camps of World War II. In August, you could stroll down Phila Street in Saratoga Springs, past the line of hotels that attracted a predominantly Jewish clientele, and hear a dozen different

European languages being spoken. Elderly Hasidim would sit with their arms on their laps, and you could sometimes see the camp numbers that were still tattooed on their wrists. It was rumored that the German government not only gave those survivors an allowance to come to Saratoga for the healing baths every summer; they even offered to give the aging men and women a handsome sum to have their tattoos removed. Those proud old men and women would sit in their rocking chairs with their sleeves rolled back, so that everyone could see that the numbers were still there—so that no one who saw them would ever forget what had happened.

One street over was Congress Park. That park had been the site of Indian encampments for many years. Abenaki and Mohawk people, "French half-breeds," some called them, came every summer from Quebec to set up tents and sell baskets to the tourists. That was long finished by the time I came along. Though there were plenty of people in and around Saratoga Springs who were descended from those Indian families that came to Saratoga for the tourists, most of them were like my grandfather. You could see the Indian in his face, but never hear about it from his lips. When I was a child, most of my own knowledge about the Indian encampment and the Indian history of our area came from the books and old documents I read in the Saratoga Springs Public Library, then located on Broadway, at the corner of that same Congress Park.

Congress Street, which ran from Broadway along the side of the huge Grand Union Hotel, was predominantly African-American. Many of the people who lived there worked for the hotels or the racetrack.

Congress Street on a warm evening in August in the 1950's was easily the most sinful and exciting place that any teenager could imagine. Bright lights, music, people laughing, nightclubs and bars, black men and women in expensive clothing. There was illegal gambling and a few other illegal things as well.

But African-American life in Saratoga Springs wasn't limited only to the glamor of Congress Street. African-American families in Saratoga went back many generations, and Saratoga Springs was known to be a place long friendly to African-Americans. There had been stops on the Underground Railroad in homes around Saratoga, hidden rooms and caves where people running from slavery could hide on their way north to free Canada. By the time I reached high school I knew all this, and I knew too that one of the most famous slave narratives of the early 1800's was written by a black man who had been born free in Saratoga Springs but was kidnapped, taken south, and sold as a slave. He spent years in bondage before winning his freedom and returning home. In many ways, being in Saratoga Springs in the summer, and being aware of all that was going on there, was like being given a history lesson.

Out in Greenfield Center, three miles from the middle of Saratoga Springs, our lives were affected by the summers in Saratoga. Not only was business four times as brisk at the gas pumps, we also added a new line of work to our lives.

To make extra money, my grandmother took in tourists from June through the end of August. The four bedrooms upstairs were almost always occupied, in some cases by regulars who came back year after year. One of them was Eddie Haviland, a trainer of horses, who came with his mother. The upstairs room to the left was always called Mrs. Haviland's room, even when she was not in it. The one to the far right, past the bathroom, was Eddie's.

I had stacks of used tickets from the races. Eddie was a big bettor and, like almost everyone involved in the professional racing game, lost far more times than he won. He always saved his losing tickets for me instead of throwing them away.

Thinking back on it, I realize that Eddie was not just making me a present of his tickets, he was holding on to them long enough each day to make sure that a protested race would not turn a loser into a winner. There were people at the track nicknamed "Stoopers," who made a good bit of money each day by bending over and picking up the tickets that people threw to the ground, tickets that sometimes paid off later.

Neither my grandfather or my grandmother ever went to the races. One could make money from the track indirectly, but that was as far as it could go. Gambling was frowned on in our family, in the same way that drinking and smoking were not condoned. It was not so much my grandfather's side as my grandmother's. The Dunhams were staunch Methodists. Cousin Bobby had once made a hundred dollars because he was a cigarette smoker. Grama's brother Orvis had said to Bobby, "I will give you one hundred dollars if you stop smoking."

"It's a deal," Bobby said. He stopped smoking that day and, a week later, Orvis gave him the money. But the next time Orvis saw Bobby, Bobby had a cigarette in his mouth.

"I thought you promised to stop smoking," Orvis said, in an indignant voice.

"I did," said Bobby. "But I didn't promise I wouldn't start again."

Orvis wanted to get his money back, but Bobby refused to give it to him. Orvis stopped talking to him.

It was the general consensus of the Dunham side of the family that Harry and Bobby were the primary examples of sinful backsliding behavior. Some said that the reason Harry drank was because of his scar. He'd shot himself with a shotgun when he was in his twenties, by accident. The gun had gone off when he was crawling through a wire fence. As a result he had a scar on his stomach that kept pulling in so that, in his later years, he looked a little like the Hunchback of Notre Dame, all bent over when he walked. As far as Bobby went—well, that was to be expected with a father like Harry. They were to be pitied.

But whenever I was with Uncle Harry and Cousin Bobby, I couldn't see any reason to pity them. The more I knew about Harry and Bobby, the more I liked them. Despite the family's numerous attempts at reformation and intervention, they stayed who they were. There was a kind of freedom in the way they lived, at odds with a good part of the polite world. Like my grandfather, they didn't talk a great deal but they always had a twinkle in their eyes—as if they knew something so well that they didn't have to talk about it.

That summer before I entered high school, I began spending even more time at Harry and Bobby's. Bobby worked as a lab technician at the hospital and did sculpture and wood carving as a hobby, sometimes selling the things he made to the doctors. He and his father were raising beagles and rabbits, and those animals were part of the reason I spent so much time at their ramshackle farm. The other part was the books.

"You read a lot. Isn't that right, Sonny?" Bobby said to me one day as I was squatting down close to Queenie, their mother beagle, who had just had ten puppies. Queenie was licking my face as I leaned over to gently stroke her four-day-old babies.

"I do," I said. I wondered why he was asking me that. Everyone knew that I was always reading—and writing too. Not everyone thought it was a good thing. I'd been told by some adults that the reason I wore such thick glasses was that I'd ruined my eyes with reading. Not my grandfather, though. Even though he found it hard to read a newspaper, he was always in favor of my being a reader and had proudly put up shelves in my bedroom to hold my ever-growing book collection.

"Then come with me," Bobby said. He turned and walked into the house and I followed him. Their house only had three small rooms downstairs and a set of stairs leading to a low-ceilinged attic. Bobby put his empty beer bottle down on the sink, next to a dozen other bottles, and motioned for me to follow him up the narrow, creaky stairs. At the top he flicked on a light.

I took a deep breath at what I saw. The floors were covered with books. Every one of them was a dime-novel paperback. Back then you could buy a pocket book for a dime or a quarter. I could see from their garish covers and their titles that every single book was science fiction.

"You read science fiction?" Bobby asked. "That's all I read."

"I do," I said. "Robert Heinlein, Ray Bradbury, A. E. Van Vogt . . ."

"Well," Bobby said, "they're all here and more. But once I've finished them I don't read them a second time. You can take whatever you want."

All I could do was nod.

From then on, whenever I went to Harry and Bobby's I always divided my time between the beagles and that attic, bringing back at least a dozen books every time I came home. My grandfather helped me put up more shelves in my bedroom. Soon they covered all my walls from floor to ceiling.

One day, when I was getting ready to go visit Harry and Bobby, my grandfather asked me where I was going.

"Uncle Harry's place," I said.

"I'll come with you," he said. "Got to pick something up."

I didn't wonder what it was. I thought only about the fact that with a car I could bring back a whole box full of science fiction books from the hundreds that still remained in that attic.

When we pulled in to their yard, though, I forgot about the books. Harry and Bobby were standing there, both of them smiling. I saw what Bobby was holding in his arms. It was one of Queenie's puppies. They were old enough to sell now, and people had been coming all that week to look them over. The one Bobby was holding was my favorite, the one I always called Sniffy.

Bobby walked up to the car and handed Sniffy in through the open window. He smiled at me and winked at my grandfather.

"You take good care of him," he said.

"Give him a good home," Uncle Harry added, placing a hand on his son's shoulder.

Once again I just nodded. I couldn't think what to say. I gave Sniffy a hug and looked at Uncle Harry. He took off his cloth cap, wiped his hand back over his hair, put the cap back on, and then smiled.

"You're welcome," he said.

Then my grandfather turned the car around and we drove home. As we drove I held my new dog carefully, thinking about how little Bobby and Harry had and how much they understood about giving.

FELLOWSHIP

One of the greatest heroes of the Iroquois people is a
person who brought the message of peace to their
five warring nations: the Mohawk, the Oneida, the
Onondaga, the Cayuga, and the Seneca. In those
days long ago, brother fought brother in blood feuds
and no place was safe. There was no fellowship
among the nations aside from the fellowship of
mistrust and revenge.

That man became known as the Peacemaker. I read about him
in books that no one else in my high school ever read. I discovered
that his best friend and the co-founder of the League of Peace was a
man named Hiawatha. Not the Hiawatha of Longfellow's poem;
Longfellow had gotten it wrong, had called the Anishinabe hero
Manabozho by the name of this great Iroquois political leader.

The fellowship formed was an important one, for Hiawatha was
a great orator and could speak the Peacemaker's message. People
had not listened to the Peacemaker—not because they disagreed
with his ideas or what was in his heart, but because of the way he
talked. This part of the story was not in The White Roots of Peace,
which Paul Wallace wrote in 1946 about the founding of the Great
League, and which I read in high school. I learned about it later.
The Peacemaker spoke strangely because he had been born with a

speech impediment, a double row of teeth. So, when he spoke, people
laughed at him.

When I reached high school I knew that I had to change. All
the things that my grandmother and grandfather had said to
me about my becoming someone had to come true. The first
thing that I did was to begin to ride the school bus again.

It worried my grandmother, but the school bus turned out
to be nothing threatening at all. At first no one would sit with
me, but none of the twenty or so other high school students
coming in from Greenfield seemed much interested in picking
on me either. They were too interested in other things—especially each other. And though it took me some time to realize it,
they were worried about going to school in Saratoga Springs.
Unlike me, most of them had gone to the little Greenfield Center elementary school—a school that my grandmother had refused to allow me to attend because it wasn't up to her
standards. But that Greenfield school went up only to eighth
grade, so the Greenfield kids were forced to come to Saratoga
Springs for high school. Those on the Greenfield bus who were
freshmen like myself knew they'd be called hicks and country
mice by the kids in Saratoga. Those who were sophomores
were still trying to be accepted. Many of them never really
were. Few of the Greenfield kids ever made it onto the varsity
teams or were elected class officers, and the highest academic
achievers all seemed to come from within the city of Saratoga
Springs.

When I see that bus again in my memory, I see the girls
dressed in skirts and dresses with so many crinoline petticoats
under them that they rustled as they walked, and two girls
could fill an entire row of seats in the bus by themselves. Those
crinolines were pretty much the fashion of the times, though
the extra bows and ribbons most of the girls wore their first

week of high school were not. The boys wore clothes that were just short of the latest style. Pegged pants, patterned shirts, most of them clearly bought from the Montgomery Ward catalog in those days before discount chain stores. "Monkey Ward" was the favorite of most of the country folks who could afford store-bought, though a great many just bought cloth and sewed clothes by hand, trying to copy what they saw in the catalog's glossy pages.

I watched what other people did at first, thinking that if I did the same things I would fit in. It didn't work too well. Somehow, whatever I wore was just different enough to make me look goofy. The color was wrong; the fit was too tight or too loose. I tried having my hair cut at the barbershop across from the high school. Barber Ed was a favorite of all the kids, a man with a quick sense of humor who knew everything going on in the high school. Barber Ed's favorite joke was to pinch someone's ear as he was cutting their hair, say, "Oops, sorry," and then drop a fake bloody ear into their lap. Whenever he cut my hair, even when it was in the style we called a D.A. (a "duck's ass," because it formed a ridge in back like a duck's tail), it was always a failure. Instead of looking like Brando's or James Dean's—his death the year before had elevated Dean's hairstyle to cult status—my hair always stuck out somewhere in a cowlick or on both sides, no matter how much I greased it with pomade. I looked like Dagwood Bumstead. Worse than being bullied, as I had been in grade school, I was ignored. And so church took on a new meaning for me.

I had been going to the Methodist church in town ever since I could walk. I loved the ministers, especially the young Reverend Donald Brant and deep-voiced, gentle Reverend Hydon, who called me "Little Joe Otter." The ringing sound of their sermons and the words in the New Testament, about caring for the little children and loving your neighbor and what you do unto the least of these, you do unto me, touch my memory still. They made me think of the way my grandparents lived . . . although it did seem that my grandmother's occasional judgments on people were more Old Testament than New. I knew the Bible so well that when I was called on to do a reading from the pulpit, I could do it by heart. For a time, I even thought seriously about becoming a Methodist minister. Reverend Hydon encouraged me in that direction, and by the time I was fourteen I was asked, now and then, to give brief sermons as well as to read from the Bible.

Better yet, as a member of the church, I couldn't be excluded from Methodist Youth Fellowship. I could get close to other kids who couldn't automatically move away from me, the way they did when I tried to sit on the curb outside the high school at lunchtime. They couldn't ignore me like the guys pitching pennies by metal shop or playing squares, a kind of handball game like Ping-Pong that we played with a small rubber ball, using the squares on the sidewalk. I *had* to be accepted at MYF. It was the Christian thing. That was good. But what was even better was that some of the girls I'd had crushes on since I was in second grade were Methodists. I could talk with them and they wouldn't be able to ignore me.

By high school I was more than just interested in girls, I was slightly crazed by them. That, I suppose, is not at all unusual for young men in their teenage years. But I was so hopelessly inept socially that I didn't have the slightest idea how to behave around them.

Although I was goofy, I don't think I was repulsive. Sometimes, in MYF, the girls would tease me. I remember one day when several girls took my hat and began throwing it back and forth, playing monkey-in-the-middle. Finally, Penny Stimsdon just held the hat behind her back. "Come and get it," she said. I started toward her and then I stopped. The two other girls were watching. I didn't know what to do. I felt my face grow redder and redder, and I knew that tears were beginning to form in the corners of my eyes. I turned away quickly.

"I don't want that dumb hat anyway. You can keep it," I said. As soon as the words were out I knew they were the wrong thing to say, just as surely as I knew that I still didn't know what the right thing would have been. I heard Penny stomp her foot, and then—*whap!*—the hat hit me in the back of the head.

"Retard," she said. Then she and the other girls ran away laughing.

I was so confused by all that was happening to me and around me in ninth grade that I hardly noticed my grandparents any longer. My grandfather seemed to know what was going on, though in his youth he had been a dark, handsome young man and a favorite of the girls. I asked him what I should do with girls.

"Don't never be rough," he said, looking over his shoulder to make sure my grandmother couldn't hear him. She walked into the room just at that moment and the conversation was ended. S-E-X, spelled out like that, was a topic that my grandmother would not have discussed in her house. "There is no need to talk about S-E-X," she said. I was on my own, even in the fellowship of the Methodist Youth.

CARING

The Abenaki people of Odanak tell this story. It was the time when the fish were running upstream. A family of four people, a man and woman and their two small children, went to the stream to fish. They kept a close eye on their little girl, but they did not pay attention to the little boy. He had his own little bow and arrow and was using it to try to shoot fish. He wandered away from his family and became lost.

When, at last, they discovered he was gone, they began to look for him. He was nowhere to be found. They went back to Odanak and asked for help. Everyone except for one lazy hunter came out to help them search. But all that they found was a place where the boy's footprints ended and the footprints of a large female bear and her two cubs began. So they knew that the little boy had been taken by the bears.

People continued to search for that boy throughout the winter, but they had no luck. The bears had gone to their winter lodges to sleep through the time of cold and deep snow. The parents were very sad, for they thought they would never see their child again.

When the next spring came, and the bears were leaving their dens, the lazy hunter decided it was time to go and find that boy. He walked along the streams until he found bear tracks. Then he found *a small arrow floating in the stream, an arrow of the little boy's. Then that lazy hunter, who for all his laziness was actually the best tracker in Odanak, found the boy's footprints. They led to a cave. He knew the boy and the bears were in there.*

The hunter knocked on the mouth of the cave with his heavy hunting spear.

"Grandmother," he said, speaking to the mother bear in that respectful way people are supposed to use with bears, "come out. It is time for you to die."

The mother bear came running out of the cave to attack the hunter, but he threw his spear and it killed her. The two young bears ran out and escaped into the forest. Then the little boy came out. When he saw that the mother bear was dead he growled like a bear and tried to attack the hunter. But the hunter grabbed hold of him and held him tightly. He carried him back to the village.

For a long time, that boy thought he was a bear and tried to escape back to the forest. But eventually he learned that he was a human being and was able to live with the people once again.

The first time my grandfather went into the hospital was at the end of my freshman year in high school. I remember my grandmother's concern and how Doc Magovern placed his hand on my shoulder.

"You're going to have to do all you can to help your grandmother, Sonny," he said. "Your grandfather has to go into the hospital and he's going to be gone for a while."

"I promise, Doc," I said. I had overheard the discussion he'd had with my grandmother while I sat in the waiting room, heard her quick indrawing of breath, and the whispered "No!" when he said to her, "Looks like it might be leukemia, Marion."

\ I knew what leukemia was, a cancer of the blood that was always fatal. My grandfather, nearly 71, was ten years older than my grandmother. I felt a fist clench in my stomach at the thought and then pushed it out of my mind. "Grampa's not gonna die now," I said to myself. "Grampa's not gonna die now. Grampa's not gonna die now."

I kept that chant going in my mind. I was used to doing things like that. There was a little chant that I had been repeating in my mind ever since I had started high school. "I'm going to be big and strong. I'm going to be big and strong." Whenever someone pushed me aside or called me a name, that unspoken chant helped me keep back the tears. Someday, I thought, those kids who are picking on me are going to want to be my friends. I'm going to be big and strong.

One awful day, not long before that visit of my grandfather's to Doc Magovern, I had gone to school wearing a new pair of pale blue slacks. My grandmother had bought them for me from a catalog. No one else in school had a pair of slacks that color. When I got off the bus they caught on the door, making a small rip above the back pocket which I didn't notice at the time.

There was five minutes before the bell rang and the doors of the school opened. Those five minutes seemed like a week when my powder blue slacks became the object of attention for a group of boys two years older than me, all of them members of the Roadrunners Club.

The Roadrunners were boys who took metal shop and made special license-plate holders for themselves with the shape of a roadrunner on the top. None of them had cars yet, but they were ready.

"Hey," one of them said, pointing at my slacks, "I thought blue was for boys!"

"Pretty color, Sonny," a second one said.

I turned to look at the boy, a lanky redhead in a T-shirt that he had rolled up to his shoulders. He was big, almost six feet tall, six inches taller than me. I'd seen him before and heard him called Red. Then I made a fatal mistake. I smiled up at him and said, "How did you know my name?" I was always forgetting that "Sonny" was a name given indiscriminately to boys, like "kid." By daring to talk directly to an older boy, I had started something.

"You talking to me, kid?" he said, staring down at me and then pushing me in the chest. "You talking to *me*?"

I retreated as fast as I could. "No, sir, I'm not."

"Then who are you talking to?"

"No one, sir."

"You mean I'm no one, wiseass?"

He stared at me again and then, more welcome than the sound of a heavenly harp, the bell rang. He turned and headed for the door of the school. I breathed a sigh of relief, not knowing that the confrontation wasn't over. It was only delayed.

Later that morning, as I walked down the hall, I felt a tug on the back of my slacks and heard a rip. I slapped my hand back and found that the small tear that I had discovered only in study hall was now six inches long. Someone brushed past me. It was Red. I kept my hand clutched over my back pocket, holding the tear together while I held my books to my chest with my other hand.

The next class was English, where I was the best student in the class. But that morning I was distracted. I didn't raise my hand to come to the board and diagram a difficult sentence. I stayed glued to my seat, leaning over to the side where my pants were torn. I was in a panic. The next period everyone went outside. I formed a plan. There was a phone booth just across the street if I could get to it. I could see it from the window of the English class. I took a nickel out of my pocket and held it tightly in my right hand.

The bell rang and I walked out of the class, one hand on my back pocket, the other holding my books. Someone bumped into me and my books went flying. As I bent to pick them up I felt another hard pull on my pants and heard the rip, a long one this time. I could feel the cool air on my thigh. I sat down, pressing my back against the lockers as I picked up my books.

I could hear people laughing. It wasn't just Red now that I had to worry about. I had read about what happens when a fish begins to bleed in the middle of a group of sharks. I looked around. No teachers were in sight, and the principal's office was at the other end of the building. I stood up and ran for the door, holding my books to my chest. People got in my way, trying to grab at my slacks and rip them further, but I lowered my head and shouldered them aside. Years later, kids who became my friends told me that I looked like a fullback breaking through the line for a touchdown as I knocked people aside. Those knocked aside included Red—who still managed to hook his hand out and grab my back pocket as he went spinning away, tearing the leg of my pants all the way down to the back of my knee.

I hit the street and was across it and into the phone booth in front of the drugstore on Lake Avenue, fifty yards ahead of any of my pursuers. In those days, all phone booths were built of solid wood. The only windows were two thick glass ones in the door. That folding door, when shut, closed the person inside completely off from the outside world. Phone booths were so private in those days that Clark Kent always went into one to change into his Superman costume. I stuck the nickel into the slot.

"Number plee-yuz," said the operator.

"Five-eight-eight-four," I said. Only a year before, all the phone numbers in our area had changed and added a digit. The old one-one-eight that had always been our number had ceased to be.

"He's in here," a muffled voice shouted from outside.

The first body slammed against the door as the phone began to ring. I braced my back against it and held it tight. Unlike Clark Kent, I knew that if I emerged from that phone booth, it would not be to fly away but to continue my unwilling striptease.

My grandmother answered.

"Hello, who is it?"

"Grama," I said, "it's me. I tore my pants and I need you to bring me another pair."

"Sonny?"

A second body joined the first trying to open the door. I pushed back even harder and the door stayed shut. I could hear swearing from outside.

"Did you hear me, Grama?"

"Yes, darling. I was just noticing that I got a package today. I think it's another pair of pants just like those new ones you wore to school. Shall I bring those?"

A third person put his shoulder to the door along with the first two. I put my feet up against the back of the phone booth. There was no way they were going to open that door. Then it registered on me what my grandmother had just said.

"No! No, Grama. Don't bring the new pants. Bring my old black ones. I'm in the phone booth on Lake Avenue. Can you come right now?"

"I'll be right there, Sonny."

By the time my grandmother arrived, the bell ending the lunch hour had rung and most of the kids had gone back inside the school. My grandmother was driving, but Grampa was with her. When he emerged from the car holding my black slacks, the last three members of the Roadrunners crew hit the road. They saw the look in my grandfather's eye.

As I came out of that phone booth, one hand holding the back of my tattered slacks, I no longer felt like a victim. The boys hadn't gotten me, and my grandparents had come to my rescue. They were always there when I needed them, always there to care for me.

Now, though, all that had changed. Suddenly, with those words of Doc Magovern's, I became the one who had to think about taking care of them.

I had to think of that. Yet all I kept telling myself were those five words, "Grampa's not gonna die now. Grampa's not gonna die now."

BOMBARDMENT

Even though the Sky Land seems far away, it is said to also be very close. There is no distance that cannot be quickly crossed in the spirit world. Our ancestors are always close to us. Oren Lyons, one of the Faithkeepers of the Onondaga, once told me that his Iroquois people always say that those who have died are no farther away than the other side of a leaf that has fallen.

There is an Abenaki story about a man who has been very ill. He wakes up one morning in his sickbed and tries to stand up. For the first time in many weeks he no longer feels weak and he manages to stand. But as he stands there, free of pain and exhaustion, he looks back and sees himself, his own body, still lying on the bed. He walks outside and sees a hill in front of his lodge. The hill looks familiar to him, though he doesn't recall ever deciding to climb it before.

As he climbs up, he feels lighter and lighter. When he reaches the top he pauses and looks down the other side. There, below him, the land looks as it did in the time of his ancestors, with great trees and clear streams and animals of all kinds. Next to a river he can see lodges and there are people in front of those lodges whom he recognizes. There are his parents and his grandparents, there are his *friends who have died. They are looking up at him and motioning for him to come down.*

He looks back the way he came. There is his own home, the home he just left behind. Next to the place where his body still rests he sees his wife and his children and the people who love him. They are talking and he can hear their words. "Don't leave us," they say. "Come back."

That man stands there on the hilltop making his decision. Then he goes down the hill. The teller of the story always stops here, and the listener must decide in which direction the man goes.

My grandfather was admitted to Saratoga Hospital for a round of transfusions. He needed blood because his white blood cell count was too high. Soon after he got there, he began to feel better. Grama visited him twice a day. I visited him in the hospital almost every day that summer, and it seemed to me that he was enjoying himself. Even though he was in a hospital bed, he acted the way he did when he was sitting in front of the station. He saw everything that went on, and when he made a comment, it was usually a funny one. All the nurses knew him and appreciated his sense of humor. After a few weeks had passed it was decided that he had improved enough to come home. But he was only home for a short time before he had to go back.

So it went. My grandfather would improve and be able to come home. A few weeks or months would pass and he would again become tired. His legs would ache and his complexion would become gray. Then he would have to be taken back to the hospital for more transfusions. I worried so much about my grandfather that I didn't always notice how my grandmother too was more tired than she had ever been before.

She had been in the hospital a year before my grandfather and, unlike Grampa, had not liked it one bit. She had vowed that she would not spend a night in there again until the day she died. She had fallen on the ice during the winter as she came up our outside steps and had strained a ligament in her knee. The doctor at the hospital, an elderly man who specialized in such injuries—not Doc Magovern—had recommended heat therapy. He placed her in a room, turned an ultraviolet light onto her leg, and left the room. Doc Magovern was in the hospital that day. When he heard where they had my grandmother, he went to the room and found her sitting there, crying. The light had been left on her for far too long, and it was burning her leg.

"My God, Marion," he said, "what have they done to you?"

Doc Magovern turned the light off. He had them bring salve for her leg and he bandaged it up. It took weeks to heal and my grandmother said that the leg still bothered her when she walked, though she always tried to avoid complaint. She had my grandfather and me to think about. I remember her saying that to me one day when I saw her leaning against the kitchen counter with tears in her eyes and I asked her if she was all right.

"I'm fine, Sonny. And if I wasn't I'd still have you and your grandfather to think about. There'll be time for my problems later."

Somehow, through it all, I continued to do fairly well in school. I no longer strove to be the best in every class, though. I tried hard only in the subjects that interested me—science courses, English and social studies, and gym class. In courses like algebra, geometry, and Latin, it was enough for me to squeeze by with the lowest possible passing grade.

I also began to develop a reputation for my sense of humor during my sophomore year. I'd discovered that I could say and write things that made people laugh. In homeroom, in study hall, and in the classes which didn't hold my interest, I'd pass notes around with funny remarks or stories I'd written on them. It earned me a trip to the office more than once, but I never got into serious trouble.

Mr. Sexton, the school principal, would sit reading one of my notes that I had passed in Mr. Lake's algebra class, chuckling in spite of himself. Then he would pull himself up to his full five feet one and sternly inform me that I needed to channel my creativity in a more constructive manner.

Although I was far from being seen as an athlete and I had never belonged to any school team, I was really good at a game we played sometimes in gym. It was called Bombardment. We would be divided up into two groups, as many as fifty on each side, and we'd use the whole gym to play. Coach Tibbetts would roll three volleyballs into the center of the gym and say "Begin!" Then the bravest or most foolhardy would rush for those three balls. The object was to get a ball and then throw it to hit a player on the other team. Any player hit was out and had to sit in the bleachers. If you caught the ball, then the one who threw it was out. You could also knock a ball thrown at you away, if you used another ball to do it.

I was never the first one out on my side. As I got better at Bombardment, I was sometimes one of the very last. I could jump over a thrown ball, dodge it, or catch it—even when it was thrown really hard. Usually at least two of the balls would have to be thrown at me at once for them to put me out. In Bombardment, people wanted me on their side.

When other kids went to the movies I would tag along with them. Uninvited, but tolerated, I would sit in the same row as a group of other boys of my age—a row carefully chosen so that it was right behind a group of girls from our class who had just happened to come to the same movie. If the movie wasn't a particularly good one, it was that much better for me. I could make remarks about what was going on up on the screen and make the other kids laugh. Italian-made movies about Hercules that starred muscle-bound American bodybuilders were popular in those days, and one of those offered a thousand opportunities for comments. Hercules and his friends would go to rescue a friend tied to a spit to be burned alive. "Wait," I would say, imitating the dubbed voice of Hercules. "We cannot take him off yet. He is not yet equally done on both sides."

My social interactions were limited by the fact that my grandmother would always drop me off at the start of the movie and be sitting outside waiting for me in the car when it was over. But slowly I was starting to make some friends.

I was still only a bit more than medium height, but at the start of my junior year something happened that made me look at myself in a different way. During lunch, the group of guys who were becoming my friends would walk down to the little store near the firehouse. It was called Lee's, named for one of the boys in our group, whose father ran the store. People liked to have me along when they went to Lee's, because I could always be counted on for a loan to anybody who was short of money.

Lee's father, Mr. Goodwin, was a little like my grandfather in that he had a dry wit and liked kids. He encouraged us to hang out there and gave people nicknames that were so appropriate they were readily accepted. One day, as we hung out, I went out the door without looking and stepped right on the foot of Red, the same boy who had torn my pants a year and a half before. Red should have graduated, but he had been held back to repeat his senior year.

He grabbed me by the shirt and threw me as hard as he could. I was off balance, but I remembered something I had learned in gym class. I tucked my head and did a perfect forward roll, bouncing back up to my feet.

"Stay down, wiseass," he said, pushing me backward. I

went down, but this time I put my hands up by my head and did a backward roll, jumping up to my feet a second time.

He stepped up and swung a fist at me. It was smaller than a Bombardment ball and not nearly as fast. I ducked it and stepped back, untouched.

"I'm going to break your damn arm," Red said. He leaped at me, grabbing my right wrist with one hand and my upper arm with the other. Then he looked at me in surprise. Under my long-sleeved shirt, my arm was thicker-boned and harder with muscle than he had expected. It was from all those years of climbing trees. I didn't resist him. I just stood there. He tried to bend my arm. He couldn't bend it. He brought his knee up and slammed my arm against it. But instead of breaking my arm he hurt his own knee.

He let go of my arm and backed up. I still just stood there.

"Just watch where you're going next time," he said. Then he walked away.

"Jumping Joe," said a voice behind me. I turned. It was Mr. Goodwin, standing at the top of the steps of his store. He smiled down at me and nodded. "That's you, all right. Jumping Joe."

And that was me, Jumping Joe. I had a nickname. That late autumn it seemed as if things were getting better and better. My grandfather came home from the hospital and didn't have to go back. It was not leukemia at all. It was pernicious anemia, and pills were all that he needed. I remember both my grandmother and me hugging him as we went in the house.

But I also remember how my grandmother had to stop and catch her breath coming up the steps. I was taking a health class then and had learned that overweight people often have a hard time getting their breath. My grandmother weighed well over two hundred and forty pounds, much too much for a woman only five feet eight inches tall. The idea of dieting was beginning to sweep America, and I began thinking of how we could put her on a diet. Then she wouldn't be short of breath so often.

I was in biology class that year and I loved it. Holger Van Aller was the instructor and he was a brilliant, sensitive teacher. Some of the kids whispered that he was close to being a pinko because he had dared to say that the Russian launch of Sputnik, the first earth satellite, was less a disaster for America than a triumph for science and mankind. In those years when the cold war was getting hotter, it took courage to say that to a group of kids who had gone through grade school with regular air-raid drills in which we learned to "duck and cover" by crawling under our desks to keep from getting killed by nuclear bombs. Mr. Van Aller had been my mother's teacher when she went to school, and he had high regard for my grandmother.

"Your grandmother, Mrs. Bowman," he told me, "is a woman of great intellect and even greater courage."

One day he asked me to stay after class to work with a special group of advanced biology students. I was so delighted that I accepted, but forgot to call my grandmother to tell her I wouldn't be on the bus. It was not a small mistake. I was still working on the dissection of a preserved fetal pig with a group of other students an hour after school had let out, when two state police officers walked into the biology room.

"Is there a Sonny Bruchac here?" one of them said, in a bored authoritarian tone.

"I'm here," I said, my voice as small as the pig in the tray before me.

"Your grandmother called to report you missing when you didn't come home on the bus. You'd better come with us."

They drove me home in their police car.

My grandmother was waiting on the porch. I had never seen her looking so upset or so frightened. But she waited until the state cruiser had pulled away before she began to speak.

"How was I to know where you were," she said. "How? How? You might have been dead. And your grandfather just home from the hospital. He's worried sick. How could you do this to him? How?"

I didn't cry. I looked over at my grandfather and saw that he was as confused as I was.

"Grama," I said, "you're wrong. I'm not a little baby anymore. I'm going to watch the station." Then I walked out of the house.

I came back an hour later, after having waited on several customers by myself. There had been no sign of either of my grandparents coming out to help me or talk with me. Grampa was in the living room, sitting in his chair. He was looking at the television set, even though it was not turned on. Sniffy, my beagle, was in his usual place under my grandfather's chair. He thumped his tail at the sight of me but didn't come out. Clearly, he had taken shelter from the storm.

"She's gone to bed," Grampa said. His voice sounded worried. I understood why. It was dark, because it was late autumn, but it was only seven o'clock. A plate sat on the table with food for me. She hadn't forgotten that, but it was the night when the Ed Sullivan Show was on. Grama never missed Ed Sullivan.

I walked back into my grandmother's bedroom and sat on the bed.

"Sonny?" my grandmother said. Her voice seemed so weak.

"I'm here, Grama. I love you. I'm sorry I made you worry."

She grabbed my hand and squeezed it so hard that it hurt. "Sonny," she said, "Sonny, I just don't know what you and your grandfather will do without me. You know what it would be like if you lived over to The Farm. Your mother always used to smile before she was married. Sonny, I'm so worried."

"Grama," I said, "it's okay. Grampa's back home now and I'm here. We're all together."

Then I leaned over her and kissed her cheek. It was wet with tears and it was warm, so warm that I knew she had a fever.

ON THE HILL

There is no word in Abenaki for good-bye. It is that way in most of the Native languages of this continent. Perhaps it is because there is no idea of a final farewell. Instead, there is a sense that those who die do not really leave us. In Abenaki, instead of saying good-bye we say Wlipamkaani, which means "Travel well." We say that those who die climb up the Star Road to find a place where the hunting is always good and the berries are always ripe. So it is right to wish people a good journey.

The highest of the mountains of New England is called by the Abenaki Wonbi Wadzoak, the White Mountain. Long ago, when there was a great flood, a white hare led the last man and woman to safety on that mountaintop while everyone else drowned. They were the grandparents of all the Abenaki people, and to this day the white hare is revered as a helper of the people. You can still find the shape of the hare incised into bark baskets. It is one of the symbols of the village of survivors known as Odanak.

That great mountain, which the Americans renamed Mount Washington, is also regarded as the starting place of the Sky Road known as the Milky Way. Wonbi Wadzoak is the last place our spirit feet step on the earth before we go out among the stars.

My grandmother was the one who handled all the organization of our household. My grandfather had no head for figures and "indoors work," as he called it. As my grandmother became more ill, losing weight and strength, he became more confused. My mother came to look over the books and see that the bills were paid. My father began coming over and helping take care of the station. I kept a wary distance from him. Although it was years since he had threatened to send me to reform school, I knew that he had never forgotten and would never forgive me for that rock I had thrown years ago.

It was January now. The 18th was my grandparents' wedding anniversary. I don't recall exactly what I got them, but it was some kind of flowering potted plant from Dehn's Greenhouse. My grandmother was sitting in her chair and she smiled and gave me a hug when I gave them the plant. But then that all-too-familiar look of pain crossed her face.

"Oh dear," she said, "oh dear." And she kept saying that.

She was never one to complain, always one to think of taking care of others. Until December, despite her flagging energy, she had still helped put on church suppers and worked on fund-raisers. But when the new year came, it only brought her more pain, so much that she no longer went to the beauty parlor to have her hair done. As a result, her gray hair became whiter each day until it was the color of snow. I sensed something in her beginning to give way, like a small crack in a dam that has finally widened to the point where it can no longer hold back the pressure behind it.

Of course, I denied it. I denied it despite the familiar frightening dreams that had come back to me, dreams I had not had since I was seven. I stood on one side of a widening chasm and my grandmother stood on the other, falling away from me, smaller and smaller and then gone. But that night of their anniversary I could deny it no longer.

At seven that evening my mother called the Corinth Emergency Squad, the nearest ambulance, though it was fifteen miles to the north of us and the Saratoga Hospital was three miles south. They wouldn't come. I tried to help, but my father and mother pushed me away. They walked her down the stairs and I followed. Grama reached out her arms to me as they shut the door to their car. I couldn't hear what she said. Perhaps it would have made no sense. They said that she was out of her head from the pain of the multiple myeloma, the bone cancer that had begun to take her life so swiftly, the cancer which probably began from that deep burn given her by the heat lamp two years before. But it seemed to me as if the words she was mouthing were these: "I love you, Sonny. Be brave."

She only spent that one night in the hospital. When they took me down to see her the next day, she was only partly conscious and she didn't know anyone. My grandfather was not a man to cry, but all the toughness went out of him as he sat by her bed and wept.

"I don't want ye to go, Marion," he said. "What be I going to do?"

A nurse told us that we had to leave. My mother tried to refuse.

"I have to be with her when . . ." she began to say. The nurse didn't listen.

"We're just going to make her more comfortable," the nurse said in a brisk voice. "You can come back later when she's resting."

As we walked down the stairs I couldn't feel the ground under my feet. I knew it was falling away beneath me. Someone bought me a sandwich. I ate it, even though it tasted like cardboard. We went into the waiting room and sat beneath a clock that kept ticking slowly, its sound like the last drops of water draining out of a broken jug. Finally, a doctor came in and whispered something to my mother.

"Oh God, no!" my mother shouted. "Not Mom."

The events of the next three days were a blur of grief for me. My father took my grandfather and me with him in his car to the Robert Hall clothing store. We had to be dressed properly for the funeral. He bought us each a dark suit. Mine was a size too large. The waist on the pants was six inches too big for me.

"It doesn't fit me," I said.

"You have to get it big so you'll have it to use later. You'll grow into it."

Decades have passed, and my waist is still two inches smaller than the waist of that suit which he forced me to wear, the suit I put into the back of my closet the day after my grandmother's funeral and never wore again. But I heard the impatience in my father's voice that day and I knew I could not complain. The person who had been my court of last resort, my protector, was gone. I looked over at my grandfather, who stood there in his suit. I had never seen him in one before. He held his arms out from the side of his body and his back was stiff, his head and chin held up high by the collar and tie.

"You look very fine, Mr. Bowman," the tailor was saying to him as he jerked on the cuffs of the pants.

Years later, when I saw pictures of young Indian men who were taken by force to boarding schools where their long hair was cut and their traditional clothing replaced by uncomfortable suits and ties that choked their necks, I recognized that posture and the look on their faces. It was the same as my grandfather's that day. Perhaps that look of an indescribable sort of loss was on my face as well.

The funeral was held out of our house. They laid the coffin on a trestle placed against the wall next to the stairs in the living room. I looked in at my grandmother's face, made up like the face of a doll. I saw that only her body was there. Her spirit was somewhere else. I went back and sat down in one of the undertaker's chairs that were lined up in neat rows. My sister Mary Ann sat down next to me.

"I went to kiss Grama," she said, "and her lips were falling away."

I didn't say anything back to her. I'd read Agee's *A Death in the Family*. They didn't bring my little sister Marge, who was five, over to the funeral. They thought it might disturb her. I understood why.

Then we were up in the Greenfield Cemetery on the hill where the Dunhams were buried, and the big headstone had their name on it. The sun was shining as the minister spoke. I didn't hear any of it, just a roaring sound in my ears. I looked out across the hills and saw children sledding down a slope half a mile away. I watched them, part of me thinking that it was a sort of sign: life goes on. Another part of me wanted the earth to open up in front of them, so that they would fall to their doom for daring to laugh and play on this day when my grandmother was being buried. Something moved on the hill above the one where the children played. I squinted my eyes. It looked like the shape of a snowshoe rabbit, crossing the patchy snow toward the forest on the hilltop.

I looked over at my grandfather, who stood next to me. We watched together as we stood there on the hill. Then he turned his face back to me. There were tears in his eyes, but there was determination in his voice as he said the only thing that he could have said that day. He whispered it in a way that made me understand what he was thinking—that he felt it should have been him and not my grandmother who died first, that he knew he wasn't as good at a lot of things as she had been, but that he was going to try his best.

"I love ye, Sonny," he said.

GROWING

There are many Abenaki stories about things and people magically growing tall. In one tale, which explains the origin of the name "Indian Summer," a man's crops fail, and he and his family face starvation. Ktsi Nwaskw takes pity on him and gives him special seeds that will grow to their full height and produce a crop in only seven days. Then, because it is when the leaves have already begun to fall, Ktsi Nwaskw gives that man a special time of year, a second summer after autumn has begun, in which those crops can grow. We no longer have those seeds, but that time, Nibun Alnoba, "A Person's Summer," is still given to us every year.

Then there is the story of a boy who is an orphan. All that he has is a little dog, no bigger than his hand. But when he goes out into the world, that little dog goes with him. Whenever he is faced by danger, that little dogs breathes in four times, grows twice as large as a bear, and saves him.

Although I had feared what would happen when my grandmother was gone, I was not forced to leave my grandfather and go over to The Farm. I was not even asked. Perhaps my parents knew how much my grandfather needed me. Perhaps they were waiting for me to admit that Grampa and I couldn't take care of ourselves and beg them to take me in. Perhaps, too, their denial of the fact that I had never lived over there before would not allow them to admit it by asking me to move in with them now. Whatever the reason, I stayed with my grandfather in the house on Splinterville Hill.

It would not be completely right to say that I stayed in the house. I stayed outside whenever I could, whether it was that winter or the early spring which followed. I spent many hours in the woods, climbing trees or just sitting with my arms around Sniffy, talking to my dog about the sorrow and confusion that I felt. Both my grandfather and I began to spend more and more of our time out in the station, only coming into the house at night to sleep and, sometimes, to eat. We moved the TV out into the station and watched *Gunsmoke* and *Dragnet*. The house seemed bigger than it ever had before. I tried to do the vacuuming and the dusting, but it was hard to keep up with it all. It took me twice as much time to do half of what Grama had done.

Grampa didn't even try. When we were in the house, he just sat in his chair and looked out the window, as if expecting a car to pull up with someone in it. He'd always sat that way when my grandmother was out at a church supper or off to a school board meeting. For a few weeks after my grandmother died people sent over cakes and casseroles, but all too soon we were on our own as far as food went. Then one day, perhaps two months after my grandmother's death, my grandfather sat up in his chair as if he had just wakened from a long, troubled dream.

"Let's have us some baked beans," he said. He took out a package of dried beans and put them to soak overnight. The next morning he drained the beans and mixed in his special secret ingredients, which included molasses. He put it all in a casserole dish and put some bacon strips on top before he placed it into the oven. When I came home from school that night we sat together at the table and ate the first hot meal that had been prepared in the house since my grandmother's death. It was literally the only meal my grandfather knew how to make, but he made it well. The next day I experimented, somewhat less successfully, with macaroni and cheese. But now we realized that there were two meals we could cook. Then, as we walked through the aisles of the A&P supermarket the next day, we made a discovery. There, in the frozen-food case, were half a dozen different kinds of TV dinners. Just heat and serve, the instructions said. And that was what we began to do.

Each day my mother came over and demanded the day's receipts from the store. My grandfather gave them to her grudgingly. To him, a dollar he was paid was a dollar he could spend. The words "net" and "gross" might as well have been Latin as far as he was concerned. My mother would pay the bills and then give him a small living allowance. She also had him sign over his Social Security check to her. After a while, though, my grandfather learned how to hold back just enough "so's she won't pay it no never mind," he said. That little bit of extra money was enough for us to go out to eat at a restaurant once a week.

I worked that summer at the Saratoga Spa, the state mineral baths in Saratoga Springs. The Washington Baths, in the same building that is now the National Museum of Dance, were part of the Spa, which had been built on the former New York State Reservation. (This was not an Indian Reservation, but a state park sited around the abundant mineral springs at the south end of Saratoga Springs.) My father had worked at the Washington Baths as a laborer, one of the last times he ever worked for anyone else, he said. He pointed out a lintel stone in the area near the Hall of Springs.

"That's the one they dropped on my leg and broke it. Then when it healed they didn't hire me back, because they were hiring married men with children first and I was unmarried and a Republican."

I was given the job in the baths, I knew, because my grandmother had been a staunch Democrat and, though Republicans dominated the local government, Democrats ran the state. My job was to work in the basement, pulling the used linen and towels out of the chutes and then carrying clean dry towels back up to be used by the patrons. My check too was handed over to my mother each week. She knew how much I was like my grandfather, who, it was said, would give away his last dollar to anyone who asked him for it. A small part of my paycheck was given back to me, the rest put into the bank. My parents kept the bankbook.

By working at the baths, I was given free admission to the Victoria Pool. It was in a beautiful building, the pool itself inside an enclosed open-roofed stone courtyard. I swam there, though, with mixed feelings. It was because of the Victoria Pool and Susie Boyle that I couldn't really smile.

The summer before my grandmother died, I had finally gotten up the nerve to go off the high board at the Victoria Pool: not just jump feetfirst, but really dive. The sting of the water from that height always hurt, because I hadn't learned how to hold my hands together so that I would enter cleanly. But just having the nerve to get up there, so high that you were level with the tops of the trees outside the building, was something I'd never dared do before that summer.

The good part about being up there was that everybody could see me, and I could also see the entrance to the girls' changing room. I waited up on the high board that August day until I saw Susie Boyle come out and head toward the pool. She was wearing a new black bathing suit. Susie had never noticed me before, but I had seen how the girls watched people when they dove off the high board. This was my chance. I waited till she was almost at the edge of the pool, then gave a loud whoop, bounced high, and launched myself into the air— my arms held out, my back straight, and my feet together. I held that pose as I fell, a perfect swan dive. I held it so tightly that my arms were still out to my sides when I hit the water, and I went down like a rocket, striking face-first on the concrete at the bottom of the pool. Something cracked. Even underwater I could hear it. I clawed my way back up to the surface, blood streaming from my nose, lips, and chin. As Ralph Marter, the lifeguard who was a year ahead of me in high school, pulled me out, I was holding my hand up to my mouth, feeling the place where my right front tooth had been broken off.

He pulled my hand away from my mouth and looked.

"Jeez," he said, "you knocked your tooth out."

I took the towel he handed me and held it against my bleeding face. I knew what was next. A call to my grandmother, a lecture on my way home, and a visit to the dentist, Dr. Benditt—whose nickname was "Bloody Benditt." The thought of all three of those things made my blood run cold. I tried to look at the bright side.

"Well," I said, my words garbled through the towel, "it could have been worse. It could have been one of my incisors."

"Are you crazy?" Ralph Marter said. "The worst thing you can do is lose a front tooth."

But Ralph Marter was wrong. The worst thing was not to lose a front tooth. The worst thing was to have it replaced—not by a porcelain cap, but by one of shiny silver. In those days, it was not a fashion statement to have a front tooth that gleamed like a headlight when you smiled.

"You'll have to wear this about eighteen months, until the

nerve shrinks back," said Dr. Benditt, wiping the blood off his smock. "Then we'll see about getting one made of porcelain."

I looked at myself in the mirror and knew that I would have to learn to smile with my mouth closed. A look back at the Saratoga Springs High School yearbooks for my junior and senior years shows how well I succeeded. In my junior year my face appears three times, in the pictures of my homeroom class, Projection Club, and Photo Club: tight-lipped in all three. In the sixteen pictures that show my face in my senior yearbook, I have that same Mona Lisa look. Maybe she had a tooth missing too.

After my grandmother's death, a strange thing happened. I began to grow. An inch . . . two inches . . . three. By May of my junior year I had almost reached my full height of six feet two inches, and my strength had increased with it. I was awkward with this new body and with the way people were acting around me. For the first time in my life, the kids who had always been bigger than me were looking up to me. I'd tried to join the wrestling team that year, but had made so few of the practices that I'd never been allowed to wrestle in a real match.

"Bruchac," Coach Tibbetts said to me, "why don't you use that big body of yours for the shot put?" So I joined the track-and-field team and spent that spring trying to learn how to throw the shot and the discus. Half a dozen other boys were better than I was, but I came to every practice and once even finished fourth in the shot put.

By the time late summer came I had decided I would try again to join the football team. I had attempted to go out for football my sophomore year. When I had showed up the first day, I was sent to the equipment room at the East Side Rec to get my uniform. I walked down the stairs into the basement. The person in the cage was Whitey Nelson. A year older than

My high school wrestling team photo, 1960

me, Whitey was one of those kids who is only a fair student and not much of an athlete, but who finds his niche as a team manager. He had looked me over, sized me up, and then handed me a broken set of shoulder pads and a pair of pants four sizes too big.

"That's all we got right now, friend. You gotta make do with them."

My face red with embarrassment, I had left the shoulder pads and the pants on the table. I went home and told my grandmother about it.

"You're better off not trying to play football," she had said. "They're just a bunch of rough boys and you might get hurt. Your grandfather and I need you here at home to help us after school anyway."

This time, though—the autumn of my senior year—was different. I stuck with it through training camp, through the bloody noses and bruises and aching muscles. By the first game of the season I was a second-string right tackle. I might even have been first-string, but the complexities of football, a game I'd seldom watched and never played, were beyond me. Each play I had to rely on the guard next to me, Bobby Clements, who would whisper as we approached the line, "Cross block, Bruchac" or "Hit the guy in front of you." Bobby's younger brother, Donny, was the starting right tackle.

Coach Tibbetts was the archetypal tough coach, a leader whose highest compliment to any team member was, "You played like a man!" However, when the coach—whom we all called "Hutch"—got excited, he talked fast and forgot things. We had two quarterbacks: Pat Svanson, who passed, and Mike Gibney, who only handed off or ran with the ball. In one memorable game, Coach Tibbetts forgot who was who and sent Mike in to throw a pass. No one dared to question an order from the coach, so Mike turned around, a little confused, to head in and call the play.

"Mike, Mike, Mike!" Coach Tibbetts called him back.

Mike turned back, hoping that the play was about to be changed.

Photo from the *Saratogian* of October 23, 1959. I'm third from the left

"Mike," Coach Tibbetts said, "you catch that ball too!"

So when the coach collared me in the hall two hours before our first game, I didn't know what to expect. "Bruchac," he said, "I'm writing down our roster for the game. What's your number?"

I hesitated. I'd thought he was about to tell me I'd been demoted to third-string. In my relief, I couldn't remember my first name, much less my number.

"It's . . . ah . . . fif . . . fifty- . . ." I knew it was something in the fifties.

"Come on, come on, lad. You want to play, don't you?"

I blurted out the first number that came into my head. "Fifty-seven, sir."

"Good," Coach Tibbetts said. "Good, good." And he was down the hall before I could tell him that I'd just remembered what my number really was. Fifty-seven was Donny Clements's number. Mine was fifty-six.

That day, I spent most of the game on the sidelines, going in only for kickoffs and for the last half of the fourth quarter, when we were ahead 21-0. But as I sat and watched, I made more tackles than anyone else on the field. The announcer called my name again and again. "And it's another tackle by number fifty-seven . . . Bruchac! That kid is having a heck of a game." It was lucky for me that Donny Clements had a good sense of humor.

I did more, though, than sit on the bench for the rest of the season. Before long, I was playing just as much as Donny played. In the game against Ballston Spa, our arch rivals, I recovered the fumble that helped us win, giving us a share of the conference championship. I also tackled their leading runner, Ducky Monaco, before he could reach the end zone. When the game was over, the final score was 13-12.

GROWING

Coach Tibbetts, who had been so excited during the game that he had bawled me out after I made each of those crucial plays, took me aside when it was over.

"Joey," he said, "you really did some growing up today. It's good to have you as one of my men."

MY GRANDFATHER'S SHOTGUN

Many years ago, a group of young Iroquois men from the Mohawk nation—who called themselves the Kanien'keha':ka, *the Flint-Place People—were going through the mountains. They traveled east until they came to a chain of lakes. When they reached the place where the water was narrowest, a bit wider than you could throw a spear, they looked across and saw there on the other side another party of men. Those men were Abenakis of the Missisquoi Nation, a name which also means "Flint Place."*

In those days, it was common for young men to go out on parties to raid the villages of other tribes, and so there was a chance those two groups might fight. But neither one really wanted to cross over and fight. They looked at each other like two wildcats staring at each other across a log.

"Come over and fight us!" one side called out.

"No, you come over here," answered those on the other side.

This went on for some time until the Abenakis began to get hungry. They had no food with them, but there were some young white pines there by the water. They began to strip the bark off and eat the pith of the pines. Pine pith can be dried and pounded and cooked as bread or eaten raw. It is a food that is high in vitamins. The white *pine is regarded by the Abenakis as a special tree, since its needles can be used to make medicine and its pith is so good to eat.*

The Mohawks saw this and began to insult the Abenakis. "You are porcupines!" they shouted. "You are Anen:taks, *eaters of bark!"*

That word stuck. From that day on the Mohawks called the Abenakis Bark Eaters, or Anen:taks, a word which became "Adirondacks," and is now the name by which the northern region of New York State is known.

My grandfather's shotgun hangs in the gunrack behind the door to my study, in the house that he built on that scorched foundation which had once supported the lives of the Dunhams. Although my grandfather never formally gave me that shotgun, at one point in my life it just became mine. It was soon after my seventeenth birthday in the fall of the year when my grandmother died. Before my grandmother's death that shotgun had always been kept in the back of the closet in my grandparents' bedroom.

When it was in the house, the gun was always unloaded. My grandfather would never have left a loaded gun around. He kept only one shell for it, hidden under his socks in the top drawer of his dresser, a shell loaded with buckshot. I found it after his death many years later, when Carol and I were cleaning out his room. Although my grandfather had killed deer when he was a young man, it had only been out of necessity. He never liked killing. "We needed 'em to eat," he said to me.

It was the Sunday after I had just played in my second football game, the game in which we beat Draper 41-0. I'd gotten a lot of playing time in that game and, as I came off the field at halftime, I looked up in surprise to see that my parents had joined my grandfather in the stands. There was an expression on my father's face that I don't recall having seen there before. My grandfather, though, was his usual self.

"See that boy there, that number fifty-six. That there's my grandson!" he was saying to the people around him.

The next day, my father came over to the station.

"I signed you up for the Gun Safety course at the Rod and Gun Club," he said. Then he hesitated. Conversations with him were like that: an abrupt statement and then a sudden pause. "If you want to take it."

"I do," I said, surprising myself with my own words.

"You pass it, I'll buy your license for you." The way he said it made me feel that he expected me to flunk the course. Instead, I went to it each week and passed easily. My father bought me my first hunting license.

"Next Sunday," he said, "I'll take you pheasant hunting." Again the pause. "If you want to go."

"I do," I said again. My grandmother had always been deeply disapproving of my father's hunting. I had grown up not only seeing Walt Disney's film *Bambi*, but also reading the book by Felix Salten. Then I had begun reading the books by writers who told more accurately of the lives of animals, books like Seton's *Wild Animals I Have Known*. I had always sympathized with the four-legged ones. On the other hand, I had been fishing now for several years, and my grandparents and I had always looked forward to the pheasants that my father presented to us each autumn for my grandmother to cook. I was the only child I know who was sent to school with pheasant sandwiches in his lunch box. Actually hunting for those pheasants myself, I reasoned, was no worse than eating them after someone else killed them. And pheasant would be a welcome addition to the diet that my grandfather and I were now consuming of beans, macaroni, and TV dinners.

In those days, where there are now housing developments in the wide rolling fields between Saratoga Springs and Albany, there used to be farms. Corn was the main crop then, and the state stocked those fields with pheasants. One field, owned by Clarence Chase, was only two miles from our house along Route 29, just past the turn to the Petrified Sea Gardens. But to hunt I needed a gun.

"You can use your grandfather's gun," my father said.

" 'Course you can," my grandfather said.

And from that point on, I did. My father and I traveled to those fields half a dozen times that fall in his green Chevy station wagon, his new twelve-gauge Browning semiautomatic shotgun with full choke in its brown leather case on the backseat, next to my grandfather's old Remington pump that I had wrapped in a green beach towel. There was an uneasy sort of truce between us. I could always feel him watching me, watching the way you watch a person who is, sooner or later, going to do something wrong. In the past I had usually lived up to his expectations.

But that first day when we hunted was different. Although my father didn't see me do it, I went down onto one knee and put my hand on the ground as we got out of the car at the edge of Chase's field. "I'm hunting you because we need you to eat," I said. We walked down the rows of corn. The first bird that flew out was a wide-winged cock pheasant that rose up cackling right in front of me. I raised the gun to my shoulder, thumbed off the safety, and shot before my father, twenty yards off to my right, could finish shouting "Mark!" It all happened in one quick, easy motion, and the bird fell.

Queenie, Dad's English setter, ran up to the bird, nosed it, and then brought it back to drop at my father's feet. My father picked up the pheasant and looked at it, admiration in his taxidermist eyes.

"Good color," he said, looking at the white ring around its neck and the bright iridescent hues on its head. There was a single drop of blood coming from its nostril. The pheasant was the size of a small chicken. My grandparents had always raised chickens, both for eggs and for eating, so I was used to seeing a bird killed for eating. But this was different. There was a clean, wild smell to the bird, not like that of a domesticated chicken. "Your bird," Dad said, handing it to me.

"You can have it to mount," I said. "I just want the meat."

"Turn around." I turned around, and my father unzipped the game pouch built into the back of my red jacket. He placed the bird inside it and then said, "Let's finish going down this row."

He turned and walked over to my right, as I reached my hand behind me to feel the warmth of the pheasant against the small of my back.

When it came to outdoor pursuits, my father had always expected the worst whenever he grudgingly involved me. Our family fishing trips had always been disastrous for me. One of the good things about hunting with him was that my sister never came along. She had never taken to hunting. Perhaps it was because my father thought of hunting as purely a man's pursuit. Perhaps it was because Mary Ann was older now, and her busy social life was more important to her.

Throughout that autumn I came to look forward to those days when we would tramp through cornfields, Queenie ranging ahead of us. After I shot that pheasant on our first day of hunting together, my father would usually be the one to take the first shot as a cock pheasant flew up at the end of a row of corn. I never saw him miss. He had badges on his hunting jacket from skeet-shooting competitions he had won, and he was the best man with a gun that I ever knew. I don't think that I fired my gun more than half a dozen times after that first shot of mine. I recall killing only one other pheasant. But the chill clean air, the crisp sounds of feet tramping the brown weeds in a frost-rimed field, even the cordite scent of gunpowder drifting in the breeze after my father shot his gun were enough for me. Carrying my grandfather's shotgun under my arm, the safety clicked on, I would walk those fields again with him gladly—fields that are all gone now, fields covered with houses and shopping malls and the macadam of airport runways for the jet planes that take me across this wide country. I know now, though I did not fully realize it then, how much my father wanted me to be with him, even if he did not know how to speak the words that might bridge the years and the pain between us.

It was not until a decade later that I would understand the irony of my carrying that seldom-fired shotgun. The irony of his speaking those words when he told me to pick up my grandfather's gun. I didn't yet know the story of the day when my father came to take me back, and my grandfather raised that same shotgun to his own head to keep me, to save me from my father's anger.

Perhaps it was a feeling of companionship on those days we spent hunting pheasants that made my father confide in me one autumn morning. For no discernible reason, he had turned to me as we climbed into his green truck to go pheasant hunting.

"You know," my father said, "your grandfather is an Abenaki Indian." He paused and I said nothing. "The Abenakis," he said, "they were so poor that they ate bark. They called them bark eaters."

I'd waited, but he said nothing more. I had looked at my father then, at his jet-black hair and his olive skin, his high cheekbones, and the epicanthic fold at the corners of his eyes. If there was ever a man who looked Indian, it was my father. Yet both his parents had come from Slovakia. As a grown man, whenever I would bring Indian friends to meet my parents, they would invariably say, "You can really see the Indian in your father." They didn't know that the only Indian in him was in his heart, a heart that was always happiest when he was alone in the forest.

I had waited that day for my father to say more about Grampa being an Indian, but he didn't. He'd broken a silence that everyone else older than me in my family had always kept. He wouldn't break it again.

Things went so well that fall with our bird hunting that my father bought me a big game license.

"We'll go up to the Gooley Club this weekend," he said. "Deer hunting."

He didn't ask me if I wanted to go and I didn't say anything. When you are seventeen, you may not be very sensitive to the feelings of your elders. I had been raised, though, by my grandparents. That had built something into me that could now begin to sense when those blunt statements made by my father were more a result of his own shyness and uncertainty around me than anything else.

I liked going to the Gooley Club. It was a private hunting and fishing club on thousands of acres of land leased from the Finch, Pruyn lumber company near Indian Lake. Most of the members of the Gooley Club were doctors and lawyers and wealthy businessmen. Belonging to the Gooley Club was a mark of status for my father, as well as a business investment—since many of the other members were customers who had their trophies mounted by Bruchac's Taxidermy.

There were mountains and more than a dozen lakes on the Gooley Club land, and it was the place where the Cedar River flowed into the Upper Hudson. I'd gone there on fishing trips a few times with my father and Mary Ann and had always felt the power of that land touching me. I was at home there and I knew, even as a little child, that I could never be lost in those woods.

For many years, that part of the Adirondacks had been familiar ground for Abenaki people. Indian Lake was named after an Abenaki guide, Sabael Benedict. Not far from there was the little town of Sabattis, named after another famous Abenaki guide of the nineteenth century, Mitchell Sabattis. My father's pack basket and his snowshoes had been made by one of Mitchell's descendants. He treasured that pack basket—which now hangs in my study.

My father was eager for me to shoot my first deer that November. We went out with a party of half a dozen others, led by George Osgood. George lived in Indian Lake and drove a school bus when he wasn't working in the woods as a guide. He was always my father's favorite guide at the Gooley.

George and my father placed me on watch near a big beech tree and put the three other men in spots further down the slope. We were to wait while they circled around the other side of Mt. Pisgah to drive the deer our way. Even if we shot something, we were to wait at our stands until George and my father came back through on the drive. They'd come from the west, so the wind would be at their backs, and the deer could smell them but not us. George knew that part of the mountain well, and he said that this year there were at least three bucks—a four-pointer, a six-pointer, and one with a big rack—along with half a dozen does.

"Now don't you shoot at a doe," my father said. His voice was stern. That stiffness—which had been missing on our pheasant hunting trips—crept back into his voice when I was with him in the company of other men. He was afraid I would embarrass him.

I nodded.

"Keep your safety on until you're ready to shoot."

I nodded again.

George Osgood was looking at me over my father's shoulder. George's face was dark and lined, much like Grampa Jesse's. His voice was gentle, and it seemed to me that George must have Abenaki blood in him too.

George Osgood nodded at me over my father's shoulder as my father barked out his stern instructions. He was giving me a message, speaking with his eyes, and I understood. You'll do all right, young fella, was the message.

"Don't you leave this stand," my father continued. "And if you do, remember that water runs downhill. You get lost, just follow the water and it'll lead you to the Cedar River."

My father turned and I watched his back disappear up the hill. George Osgood followed, with his .22 rimfire rifle, the only gun George ever used, cradled comfortably along his right arm.

I scuffed the dry leaves away around my feet so that I wouldn't make noise when I shifted my position. Then I leaned back against the beech tree and waited. I felt comfortable, hearing the noises of the forest return as the sounds of walking men grew fainter and fainter.

For a long time, I watched and listened. There was the faint sound of the wind and the rattling of dry leaves as they fell. I heard the squeak of a hunting shrew and saw its tiny gray body scuttle out from under a dead log and disappear again into the leaves. A chickadee came fluttering in and landed on a branch near my shoulder.

Then I heard a person cough. It was Dr. Niles, a surgeon from Albany. He'd been placed on watch fifty yards down from me. His feet began crunching the leaves and breaking twigs. Unlike me, he'd grown tired of waiting and was trying to find a better spot. I could see why George and my father referred to him as Nervous Niles. I looked at my wristwatch. An hour had passed since my father and George had gone.

Dr. Niles's footsteps went farther and farther away till they could be heard no more. It grew silent again. Then I heard another sound like the howling of a wolf. It was George Osgood, making noise to get the deer started our way. From further upslope and just as far away, I heard a distant sound of barking like a dog's. That was my father. I waited.

Then I heard the sound of running feet. I looked toward that sound and two does came out into the clear line of sight below my stand. Does always are the ones to go through first when you make a drive. I knew that from the books I'd been reading about hunting and from the countless issues of *Outdoor Life* and *Field and Stream* that my father had given my grandfather. My father got those magazines free because he advertised in them. I'd been reading them since I was seven. One doe lifted her head and swiveled her ears in my direction.

"Hello," I said. The doe raised her tail up like a white flag and crossed the clearing in three leaps, followed by the second female. I listened closely. I could hear other feet, not running as swiftly as the does'. It was probably one of the bucks. I couldn't see it, but I could tell by the motion of the small beeches and hop hornbeam bushes and by the sound of its hooves in the dry leaves that it was passing right by the now-deserted stand where Nervous Niles had been placed. I smiled.

That was when the second buck, the one with the big rack, stepped out of the brush. The 30.06 was on my shoulder, and I laid the open sight across his back, lowered it slightly so it was centered in one of those spots I had seen drawn on the picture of a deer in a sportsman's magazine. But I didn't take off the safety. I lowered my gun.

"Go home," I whispered. The deer ducked its head, as if it were bowing to me, backed in the brush, and was gone, heading down the slope past the deserted stand to safety.

Again, for a long time, things were quiet. I heard a shot

from the west. The pop of a .22. Then I heard the boom of my father's .308. I waited. My father was the first to appear. He came up to me.

"Did you see anything?"

"Nothing I could shoot," I said.

"We drove two nice bucks right through here," he said. He sounded suspicious.

"I bet they went down by where Dr. Niles was supposed to be," I said. "I heard him walk out of his stand about half an hour ago."

George Osgood came up to join my father, two of the three other hunters with him.

"Can't find Niles," he said.

"Gee-zis," my father said. "He's gone and done it again. Now we have to find him."

"I'll do it," said George. "You and the boy can follow that one we wounded."

A small deer had tried to circle back. George had shot at it once with his .22, and my father had taken a second shot at it from two hundred yards away as it passed below him. They were certain that both shots had hit but that neither had been enough to kill the deer. They'd seen blood and planned to track it after picking us up.

"I'll go with you," said one of the men to my father. It was Ed White. He owned a Cadillac dealership in Schenectady.

"Fine," said my father. "But let Sonny here take the shot. It'll be his first deer."

I said nothing as I followed them. The blood trail was easy to locate. A little snow had fallen, and where the deer's tracks crossed those patches of pure white the blood was a crimson line. My father picked up a wide yellow beech leaf that was speckled with red and held it up to his nose. "Gut shot," he said. "Been eating chestnuts, you can smell it."

We walked over one hill and then another and came into the edge of a small cedar swamp. That was as far as the young spikehorn buck had been able to run. I saw it lying down, partially concealed by a little cedar tree. Its head was up and it was still alive, but breathing hard. You could see the small hole punched by the .22 just behind its nostril.

George Osgood had tried for a brain shot, but missed. George always liked to shoot a deer in the head because he wanted the heart. "The best eating in a deer," he said. The round from my father's .308 had struck the deer far back in its belly, a wound that would eventually have killed it, but not quickly.

My father walked up to it. Ed White had pulled out his bowie knife.

"I can just cut its throat," he said.

My father held up his hand.

"This is Sonny's deer. He has to shoot it." He looked at me.

"Just lying there like that?" I said.

My father walked up to the deer and kicked it hard in the rump. I felt as if I had been kicked. The deer jumped up and ran ten yards before stumbling back down again onto its knees below two white birch trees.

"Shoot it," my father said. "In the neck so George can have the heart."

I was embarrassing him. I raised the 30.06 to my shoulder and pressed down on the safety. I aimed carefully at the shoulder and spoke without making any sound. "I'm sorry." It was all I could think to say before I pulled the trigger and killed the only deer I ever shot.

A REAL WRESTLER

I went to my thirty-fifth high school reunion. It wasn't easy for me to be there, because until the night before the banquet I'd been in the Midwest. There I had been the first keynote speaker at a Native writers' conference in Oneida, Wisconsin. I had gone there with my older son, Jim, but couldn't stay for the whole conference because of my reunion. I flew back, leaving Jim at the conference. In my pocket was a small Dream Catcher, a present from the Oneida Nation.

I'd been asked to say a few words to my classmates, and I did. I reminded them of all the things that had happened since we had been high school seniors—cellular phones, color TVs in every home, the first landing on the moon, photocopy machines, fax machines, personal computers, disco, reggae, rap, and hip-hop. With all these new ideas and new words, it sometimes was hard to believe we were still speaking English.

"But there are some things," I said, "that still remain the same. Honor and loyalty, courage and love and memory. Let's hear it for memory." And everyone applauded.

"Jumping Joe!" someone yelled.

I looked over at Carol, who was sitting in the back of the room. She smiled at me and nodded.

A REAL WRESTLER

All that evening people came over to talk to me. Some spoke about my unexpected emergence as an athlete in my senior year and how I went on to wrestle in the Nationals for Cornell University. Some said they had been reading my books, seeing me on TV, or hearing me on radio.

Maude Gailor took my hand. "Your work," she said, "inspired me to become a storyteller." She had just gotten back from Ireland where she went to seek out her relatives and her own Irish traditions. Now she was part of a group telling Irish-American stories.

James Parham—even taller than I remembered, but with a distinguished goatee—put his arm around me. "Joe," he said, "I have followed in your footsteps." James had entered the academic world. He had a Ph.D. and was a professor at the University of Pittsburgh. He reminded me how his had been the only African-American family in Greenfield and how the two of us had gone out for football for the first time in our senior year. He told me too about his two tours in Vietnam and about basic training in Oklahoma.

"When I got to Oklahoma," he said, "I was surprised. I'd always expected, when I left Saratoga, to be the low man on the totem pole. But it wasn't that way in Oklahoma. Way down there on the bottom were the Indians."

Wendy Cote poked me in the ribs. "I was teaching a course in Native American studies in California. I bought a book in the Nature Company," she said, "and I was halfway through reading it before it dawned on me that you were the one who wrote it. I read your bio, and when I saw it said you were a member of the Abenaki Indian Nation, I said to myself, 'No way—he's a Slovak, just like me!' " Wendy paused and leaned closer. "You know," she said, "on the other side of my family, all they would say is that we were French-Canadian. Just like your grandfather." She held her arm next to mine. "See how dark my skin is too?"

Wendy held one of my books in her hand, held it open to the picture of an Abenaki man surrounded by the spirits of the animals.

"You see," she said, gently placing her hand on the picture, "that's me."

I looked around the room, seeing the faces of middle-aged men and women, some of them grandparents. Yet I also saw, in their faces and in their laughter, the same faces of those young people I'd gone to high school with, faces that still held on to memories and dreams.

I thought about the journeys of self-discovery each of them had taken in the years since high school and I thought about my own journey toward my Indian roots. I thought about the countless hours that I began to spend in research about Native American life while I was in college—though in those days there were no courses taught in Native American studies and everything I did, I did on my own. My first published poem at Cornell had been about the deer I shot. The form of that poem had been shaped by translations of traditional Native prayers of forgiveness to the animals they killed, which I had read in Bureau of American Ethnology volumes published at the turn of the century.

I thought of my first visits to Onondaga while I was a graduate student at Syracuse and how, after three years of teaching in West Africa, I returned home to Greenfield Center and began doing poetry in the schools programs in the reservation schools of New York State. In those years in the early 1970's I always learned more than I taught whenever I went to work with the Native children of Onondaga or Akwesasne, Cattaraugus or Salamanca. When I began publishing a literary magazine called The Greenfield Review *in 1970, I looked for work by others like myself, people who were seeking out their Native roots along the word trails, people who were unafraid of being Indian in an America which ignored or stereotyped them. Many of those young Native writers became my close friends. Year after year I continued reading and researching, traveling to seek out Native elders to listen to them, publishing the work of others, writing and teaching. I found myself meeting again the Indian people I'd first met in my childhood when I went to Frontier Town and the Enchanted Forest and the Lake George Indian Village—Ray Fadden, Swift Eagle, and Maurice Dennis. Gradually, they became my teachers. They led me to Swanton and Odanak, to connections to my Native family that the generations before me had tried to hide.*

The steps I took on my journey were slow, sometimes along trails that I couldn't really see until I had been on them for years, but I continued on. I had learned that from wrestling. Out there on the mat, all alone, if you give up you lose. All that you can do is stick with it.

Ray Waldron, the wrestling coach, had been one of the assistant coaches for football, and it was Ray who encouraged me to try for the team. I'd proven something by going out for football and sticking with it. I had a sweater with a varsity letter on it, and somehow, people who had seen me as an egghead only a year before now saw me as a jock and as an unlikely blend of athlete and intellectual. It was confusing to many of them, but not as confusing as it was to me.

The only one who was never confused about it was my grandfather. He was behind me every step that I took.

"Ain't no need to worry," he said to me. "I know you kin do it!"

He went with me everywhere, including the restaurants where the kids went to celebrate on Saturday nights after the games. It wasn't as it might have been if a mother or father had been along. Grampa was as full of mischief as any of the kids my age, teasing, laughing, and every now and then saying a gentle word where one was needed. The other kids called him "Jess," and whenever I was invited somewhere they'd say, "And bring along your grandfather!"

My grandfather also kept a close watch on me, ready to give

me space if he thought I needed it, especially when he felt I might be making some progress in developing a relationship with a girl. He needn't have worried. As far as the opposite sex was concerned, I had fewer social skills than Johnny Weissmuller playing Tarzan. It wasn't that girls disliked me. I now had many friends who were girls. They were friends who laughed at the stories I wrote for them, asked me how other guys felt about them, but always said no whenever I got up the courage to ask one of them to go with me to a movie. I had graduated from the category of Creep to Big Brother. One of the responses that I often got was, "You'll find the right girl some day, Joey, just you wait. And she'll be lucky to have a wonderful guy like you."

I threw all my energy into wrestling. In those days, there was no such thing as a weight limit when you wrestled as a heavyweight. I weighed just two hundred pounds. The starting heavyweight, Ed Maderassey, weighed eighty pounds more than I did. To be on the team, I had to beat him in a wrestle-off.

In football, you are only one of many people on the field. One little mistake on your part may go unnoticed. But in wrestling there are only two people—you and your opponent. Every move you make is watched. Few things can build character and self-awareness the way wrestling does. And few things can make you more nervous than waiting for your match to come up! There were four other wrestle-offs that day. Mine was the last.

My grandfather had been delighted when I told him I was going to try to wrestle. Since I was six years old he'd been a fan of professional wrestling. It was the only thing on television that he liked as much as *Gunsmoke*, and when there were professional wrestling matches at the Convention Hall in Saratoga, he'd take me with him. I had an autograph book that had been signed by all the famous wrestlers who'd come to Saratoga—

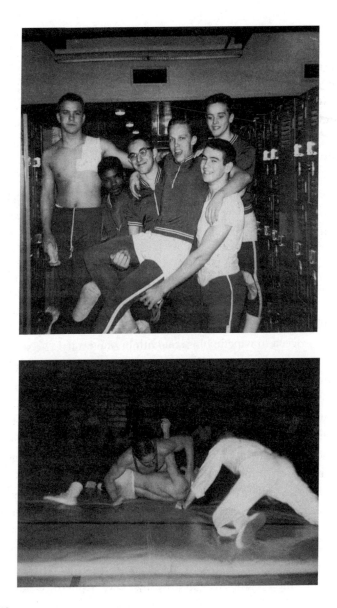

"Supporting" my high school wrestling team. I'm the third from the left, *top*, and pinning one of my opponents, *bottom*

Lou Thesz, Killer Kowalski, Antonino Rocca, Yukon Eric. My grandfather remained convinced throughout his life that professional wrestling contests were the real thing, rather than carefully-scripted athletic morality plays in which good guys like Roy McClarity and Danny O'Shocker were supposed to win.

One of his favorite wrestlers was a man Grampa called "The Chief." The Chief would be thrown around the ring, body-slammed, kicked, and eye-gouged. He'd absorb more punishment than it seemed a human body could withstand.

"Just watch," Grampa would say, "he ain't mad yet."

And Grampa was right. Finally, something would get The Chief angry. He would stand up tall and throw the other man off him. Then he would do his "war dance." The other wrestler would cower back in fear—and rightly so, for The Chief would then proceed to wipe up the mat with his adversary.

"You see," my grandfather would say, "you don't never want to get an Indian mad."

That day in my first wrestle-off, as I looked across the mat at Ed Maderassey, I felt for a moment as if I was six years old and my opponent was Yukon Eric, who billed himself as "the logger from the last frontier," and who was built like a giant tree. Ed Maderassey was as broad as a barn, it seemed; his legs were huge, and when we had worked out together in practice and he had put his weight on me in the spin drill I'd felt like I was under an elephant.

Then I thought about my grandfather. He wanted to see me wrestle, and the only way that was going to happen was for me to win today. I looked at Ed Maderassey and I felt angry. There was a little smile on his face as he shook my hand. He wanted to prevent my grandfather from ever seeing me wrestle. I smiled too, and my silver front tooth gleamed. Coach Waldron blew his whistle. Maderassey and I surged together. We locked up and pushed back and forth. Then I thrust his arms up off my neck and dropped in to try a double leg take-down. The weight of the world came down on my back, but I pulled in with my arms, heaved up, and found myself on top.

"Two points, take-down!" Ray Waldron shouted.

Maderassey hooked my arm and rolled. A year before, he had tried that same move on Brett Haskell, the wrestler from Ballston Spa who everyone knew was the best heavyweight. He'd won the regional tournament and the sectionals two years in a row. Haskell was as big as Maderassey, and the only defeat in his whole career had come when Maderassey rolled as Haskell was taking him down. Haskell had ended up briefly stuck on his back and the referee had quickly—too quickly, perhaps—slapped the mat for a pin. Haskell had later avenged that one defeat by pinning Maderassey in less than a minute in the regional tournament.

I felt myself going over as Maderassey rolled, but I rolled with him, rolled through, heaved, and ended up with him on the bottom again. Ray Waldron's whistle blew. It was the end of the first period. Somehow, two minutes had flown past.

In the second period, we began with me down, Maderassey on my back. The whistle blew and I did the only other move I had really learned, aside from the double leg take-down. I did a switch, sitting out, throwing back my right arm to grab Maderassey's giant leg, then turning.

"Two points, reversal!" Ray Waldron called out.

I ended up winning my first wrestle-off. Though I didn't know it, I would never lose a wrestle-off. I would go on to wrestle for four years at Cornell University and, apart from a few times when I was injured, I would always be the starting heavyweight. But except for one, there was no match that was more important for me than the first win I earned that day. Watched only by my coach and my teammates—on old-fashioned canvas mats that slid apart as we wrestled on the floor of the high school cafeteria, so that our elbows and knees hit the hard linoleum—I became a real wrestler.

32 TESTS

The people were hungry. This was long ago, so our cousins the Anishinabe say. A young man went into the forest and prayed to Gitchee Manitou for help. He wanted to do something for his people. Then he sat and waited for a vision. He waited and waited, and after waiting a long time he slept. In his dream he saw a tall, straight warrior dressed in skins which were as green as the grass. That tall warrior had hair that was as yellow as the bright sun.

"You will wrestle me," said that warrior. "My name is Mondawmin. If you beat me, your people will be fed. We will wrestle until we hear the heron's cry at the end of the day."

When the man woke, there before him was Mondawmin. He sprang up, and the two began to wrestle. They wrestled all through that day. Neither could defeat the other. When the night came the heron gave its loud cry and they stopped wrestling. When the second day came they wrestled again, and neither could win before the heron's cry called an end to their contest. It was the same on the third day.

But on the evening of that third day, the man dreamed again. In his dream Mondawmin spoke to him.

"Tomorrow," Mondawmin said, "you must defeat me. You will

*throw me to the ground. Then you must bury me. Keep my grave
clean, and guard it from the animals and the birds. If you do this,
you will see me again and your people will be fed."*

*When the fourth day dawned they began again to wrestle. Just
as before, it seemed neither could win. However, just as the sun was
about to set, the young man lifted up Mondawmin and threw him
to the ground so hard that the life seemed to go out of him.*

*The man remembered his dream. He buried Mondawmin and
kept watch over the grave. He kept it clean and kept away animals
and birds. A plant he had never seen before began to grow from the
grave. It was as green as Mondawmin's buckskin clothing. It grew
and grew until yellow hair, as yellow as Mondawmin's hair, appeared on top of it. All along it were ears of corn, the first corn. That
corn fed the man's people. That corn, which the Anishinabe call
Mondawmin, was Gitchee Manitou's gift to the people.*

My first real match was not an easy one. It was against Ballston
Spa. I still remember sitting in the very last of a line of metal
folding chairs in the gymnasium of the Ballston Spa High
School. My grandfather had not shown up at the match. He'd
planned to find someone to watch the station for him and drive
down, but he was not there. I was glad of that. I didn't want
him to see me get beaten. Across the floor from me, looking
supremely confident, was Brett Haskell. He had laughed as we
shook hands. I knew it was meant to intimidate me. Kids from
other schools had refused to wrestle Brett Haskell after he had
shaken their hands. His laugh had been contemptuous, and his
handshake had been an attempt at a bone-crushing clamp. But
I had smiled back at him, showing my silver front tooth, and I
had pushed my hand firmly into his, so that my thumb touched
the back of his wrist.

Our match was a short one. I tried to take him down and

failed. The next thing I knew, I had lost my balance and I was on my back. The mat was slapped and it was all over in a little more than a minute—longer than my coach or teammates had expected.

"By gosh, you went after him, Bruchac," Coach Waldron said.

When I got off the bus at the high school that evening, I was ready to hitch my way home. It was what I had done all through the football season, for there was no such thing as a late bus for athletes in those days. Many of the other Greenfield kids didn't go out for sports because of that, and I'd walked all the way home after football practice, a distance of five miles, many an evening.

This time, however, my mother was waiting for me. I walked over to her car, feeling uncertain. Mom had been trying to play the role of a mother for me since my grandmother's death. The only problem was that sometimes she had no idea how to do it.

Only six months before, she had inadvertently sabotaged my first driver's test by insisting that I had to take it in her car rather than my grandfather's. On our way down to take the test, she had insisted on driving, even though I had a learner's permit. She took a corner a little too close and ran the right front tire hard over the curb as we turned onto North Broadway, where the test was being given.

"We're ready for him to take his test," she said to the severe-looking man with the clipboard.

"In that car?" he said.

"Yes, why not?" asked my mother.

"You have a flat tire," he said. "Right front."

"We'll get it fixed," she said.

Not now, we won't, I thought. But I got out the jack and tire iron, took off the tire, rolled it half a mile to the nearest gas station, got it patched, and then brought it back.

The examiner was waiting, tapping his clipboard with his pencil. The way he tapped that clipboard was not a good sign. He watched as I put the tire on.

"We're ready," said my mother. The examiner looked at his watch and sighed. I counted the glance and the sigh as two more signs that this was the day I was probably not going to pass a driver's test. Then my mother sealed my fate. As the examiner climbed into the passenger seat, she opened the back door.

"Can I come along?" she said.

No, I thought. No, no, no, no.

"Yes," he said, and then he smiled. I knew I was doomed.

I'm not sure how many things I did wrong or right. I only recall my mother's constant, nervously helpful comments from the back.

Those comments ranged from "Watch out for that car!" to "Isn't a four-point turn good enough?" to "Can't he try that twice? I'm sure he can do better." I gripped the wheel tighter and tried not to scream. The failing slip that he placed in my hand at the end of the ordeal was actually a relief. At least it was over. When I retook my test several weeks later with my grandfather's car—while Grampa sat smoking his pipe and waiting for us to come back—I had no trouble at all.

I walked over to my mother's car.

"Get in," she said, her voice strained. "We're going to the hospital."

"It's Grampa," I said.

"How did you do in your wrestling?" Her voice was nervous, as if she was not certain how I was going to react.

TESTS

"I lost. Is it Grampa? Tell me!" My hand was on the door. I was ready to open it and start running if she didn't start the car. The hospital was just across town, less than a mile away.

"He needed some tests," she said.

She reached out her finger and pressed the starter button on the dashboard.

By the time we reached the hospital, though, we found my grandfather waiting for us at the door.

"They ain't keeping me here," he said.

"Pop," said my mother, "they said they had to do some tests."

"Let 'em do 'em on someone else. I already missed Sonny's first match because of them. I tole Doc Magovern I was going home and he said, 'Wull, Jess, if that's what you want to do, you do it.' So I'm doing it."

My grandfather climbed into the back of my mother's car. I turned around to look at him and he reached out both his hands and took me by the shoulders. I tried to talk, to tell him how glad I was that he was going home, to tell him how sorry I was that I had lost my match. There were tears in my eyes.

"Grampa," I said, "I wanted you to be proud of me, but I lost."

"Sonny," he said, "no way I can't be proud of you."

At my next match a few days later, my grandfather was there. He stood up and shouted as I won my first match, using more strength than skill to pin a kid from Albany Academy who was two inches taller than me. I jumped up as soon as the referee slapped the mat and then did a forward roll.

By the time of the regional tournament, my grandfather had watched me do that forward roll many times. He had come to almost all my matches and had never seen me lose. I was no longer winning on strength alone, but had developed balance and learned more moves. I still, however, grinned a silver-toothed grin when I was on the mats. Years later I would be told by a boy who had attended another school that some kids thought I wasn't quite right in my head back then—with that crazy grin and all.

I was looking forward to the tournament. It would be a chance to wrestle Brett Haskell again. To do it, though, I had to win my way through to the finals, and there was some doubt that I could do that. Unlimited was the other name for my weight class and it meant just that. Some of the contestants in my division were behemoths.

My father had mentioned that to me just a week before the tournament, when he asked me to come over and help him load some deer hides into his truck. Asking me to do work for him was his way of getting me in a position where he could give me advice. Like my mother, he was trying to do more parenting now that my grandmother was gone. I sensed that. So, whenever he would call and say, "Get over here," I would do just that.

As I helped him load those hides to take to the tannery, he might, for example, say, "You know, if you get in a fight, you hit the other person first before he can hit you."

I nodded, knowing that was advice I would never take. I'd discovered a better way than he suggested. The few times people had tried to fight me since I'd gotten big, I did one of two things. I either let them hit me and then smiled at them when they hurt their hand, or I just caught their punch with my palm in midair. I never hit anyone back. I didn't like to hurt people. After a while, people stopped trying to fight with me.

Other times, my father might actually be asking me for help. Although she was two grades behind me, my sister Mary

TESTS

Ann was extremely popular with boys. That troubled my father deeply. He tried to keep her from dating, but she found ways to get around him. It had been that way for several years now. Almost every boy who had agreed to sign my junior yearbook—aside from a few friends like Wit Richmond, Jeff Perkins, and Billy Strauss—had only done so because they wanted to get on Mary Ann's good side. "Take care of your sister," some wrote. "How did you get such a beautiful sister?" wrote others. Mary Ann had been a finalist in the Miss Saratoga contest.

In my senior year, my grandfather had become Mary Ann's ally. Instead of coming to my parents' house to see Mary Ann, boys would come to the station. Then Mary Ann would come over, "to see Sonny and Grampa," and rendezvous with her boyfriend. If my grandfather saw my father's car coming—and Dad made regular checks on Mary Ann—he would whistle, and Fred Clark or Tom Furlong would hide in the men's room at the station. They were afraid of my father and were sure he would beat up any boy he ever caught holding hands with Mary Ann—and shoot any boy he ever caught kissing her.

My father knew something was going on, even though he never accepted that he was powerless to prevent it. "Why don't you just beat up that Fred Clark?" he would say to me, his voice full of anger. "He won't leave Mary Ann alone."

Although my father was able to show more love directly to my younger sister Marge than he could to myself or Mary Ann, by the time Marge reached her teenage years he was just as overprotective of her. "I was a bird in a cage," Marge said.

That one day as we loaded untanned hides into the truck, the smells of salt and raw flesh and hair clinging to our hands and our brown work shirts, my father tried to talk to me about wrestling. He was afraid that I was getting too proud of myself.

In some ways, in those years, my successes were harder for him to understand than my failures. He'd never expected me to succeed.

"Now there's some of those wrestlers from other schools that are awfully tough," he said. "You just can't expect to beat them all."

"Uh-huh," I said, swinging another deer hide up to him as he stood in the truck, pressing the skins down as he loaded them, his feet moving in delicate balance, a long-practiced dance of death on top of those mortal remains of three hundred animals.

"That's right," he said. "I got a friend up in South Glens Falls who says there's a wrestler there no one can beat. Why, that boy weighs three hundred and twenty pounds! What's wrong? Why are you shaking your head? Don't you believe me?"

I held up a hand. "Dad," I said, feeling an embarrassment I didn't understand, "I'm sorry, but I just pinned that three-hundred-twenty-pound wrestler from South Glens Falls yesterday in a scrimmage."

My grandfather sat in the front row during the Western Conference Tournament. He cheered me on as I won my first match, my second, and my third.

"That there is my grandson," he hollered. "Pin 'em, Sonny."

Two months had passed since I had faced Brett Haskell for the first time. For all that I had learned, it might have been two years. He didn't laugh when we shook hands, but I still flashed my silver smile. We circled and I shot in at him with a double leg take-down. When he countered me and tried to spin behind, I stood up and turned, locking him in a bear hug. We went off the mat together, neither one of us taking the other down. I looked up at Grampa, squinting to see him in the stands. Without my glasses, he was a little blurred, but I could see that he was grinning. I winked at him and then the referee signaled us to start once more.

By the time we reached the third period, the score was tied. It was three to three. Each of us had scored a two-point take-down. Each of us had scored a one-point escape. It was my turn to start on the bottom. I got down on my hands and knees and tensed my back. Brett Haskell put one hand on my left elbow and his right arm around my waist. The referee blew his whistle, and I rocketed up in a perfect stand-up and turn-out.

"One point!"

I was ahead. The seconds were ticking down in the match, and I was one point ahead. But I knew I couldn't stall. I had to keep on the attack. I circled, grabbed Haskell's arm, pulled, and then shot for my take-down. But he flailed his arm back across my face, hitting me in the eyes. It was unintentional, I'm sure, but it blinded me for a split second. In that split second, Haskell drove his shoulder into my side and forced me onto my stomach.

"Two points! Take-down."

All of his weight was on me. He wasn't going to try to pin me, just to hold me down and ride me out so that he could squeeze out a narrow win. Only twenty seconds were left. And I heard my grandfather's voice.

"Come on, Sonny," he was shouting, "you kin do it!"

I sat back, pushing with my hands. He was trying to break me down, but I wouldn't let him. I could feel all that my years of climbing trees had given to me. I felt as if a bear's strength had come into me, and I growled like a bear as I forced my way up.

Ten seconds now. I thrust a foot out, as if about to do a stand-up move again, knowing how Brett Haskell would react. He shifted his weight to pull me back. I let him pull me and then sat out into a switch so quickly that he sprawled onto his belly.

"Two points, reversal!" And the buzzer sounded. It was over, and I had won the Western Conference Tournament.

"Jumping Joe!" people were shouting. "Jumping Joe! Jumping Joe!"

I did my forward roll and leaped up. My grandfather was on the mat with me, hugging me so hard that I thought he would crack my ribs, as the referee raised my hand in victory.

"I knowed you could do it. I knowed it," Grampa said.

"I did it for you and Grama," I tried to say. I don't know if my lips said it, but my heart said it.

Brett Haskell was shaking my hand. "Good match," he said. "But you only won 'cause I was tired. I went to New York yesterday. You won't beat me in the sectionals."

I looked at Brett Haskell, and what I saw was not a bully or an unbeatable monster. I just saw a big kid of my own age, a big kid who looked really sad.

I shook his hand back. "It's okay," I said. "You'll beat me next time."

Then I turned and put one arm around my grandfather's shoulder and my other arm around Coach Waldron. I'd won my victory.

Many years have passed since that tournament, but the trophy I won that day still sits on the shelf in the living room of that old house where I was raised. There are other trophies there that I went on to win in later years. But no trophy or award that I've been given means more to me than that small metal figure of a wrestler, arms held out as if ready to begin again a match that would reward an old man's pride and prove that a small boy's dreams really can come true.

GETTING READY TO GO

*The Navajo tell a story about the hero twins, the
children of the Sun. The hero twins were raised by
Changing Woman and did not know who their father was. So they went to seek him out. He did not
know them when he saw them, and he tested them.
Those tests were dangerous, but they passed them
all. Then their father gave them weapons to use to
fight the monsters that threatened the lives of the people.*

Shonto Begay is a Navajo storyteller and artist. He and I were
at a conference this year, and as I looked at his paintings and listened to him talk, I felt that old familiarity, that calm I feel when
I'm hearing the old stories told. When I'm hearing voices that come
from the heart of the land, I hear my grandfather's voice. When I
left for college, I kept listening for that voice. Whenever I met Native
people, I would listen to them for a long time. After a while I would
tell them that I was part Indian. I sometimes told that to non-
Natives, too, but I knew that was riskier. You could never tell how
white people would respond.

In college I wrote a poem about that. It was called "Notes of a
Part-time Indian." I wrote it long before I heard the story of the
hero twins.

Sometimes I tell people
that I am half Indian.

Some laugh.
A woman from Oklahoma said
"But Indians are so dirty."

Others ask me "which half?"
But when I point at the sun
no one understands.

Few things go faster than your senior year in high school. But there were more surprises for me along the way after winning that wrestling championship. I was continuing to do well only in the courses that I liked best—English and social studies in particular. I sat in the back of the room in Miss Wells's English class. She had been my mother's English teacher too. I had a game that I played there. Miss Wells loved to read poems aloud, classics of American and English literature, as well as the more modern works of Robert Frost. Whenever she started reading a poem from the text, I would begin to recite from memory the last ten lines of it aloud, though not loud enough for her to hear. It created a great deal of interest in poetry in the class as my classmates would listen to Miss Wells in front and me in back. Either Miss Wells never noticed or was amused by it herself. She never stopped me from my last line recitations.

Sometimes, though, she would say, "Joseph, I'd like to have you do the next one. Would you please give us ⌣ . ." and then she would say the name of the poem she had in mind. Whatever it was, whether it was "The Highwayman" or Frost's "Stopping by Woods on a Snowy Evening," I would then stand up and recite it from memory—with the appropriate dramatic gestures.

I was good at memorizing things. I memorized the routines

of my favorite comedians. Jonathan Winters was the one I liked best. It would be a decade before Winters himself, who influenced a whole generation of manic stand-up comedians, would talk openly about the fact that he was Indian. My favorite of all his routines was the one in which a wagon train crossing the plains is attacked by Indians. Just in the nick of time, the cavalry arrives and charges. Then there is silence until a bugle is heard playing a familiar army tune. The bugle sound ends, and then we hear: "Not bad. First time play white man horn."

In Mrs. Lake's social studies class I had a perfect average. One day, Mr. Lake stopped me in the halls. Mr. Lake was a tall, friendly man with a deep voice. I'd always liked him, even though he was teaching algebra, a course in which I had no interest and only received mediocre grades.

"Bruchac," he said, resting one of his big hands on my shoulder, "my wife says you're not a dummy. She says you're her best student. Why can't you do the same in my course?"

I can't recall my exact words, which I spoke quickly so I could escape his grasp. Embarrassed, I blurted out something like, "I'm just not real good in math." But after that I raised my average in his course by ten points.

No one said anything to me about going to college. My grandmother had always assumed that I would get a college degree, but the world of higher education was as far away from my grandfather's thoughts as landing on the surface of the moon. My parents talked about college plans for Mary Ann, who was still at the very top of her class academically, but nothing was said about sending me to school.

I knew, though, what I wanted to do. I wanted to go to college and become a naturalist. Then I would live outdoors and write about animals. Maybe I would travel to places like Africa.

But I would always come back home to my grandfather.

One day as I walked down the hall after school, I noticed the door to Mr. Casey's office was still open. Mr. Casey was the guidance counselor. I stuck my head in to say hello. As I did, I saw a new poster on the wall by the door. CAREERS IN WILDLIFE CONSERVATION, it said. It was an advertisement for the Cornell University School of Agriculture. I was reading the poster when Mr. Casey walked in from the other room.

"Interested?" he said. The tone of his voice showed that he knew I was.

"Yes, I-I-I want to be a naturalist."

"I'll help you fill out an application."

It was the only application for college that I sent out. It had been dropped into my lap just at the time I needed it. Because the School of Agriculture was a state school, it was tuition-free for New York residents such as myself, although there were still fees and room and board to pay. I told my parents I was applying to Cornell. I had to do that because I needed them to fill out a financial form. They were skeptical.

"It costs a lot to go to college," my father said.

"It's tuition-free," I said, but he shook his head.

"There's still an awful lot of expenses there."

Later, Mary Ann spoke to me about it. "Daddy doesn't just think it's too expensive. He's also certain you'll just flunk out as soon as you go to college," she said.

"I understand," I answered. I was used to that kind of reaction, and I was determined not to let it happen.

In the end, I was able to send in my application, in part because my parents thought I would never be accepted. And even if I was, there was the question of paying for it. I had earned a few hundred dollars through summer work—money that my mother had banked for me. Aside from that, my grandfather and I had only a few dollars a week to live on.

"I want to go to college, Grampa," I told him.

"I'll miss ye, Sonny," he said, "but you'll do fine."

One afternoon, after the end of wrestling season, we had an assembly program. I was busy in track now, with the discus and shotput. I seldom took first in our meets, but I was always in the top three. I was thinking so much about track that I had forgotten about the assembly that Friday, even though the other kids were buzzing about it in the halls. It was the scholarship assembly.

Years ago, college scholarships to New York State schools were called Regents Scholarships. They were not given to every student based on financial need. In the 1950's and 1960's, these scholarships were awarded on a competitive basis. Every student in New York who hoped to go to college took a standard examination. Only the top scorers in each county would be awarded Regents Scholarships.

I sat next to Wit Richmond and Jeff Perkins.

"Jumpin' Joe," Wit said, "good luck this afternoon against Johnstown."

"Jess is going with us tonight, isn't he?" Jeff said.

"Yup," I said, "Grampa will be there."

"All right!" said Wit.

The assembly had already started as we were talking, and the names of the scholarship winners were being read. Suddenly, Wit and Jeff both stared at Principal John Sexton, who had just announced a name. People started clapping.

"Please," Principal Sexton said, "hold your applause till I have finished." But people kept applauding. Some were yelling something.

"No," Wit said. "Son of a gun!"

Jeff was shaking my arm. "Did you hear that? Did you hear that!"

And that was when I realized what people were yelling.

"Bruchac! Bruchac! Jumping Joe!"

My name had been called for a Regents Scholarship. I was going to be able to go to college.

I went to the track meet in a daze. Before I left on the bus, I'd called my grandfather and told him the news about my scholarship, but all he said was "I'll meet you there." There was something funny about the way he said it.

The meet was at Johnstown. Shot put was first, and I threw the twelve-pound ball forty-four feet. It was my best throw that year and it was enough to give me second place. But my grandfather wasn't there yet. I was disappointed. My only other event was discus, and I didn't stand a chance to place in it. I didn't know how to do the spin, and in those days we got very little coaching. Most of what we learned we taught each other. I

The track-and-field team in the spring of my senior year in high school
In the back row I'm fourth from the left, and Coach
"Hutch" Tibbetts is at the far right

was able to hit only one hundred and five feet. In this meet it wouldn't even be enough for fourth.

My first throw was my usual one hundred and five. Ten feet behind the person in third place. Twenty feet behind the leader. I got up for my last throw. I held the discus and swung my arm back, and then someone honked a horn right behind me. I stopped and turned to look. A beautiful new gold Plymouth with high fish-tail fins had pulled up next to the field. My grandfather got out of it, his hand still on the horn. He honked it again.

"Sonny," he yelled, "this here is your car! Your father just bought it for you."

"Ya-hoo!" I shouted. I swung my arm back and heaved the discus. It spiraled through the air, farther and farther. It looked as if it was never going to stop, but when it struck the ground it had flown one hundred and twenty-eight feet. I ended up in second place.

That car was, I believe, a sort of acknowledgment on my father's part. With the news of my Regents Scholarship he was willing to provide the extra support needed to send me to school. Shortly after that, I received an acceptance from Cornell.

What I didn't know was that my grandfather had signed over all of his property—his house, the station, and the two acres of land they stood on—to my parents. I'm not sure if he knew what he was doing. He always said to me that the house and the station would be mine one day. My grandmother had told me that she had written her will and my grandfather's in such a way that there would be no doubt I would inherit it all. But I think my grandfather knew what he had to do so that my parents would help me go to college. Even though I was going away, he was going to give me all that he could give.

SUMMER'S END

As I walked outside, my grandfather was standing in the carport where, so many years ago now, he had pumped gas for customers. He was pointing down at the ground.

"Watch out there, Sonny," he said. "You be careful where you walk."

I looked where he was pointing. There was a rattlesnake there, not coiled, but going back slowly across the muddy ground, leaving behind it a curving track on the earth. It was beautiful, its diamond-patterned scales that bright color a snake only has shortly after it has shed its old skin.

Garter snakes and the little green grass snakes had always startled my grandfather, even though those little creatures would frantically seek shelter whenever they encountered a person. But he stood there calmly, watching with me as that rattlesnake crawled away from us. Little things could sometimes upset Grampa, but the big things—the powerful ones that held the potential for danger—those never bothered him. As we watched, I remembered how the rattlesnake was always respected by the Abenaki people for its bravery. It would warn you before it would strike and give you time to move away. All it wanted to do was to defend itself and the place where it lived.

SUMMER'S END

"I'll be careful, Grampa," I said. That was when I woke up from my dream. There were tears in my eyes, and I was remembering a story that I heard from my grandfather's brother, Jack Bowman—a story that goes back a long time.

Jack lived most of his adult life with his wife, Kathy, in a little house near Lake George. Jack worked as a groundskeeper at the big Sagamore Hotel on the lake. Further up the lake is Brown Mountain. There are still rattlesnakes there and, to this day, they swim out from the cliffs at the base of Brown Mountain to reach the little islands. No one ever seems to get bitten by them. There's a hundred times greater chance of being struck by lightning. But every year the rangers take a half dozen or so rattlesnakes off the islands—where there are public campsites—to relocate them back on Brown Mountain.

Long ago, the story goes, one of our ancestors, an Indian or a Frenchman, was in a canoe on the lake. He had rested his paddle for a while and drifted there under that cliff. When he tried to lift his paddle again, it felt heavy. He raised it up, thinking that a branch had been caught on it. But what he saw was a six-foot-long rattlesnake crawling up that paddle, almost as swiftly as a ripple of light, right into the boat with him. The man sat there, trying not to move. A quick motion might frighten the snake and make it strike.

But the rattlesnake crawled unhurriedly into the other end of the canoe. It coiled up, lifted its head, and looked first at the distant shore, then back at the man.

The man understood. He began to paddle back toward the shore. As soon as his canoe touched land, that big rattlesnake flowed out onto the shore and was gone.

As soon as I had a car that was more or less my own, I had a new kind of freedom. I say it was more or less my own because it was given to me with a whole ball of strings attached to it by my father. I was never to take it out of town. Each morning he would check the odometer to make sure that I had not gone over the allotted mileage. I was never to have more than three other people in the car with me. And, in the fall, I was not going to be allowed to take it with me to college. It didn't matter. It was a new car and it was sort of my own. Maybe, I thought, it would open up a whole new social life for me. With a car, girls might go out with me. Girls, I was told, liked to ride in new cars.

And that turned out to be right.

"Want to go for a ride with me after school in my new car?" I would ask one girl after another. There were a lot of girls who were friends with me my senior year in high school. Not only was I an athlete, I could always be counted on to help them with their English or social studies homework.

"Sure," they would say. After school they would climb into my car and we would go riding. The girl would sit on her side of that wide front seat, a seat that began to feel as wide as the Grand Canyon to me, while I sat on the other. We'd talk about school and I'd make jokes. We'd drive around Saratoga Lake or out through Yaddo. Sometimes I'd stop at the Dairy Queen and buy us both an ice-cream cone.

Finally, after an hour or two, the girl would say, "I have to go home now."

"Okay," I'd say. Then I would drive her to her doorstep. She would gather her books up into her arms while I walked around and opened the door for her.

"See you in school," she'd say. Then she would brush by and be gone.

And that was how it went. I was too polite and too shy to try, as the other guys put it, "making a move." I hoped that, just like in the movies, one of those girls might sit really close to me or ask me to put my arm around her. Hope, however, was still several years removed from reality for me.

On the other hand, I can't say that no one ever "made out" in my car. "Making out" involved a good deal of hugging, kissing, and various fully-clothed body motions on the part of a young man and a young woman. "Heavy petting" was the next stage, in which articles of apparel might be somewhat disarranged and certain strategic areas tentatively touched by a boy until the girl said "No," and pulled his hand away. Both "making out" and "heavy petting" were as theoretical for me as the splitting of the atom. I knew such things could be done and could have written an informative essay on the subject, but I had no practical experience and none of the necessary training. Unlike my friends.

"Joe," one guy might say, "I got a date. Want to come along?"

"Sure," I'd answer. Then we would double-date, my friend and his girl with me and my car. I'd go with them to the movies and then drive around or sit at our favorite parking places, listening to the radio in the front seat while my friend and his date "made out" in the back. I'd always tilt the rearview mirror so that they would have privacy as I sat, softly singing along with the music. I knew the words to every popular song.

At the end of the evening, I would pull up in front of the house where the girl lived. The two in the back would get out while I sat in front, my eyes forward. Sometimes, the girl would come around to my side, put a hand on my arm, and say "Thanks, Joe, you're great!" On a memorable night, one girl actually leaned over and kissed my cheek. "Joe," she said, "someday you are going to make some girl a great husband."

I finally had my silver tooth replaced by one that looked real the week before graduation.

"The root has shrunk back enough," Dr. Benditt said, as I spat blood into the water swirling in the sink next to the dentist's chair. "Time for the crown."

I went to the Senior Prom actually able to smile with my lips parted. But I was not destined to do much smiling. My date was one of my sister Mary Ann's friends. Mary Ann had set it up for me; we were double-dating with her and Tommy Furlong. Mary Ann's friend sat in the well-worn place at the far end of the front seat near the passenger door in my Plymouth. Her boyfriend was in the navy, and she spent the whole evening talking about him and about all the things the two of them planned to do together when he was on leave. She agreed to stand next to me for the obligatory Senior Prom picture, but she wouldn't dance with me. At her request, we dropped her off early. Then we drove slowly around Saratoga Lake until it was time for us to drop Tommy off and for me to go back home.

When my sister and I finally pulled in to the driveway in front of my parents' house they were waiting, my father looking at his watch and ready to check the odometer to make sure I hadn't gone over the allotted miles for the night. It made me angry, seeing him standing there like that after I'd had one of the worst nights of my life. I slammed on the brakes and then leaned forward to pound my fist on the dashboard, making a dent in the solid metal.

My parents ran up.

"My God!" my father shouted. "What's wrong?"

Mary Ann got out, a disgusted look on her face. "We just killed a dozen people," she said.

"Oh, no!" my mother screamed.

"How the hell did you do that?" my father shouted, his voice several decibels higher than I'd ever heard it before, his worst fears about me finally realized.

I got out, looked at them, and shook my head.

"Stop it," I said to them. "We didn't kill anyone. I just had a lousy date. Okay?"

There was a moment of silence then, but it wasn't okay. As Mary Ann went into the house, both my parents shouted at me about worrying them to death.

"How could you do this to us?" my mother screamed.

"I didn't get you a car for you to do things like this," my father yelled.

I put the keys to the Plymouth into my father's hand.

"The car is yours, Dad," I said. "Keep it."

Then I turned around and walked away from them. I walked, still wearing my rented tuxedo and cummerbund and pink carnation, into the darkness along the lane that led from their house. No one followed me. I walked back home down Middle Grove Road, toward the lights that were still burning above the gas pumps at Bowman's Store.

My grandfather got up from his chair in front of the station as I walked past him without speaking. He turned off the lights and shut the door to the station and then followed me into the house. He found me sitting on the couch, my arms around Sniffy, who had leaped up and thrust his nose against my cheek. As I sat there, tears streaming from my eyes, my Grampa sat behind me, patting me on the back, not saying a thing nor asking any questions. I closed my eyes, feeling as if all the love I was ever going to know in my life was there in that room with me.

The next day was a Sunday. On Sundays I was always the one to open up the station. When I walked outside, the Plymouth was parked there, the keys in the ignition. There was no note, and neither my father nor my mother said anything about it. But, throughout that summer, my father still checked the odometer regularly to see how many miles I'd put on the car.

That summer went faster than any summer I can remember. I earned money parking cars at the racetrack and working in the state park. I drove my friends to drinking parties that we would hold on deserted roads or late at night in unused camping areas along Geyser Brook. All of us were underage for drinking, but as the biggest guy I was always the one sent into the stores to buy beer. I didn't drink it myself, but I would take the money from my friends, pick up the six-pack, and deliver it to them.

Lake George, which was thirty miles away, was also a popular place to go. It was, indeed, out of town and my father's ban on out-of-town trips with the car was still in effect. But I ignored it, loading as many as eight of my friends into the Plymouth, heading north to go to the clubs where they had live music. We had discovered that the odometer of the Plymouth would actually roll backward when the car went in reverse. So we would drive home backward along dirt roads to keep within my father's arbitrary allowance of miles. Though I would not realize it until years later, as we drove backward along those roads, driving as if we were going back in time, we went right past the house where my grandfather's brother Jack was living.

I was busy all the time, and there was only one sad moment that made the rapid disappearing of the days stop for me. One morning, when I went outside, I noticed that Sniffy had slipped free of his collar. We always kept him tied to his doghouse under the big blue spruces whenever we left him alone outside. The State Road was just too dangerous.

My first thought was that he had been killed. I looked up and down the road. There was no sign of a small black-and-tan body with white markings. My grandfather looked for him all that day without finding him. The next day, my mother called.

"Your father saw a dead dog on the roadside down at the end of Mill Road," she told me. "It might be yours."

My grandfather and I drove down to the end of Mill Road, where it intersected 9N a mile below our house. A little black-and-white-and-tan beagle lay there. He had been hit hard by a

My high school graduation picture, class of 1960

truck and thrown, it seemed, a long way over onto the shoulder. He was bloody and torn by the awful impact.

My grandfather took a burlap bag out of the car.

We carefully put the small, broken body into the bag and drove back home. I dug a deep hole by the edge of the woods past the end of the garden and buried him there.

"I'm going to miss him," my grandfather said.

I nodded. I wasn't thinking of the fact that I was soon going away to college and that everything would change for my grandfather with my departure.

"We can get another dog," my grandfather said, after a while. It was what we had always done in the past. This time, though, I shook my head.

"I'm going away soon, Grampa," I said. "Don't you remember that?"

"I surely do," he said.

"So there's not time for me to have another dog. And I don't want another dog," I said. "I want my dog. I want Sniffy."

"I understand, Sonny," my grandfather said. And he did understand, much more than I did then.

CLOSING THE CIRCLE

There is a special kind of bond, they say, between those whose spirits are connected. You can feel each other from far away. "I don't ever write to the people I care about," Dewasentah said to me, as I sat with her in her kitchen in Onondaga. "That way the telepathy is stronger."

It was that way with Swift Eagle, who was long a friend and teacher to our family. My second son Jesse and I were pulling into our driveway one day. Jesse was seven years old then. I stopped the car, and then we turned and looked at each other.

"Swifty," Jesse said.

"Yes," I answered.

And though neither of us had known before then that Swift Eagle had been taken ill and was in the hospital, we both knew at that moment that his spirit had left his body and we would not see him again in this lifetime.

The next morning a phone call came with the news that Swifty had died the past evening. Jesse and I were both crying as we went into my older son Jim's room to wake him up. But Jim was already awake and sitting up in bed.

"Swift Eagle has died, hasn't he?" Jim said, before we could say anything. "He came to me in a dream last night. He asked me if I

still had what he gave me—that little canteen. I said that I did, and then he was gone."

It is said that in the old days people knew when they were going to die. They saw it coming from a long way off, or they just plain chose the day when they would go. I was told that one way it was done was to seek the Spirit of the North. When a man or a woman knew it was their time, they would leave the village and walk up into the hills. They would walk high into the Kaydeross Range that rises above Greenfield Center, until they came to a certain place they had chosen long ago. There they would sit and watch their last sunset. Then their spirit would start its walk up into the stars. And the birds and the animals and the stones and earth of the mountain would take back their flesh and their bones.

But if they were too weak to make that walk and no one would carry them to that place they had chosen, then they would just close their eyes. They would know that the time to close the circle had come, and they would go to sleep.

When I left that fall for Cornell University, I didn't know how long a journey I was about to embark upon. I thought no further than going to college and getting the degree that would enable me to become a naturalist. Perhaps I could become a ranger in a national park. I'd worked two summers as a nature counselor at Skye Farm, the Methodist Church summer camp near Warrensburg in the Adirondack Mountains to the north, and I knew that I wanted a life that would not confine me to a city or an office. I knew that I could write well, and I thought about that as being part of my work someday. But I know that I did not think as much as I might have about what my leaving meant to my grandfather.

I wrote him regularly. I tried to keep my letters clear and simple. I'd taken with me the big gray upright typewriter that had been my grandmother's. By typing my letters, I thought it would be easier for Grampa to read them. My sister Mary Ann wrote me with news of her life in high school, telling me what people were doing.

"Daddy still says that you won't be gone long," she added. "He is sure you'll flunk out."

I didn't answer that. I only wrote back about what life was like in the freshman dorms, about the difficulties of living with a roommate, and about going out for the college wrestling team as a walk-on. Though it was just my second year of wrestling, I won a place on the Cornell team as the heavyweight. I won all but two matches that year and finished third in the Freshman Eastern Tournament. I was the varsity heavyweight wrestler for the next three years until a neck injury ended my career, two weeks before the National Tournament, in my fourth year at Cornell.

Two weeks after arriving at Cornell, I checked my mailbox and found a letter that surprised me. I recognized the handwriting, which was scrawled all over the front of the envelope, laboriously spelling out my name and my address. I pressed the letter to my forehead and then I opened it. It was from Grampa. It was difficult for him to write anything more than his own name. Now that Grama was gone, he always had people write their own names and what they'd gotten in the black account book he kept for people who had charge accounts at the station. But he had written me a letter.

"Dear Sonny," it read. "How be you? This be your Grmpa. I be fine. Wethur warm. Mis you so much. You do good. I be fine. Doc say. I love you Sonny."

Those words filled the top half of the page. The bottom half was filled with X's and O's. Each X stood for a kiss. Each O stood for a hug. I could feel his strong old arms around me as he made each of those marks, wrestling with the pencil he used

On the wrestling team at Cornell

to write his letter. I could see marks on the paper where he had borne down too hard and broken the lead. Then, after pulling out his jackknife to sharpen the pencil (he never used a pencil sharpener), he had started again. I knew how stiff his fingers had become with arthritis. He could still hold a hoe or a shovel, or pump gas, but it hurt him to grip something as small as a pencil or a pen. And the words, forming them, putting the shapes of letters on a page, that too could not have been done without concentration, without pain. I could see how furrowed his brow was as he bent over the dining-room table, writing one letter at a time. Only now and then taking a break to drink from his coffee cup. (There were brown coffee stains on the page.) Even before those X's and O's were drawn in at the bottom, that letter was filled with the gift of more love than any letter I had ever received before. It was, I believe, the first letter my grandfather had ever written.

From then on he wrote to me twice every week. His writing and spelling improved some, but not much. I don't think he used more than a hundred different words in all the letters he sent me—and there were dozens of them over the years. I kept them all.

He visited me at college. Not often. Once he was able to get friends of mine to drive the two hundred miles out to Ithaca with him—though he had to do it on the sly. My father's restriction about not going out of town with the car applied to my grandfather as much as it did to me. When he got back home, as he later told me, "there was hell to pay." But though my father and mother were upset, my grandfather knew how to respond. He stopped talking to them. Not just for a day, but for a week. His silence continued until they asked him if he'd like to go with them on a trip to Ithaca to visit me at Cornell.

Important as his letters were to me, my grandfather was no longer visibly at the center of my life. Too many other things were happening to me. When I came home for vacations, Grampa and I would still do things together, but it would only be for a few days or a few weeks. Then I would be back at school again.

Yet Grampa could still make things happen for me. One day, during my sophomore year, I got a letter from him that surprised me. I read the line which had given me that surprise over and over. Finally I could stand it no longer. I called him on the phone. He answered on the third ring.

"Grampa," I said, "it's me."

"Hello, Sonny. When you coming home?"

"Next weekend, Grampa. But I got your letter. What did you mean when you wrote in it 'Yer dog is fine'?"

On the other end of the line my grandfather started to chuckle.

"Guess you better come home and see, Sonny," he said.

When I got off the Greyhound bus in Saratoga Springs, Grampa was waiting for me in the Plymouth. I noticed it had yet another dent in the front bumper. I hoped that didn't mean that Grampa had rear-ended another state trooper at a stoplight. That was what had caused the dent on the right side of the bumper. Somehow, after it had happened, the state trooper had ended up apologizing to my grandfather. "He seed the right of it after I tole him you wasn't supposed to stop on a yellow light," my grandfather had said to me.

Grampa got out of the car while I was still eyeing that new bump.

"Parking meter," he said. "I tole them they oughtn't to have put them so dang close to the curb." He grabbed my bag out of my hand and threw it into the back of the car. "Let's get home. Somebody's waiting."

And that was all that he would say as we drove the three miles to the house. But as soon as I opened the front door, a small furry body leapt off the couch and began running around my feet. Growling in mock anger as he pulled at my pants leg, barking and licking my face with joy as I knelt down to pet him, it was Sniffy—my dead dog!

I looked up at my grandfather. He looked like the cat who had swallowed the canary.

"How?" I said. I couldn't think of anything else to say.

"Jes' run off and got lost," my grandfather said. "A beagle 'ull do that, start to chasing something. Dan Atwell tole me

My younger sister Marge with my resurrected dog, Sniffy, in 1961

he'd seen a dog looked jes' like mine over to the other side of town. So I run over there and there he was." Grampa laughed. "They was calling him Beau, but when I yelled 'Sniffy!' he run right over and jumped in the car. They couldn't get him out no-how, neither. He jes' growled at them when they tried."

He reached down and patted Sniffy's head. Sniffy rolled over on his back so that Grampa could stroke his belly. "Don't nobody want to try to take ahold of me when this dog is around," he said.

"But what about the dog we buried?"

"Guess it was somebody else's. Always thought that dog

what was kilt was a little too small, but you was so sad there wasn't nothing I could say." My grandfather smiled as I picked Sniffy up and hugged him to my chest. "Tole you yer dog is fine, didn't I?"

But I had to leave Sniffy behind and go back to college. Knowing that he was there to keep my grandfather company made it easier for me to leave him. By my third year at Cornell even more things were happening. I had met Carol and, within a few months, we were engaged to be married. My circle of love had grown wider. And I had taken a course in creative writing and realized that, even more than being a naturalist, I wanted to be a writer. I wanted to write about the natural world—and the more I wrote, the more that writing led me into a quest for my own Native ancestry. My poems, unexpectedly for those who thought of me as only a jock at Cornell, began to appear in the *The Trojan Horse*, Cornell's literary magazine. So I transferred from the School of Agriculture to the School of Arts and Sciences. It meant an extra year of college to fill out a major, but I was prepared to do that. I took out a student loan to cover the costs of my tuition.

My father wrote me, saying that he would not support me if I got married. I wrote back, thanking him and my mother for the help they'd given me, but telling him that Carol and I would go it on our own after we were married. And we did just that. I only discovered years later, in talking with my sister Marge, that my father continued to tell everyone that he was paying all of our expenses. That was not true. Dad wanted people to think he was taking care of us. That was a matter of pride for him. But our rent, our food, our car insurance, and all my costs for attending college—aside from my scholarships—were paid for out of our own pockets, from the jobs that Carol worked and the money I earned when I was not in school. Our

A wedding picture with Carol's grandparents, Isabel and
Edmund Worthen (*at left*), and Grama Bruchac with Grampa Jesse

wedding took place at the end of my fourth year at Cornell. We
were married in Anabel Taylor Chapel on the Cornell campus,
and my grandfather was there.

"I loves you both," he said. "I be waiting for you. You'll
come home."

But, though my grandfather expected us to move in with
him when I finished my degree at Cornell a year later, it was

At Syracuse University in 1965

not to happen that quickly. I would go on to Syracuse University on a Creative Writing Fellowship. The Onondaga Indian Reservation was only a few miles from the university. I had an old Harley-Davidson motorcycle, and I would ride it out to the rez where I'd talk with elders, beginning a friendship with Onondaga and her people that has lasted over three decades.

Whenever I came home, I showed my grandfather the poems and stories I had published. Many of them were about my search for my Native heritage. He always approved of them, yet he still never openly acknowledged or talked about his own Abenaki ancestry to me.

I was involved in those years with the civil rights movement and I was opposed to the Vietnam War. I marched on Washington, and I was with Martin Luther King Jr. and James Meredith in Mississippi. I didn't believe it was right to kill other human beings. Life was too short and too precious for that. Carol agreed with me. At the end of my master's degree program at Syracuse, we joined a volunteer teachers' program called Teachers for West Africa. For the next three years we lived in Ghana, working at Keta Secondary School. When we left America, in a time of great national turmoil, we were not certain we would ever return.

During the summer after our second year in Ghana, our first son was born, the first firstborn to survive in four generations. We named him James. I would not name him Joseph, as my father and his father before him had been named. It was time to begin again and not repeat the old mistakes. We went home that summer and stayed with my grandfather. The years of being haphazardly cared for by an old man living alone had taken their toll on a house which had already suffered its share of injuries from the years that my grandfather and I were there without my grandmother. Carol looked at the holes in the walls, the living-room rug that was thick with dirt, the uncleaned windows, and the upstairs rooms that were piled high with furniture.

"How could we ever live here?" she said.

I didn't know. Yet we both felt something calling to us there. We spent a third and final year in Ghana and then, somehow, we came home.

My grandfather was waiting. He welcomed us and he welcomed Jamey. I have pictures in our album of the two of them together, both of them always smiling—except for the picture

Carol and me in Ghana with James in September 1968

we took one day when we had a picnic in the backyard. In that picture the two of them lie together on a blanket, curled up in peaceful sleep.

"I knowed you'd come home," Grampa said. There was a glow about him when he said that, as if a sort of peace had settled within him, like a grouse settling into a cedar tree for the night.

Every now and then he would say, "I got something to show you." Then he might take Carol or me down into the cellar. "See that there valve?" he'd say. "That's to fill the radiators. When I go, I want you to know about that." Another time he might take me out to the Little House. "See that there rocker?" he'd say, pointing at an old chair with its stuffing falling out. "That there's a Lincoln rocker. When I go, I want you to know where that is. You'll want to reupholster that someday when you got the money."

We laughed about Grampa's "When I go's," but our time with him there in the old house on Splinterville Hill was to be short. Six months after our return from Africa, he went into the Saratoga Hospital. He had fallen on the ice and broken a hip. The hip healed quickly, but pneumonia set in.

Carol and my mother and I were sitting around his bed. He looked at us and spoke.

"I'm going to bed now," he said. "You go home. I'll be all right."

My mother thought he was delirious. "Pop," she said, her voice choked, "you're already in bed."

My grandfather laughed. "Flora," he said, "I know where I be. I mean I'm jes' goin' to sleep now. You all go home."

We did as he said. We left the room. He died before we were out of the hospital.

Doc Magovern spoke to Carol and me later that day. He placed his hand on my shoulder as he spoke, and I could see

Grampa and James, at age 13 months, July 1969

that my grandfather's passing weighed heavily on him too. Somehow, although he had always seemed as solid and indestructible as a tall oak tree, Doc Magovern had gotten old himself.

"Your grandfather was a special man," he said. "You know, he had enough things wrong with him to kill ten younger men. He had cancer in his lungs, anemia, and arthritis. But he was determined to see you two and that great-grandson of his come home to that house. He was just waiting for you all to come home."

"Doc," I said, "we understand. We'll be staying there." There at Bowman's Store.

And we've stayed to this day.

AFTERWORD

It is a warm day in September. I'm sitting in a cabin up in the Kaydeross Range, on the southeast shoulder of Glass Factory Mountain, a mile from Cole Hill, where my grandfather Jesse Bowman and his twelve brothers and sisters were born. Just down slope behind me is Bucket Pond, where my grandfather told me he used to fish as a child. Although our primary residence remains at Bowman's Store, Carol and I now spend a great deal of time in this place, away from traffic and telephones and the many daily interruptions that come from living on an intersection.

This place, though, is another kind of intersection. Ridge Road, which now dead-ends at our driveway, is one of the trails the old people used to walk long before the homesteads and sheep farms and camps and the eventual reclamation of the hardscrabble hills by the northern forest. It was, Don Bowman tells me, one of the routes taken when old men or women decided their time had come to walk the Sky Trail. Before they became too feeble to care for themselves, before their lives could become a burden, they would slip away from the longhouse or wigwam to seek the Spirit of the North. They'd reach the highest hill their legs could carry them to, watch one last sunset, then turn their last breath and their eyes toward the stars. When their children found their bodies, they would bury them there.

*   *   *

It is fascinating to consider how many things come from one action, from feelings of identity or identification. The slow discovery of our Abenaki blood has led to so many things for me and the members of our family. Just last weekend, before an audience of more than 3,000 people, my little sister Marge (now six feet tall), my son Jim, and I told traditional Abenaki stories at the Corn Island Storytelling Festival in Louisville, Kentucky. When Jesse, my younger son, was working toward his Bachelor's degree at Goddard College, his thesis was the creation of a syllabus to teach the Abenaki language. Marge, Jim, Jesse, and I have performed together on many occasions as The Dawnland Singers, sharing traditional Abenaki music and songs of our own composition.

One of the things I am often asked by people who have read *Bowman's Store* is this: What happened to my father and mother after my grandfather's death in 1970?

My parents have now both passed on. My father had his first major heart attack in 1983. He was told that he needed bypass surgery. He refused it. A pacemaker was installed, but it was hard for him to work as he'd done before. His voice was gentler now, and he and Mom began to go out for their meals. They came to all the sports events their grandchildren were involved in, and I'd sometimes see their car parked near the fence of the East Side Recreation Field, where they could watch kids they didn't know playing Little League baseball.

My father's final heart attack came two and a half years after the one that put him in the hospital. He got up and told Mom they needed to go for a ride. They visited all of their favorite places and they went to dinner at a restaurant they both loved. As he stood before the cash register, waiting to pay their bill, he suddenly fell.

For the next 12 years we were Mom's primary caregivers. Even though she said she didn't want to live after Dad was gone, Mom proved to be as tough as Grampa Jesse. She survived four major surgeries, at least two strokes, and three heart attacks.

At times Mom would talk some about the past with my sister Marge or Jim or me. Marge was becoming deeply involved with our Native heritage herself and would lose patience with Mom when she referred to me as "your brother, the Indian."

"What about me, Mom?" Marge asked.

"Well," Mom said, "I guess you're as Indian as he is. And your grandfather was Indian. But I'm not."

And yet she was. The protective distance Mom tried to keep between herself and that painful ancestry grew less over the years. She actually took the time to explain, first to Marge and then to Jim, how many of the families who lived around us in Greenfield also had Indian blood. A surprising number of them, like our family, were a mix of Indian and Slovak, two despised minorities finding comfort with each other.

Mom also looked at the land—more than 80 acres—that had been her family's and then hers and Dad's. Before she could no longer drive a car, she went to a meeting about protecting land from development. Even though the property was worth a great deal as real estate, she made her decision and refused to be swayed from it by anyone. In 1991 the entirety of her property was placed in a conservation easement with the Saratoga Land Conservancy. It was the first in our county, and *The Saratogian* ran a front-page story with Mom's picture. "FOREVER WILD," it said beneath her picture. She framed the article and hung it on her wall next to the television. "That's me," she said, "forever wild."

Today that land is the home of the Ndakinna Education Center, where our son Jim and his staff teach Native outdoor skills. A sign by the trail leading up into the field reads: MARION BOWMAN BRUCHAC MEMORIAL NATURE PRESERVE.

Mom's last heart attack came in the fall of 1998. She needed round-the-clock care and was moved to a nearby nursing home, where she passed away in early 1999.

* * *

So many things come from memory. One of the people I will always remember is Alice Papineau, who left this life in September 2000. The Clan Mother of the Eel Clan of the

Onondaga Nation, her Iroquois name was Dewasentah. One of the elders I have loved and admired most for more than 30 years, Dewasentah was the one who, one autumn day while I was doing my annual residency at the Onondaga Nation School, handed me a package with an eagle feather and a small lacrosse stick in it. On the envelope was written a name: Gah-neh-go-he-yoh.

"I thought you should have an Onondaga name," she said to me, "because of your writing and all the work you do with our people. That name means 'The Good Mind.' The Creator has given you a special gift and that name is about that."

Gifts. It seems as if all our Native American traditions believe in gifts. Each person is born with a gift from the Creator, some special ability he or she can use for the good of the people. By using the gift in that way, by giving back, the person's own life is made happier and stronger. And the more one returns that gift, the more gifts will be given in return. But if the person becomes confused, lost in individual greed or self-pity, that gift may turn against him or her. Giving is the key.

One of the things that I was given is a good memory. Memory is a wonderful and mysterious thing. I've met many people who say they have bad memories, that they can't recall anything about their childhoods. Part of it may be that deep inside they don't want to remember or they are afraid of their memories, but such reticence or fear of memory has never been part of me, even though my memory has sometimes set me apart. In grade school, for example, I was the kid who always remembered every answer and was the first to raise his hand with it. Some thought I was showing off and resented me for trying to be a teacher's pet, but that wasn't it at all. I had to do it. The memory itself compelled me to share what I knew.

It is thanks to the gift of memory that I was able, over the years that followed, to learn so much from so many Native elders. I'd learned by then that it was fruitless to ask my parents or my grandfather to tell me more about the Indian heritage I now knew was mine and burned to know more about. Every direction I turned in my own family, I met with frustration. Either they didn't know or they weren't about to tell me. But whenever I met other Indians, especially older people, all I had to do was show them I was ready to listen and they would start talking. I heard stories of their lives, the histories of their people, songs, and traditional tales. By the time I was in graduate school at Syracuse University and riding my motorcycle out to Onondaga to sit with Dewasentah and her mother in their Onondaga Trading Post, I was hearing so much that I wasn't sure I was taking it in. But it seems I was. All I have to do is start thinking of those times and the memories flood back. A name, a word, the smell of cedar smoke on the wind, the breath feather of an eagle hung in a blackberry bush near a roughly varnished wooden back door—that is all it takes to summon a memory.

That gift of memory has made me a writer and a storyteller. And because I am the one who does remember "the words to all the songs," I will continue sharing that gift.

Peace,
Joe
September 2000

JOSEPH BRUCHAC, of Abenaki Indian and Slovak descent, is a writer, poet, and storyteller. He is the author of numerous award-winning books for children and adults, including the *Keepers of the Earth* series and Lee & Low's *Crazy Horse's Vision,* a winner of the Parents' Choice Award. Bruchac earned a B.A. from Cornell University, an M.A. from Syracuse University, and a Ph.D. from Union Institute of Ohio. A Rockefeller Fellow and an NEA Poetry Writing Fellow, he was the 1999 recipient of the Native Writers' Circle of the Americas Lifetime Achievement Award. In addition to being a writer, Bruchac is editor at Greenfield Review Press, a literary publishing house he co-founded with his wife, Carol. They live in Greenfield Center, New York, in Bruchac's childhood home.

To find out more about
Joseph Bruchac, visit
www.leeandlow.com/booktalk